Bringing the Market Back In

The Political Revitalization of Market Liberalism

John L. Kelley
Associate Professor of History
Shawnee State University, Ohio

For Richard Sincere
John Kelley

NEW YORK UNIVERSITY PRESS
Washington Square, New York

First published in the U.S.A. in 1997 by
NEW YORK UNIVERSITY PRESS
Washington Square
New York, N.Y. 10003

This book is printed on paper suitable for recycling and
made from fully managed and sustained forest sources.

Library of Congress Cataloging-in-Publication Data
Kelley, John L., 1944–
Bringing the market back in : the political revitalization of
market liberalism / John L. Kelley.
p. cm.
Originally published as a doctoral dissertation (Ohio University).
Includes bibliographical references and index.
ISBN 0–8147–4688–8
1. Libertarianism—United States.   2. Libertarian Party.   3. Free
enterprise—United States.   I. Title.
JC599.U5K43 1997
320.51'2—dc21   96–53059
                                                      CIP

Printed in Great Britain

Contents

Preface and Acknowledgements

The thirties and forties saw the establishment of a long-lived consensus in the United States that unrestrained capitalism was a failure. It apparently suffered from cyclical instability, a tendency towards monopoly, an inadequate provision of public goods, and an inequitable income distribution. As the American political culture never would accept a socialist order, reformers ultimately settled on what has been variously called the mixed economy, "via media," or the "vital center": a regime of regulated capitalism, interest-group liberalism, and Keynesian macro-economics.

This Vital Center liberalism was most self-celebratory during the mid-1960s, just before its crisis. Confident that the "New Economics" could drive the economy to higher levels of productivity, that the resultant "social dividend" would provide for an expanded social welfare state, and social science knowledge would permit the therapeutic state to solve problems of racial justice and residual poverty, President Johnson simultaneously launched domestic wars against poverty, social blight, and racism while escalating in Vietnam.

This reform activism, paradoxically, reached its apogee not during the Johnson years but with the Presidency of Richard Nixon. As Joan Hoff has recently noted, the Nixon administration exceeded the record of the New Deal and the Great Society in the areas of affirmative action, social welfare spending, and social regulation. This activism overloaded the Vital Center order, generated unbalanced budgets and stagflation, spawned new "rent-seeking" special interest groups, and produced a regulation of business and the civil society so substantial that even many liberals were prepared to reconsider their enthusiasm for an expanded state.

The "crisis of confidence" of the Vital Center paradigm gave the advocates of a rejuvenated classical liberalism (what I call "market liberalism") an opportunity to promote an alternative vision of the good society. This revival of what was once thought to be a dead tradition could be seen in the expanding influence of the Austrian, Chicago and Public Choice schools of economics and the development of the related libertarian movement. Because the excesses of Vital Center liberalism generated powerful dissatisfactions, the market liberals, now armed with research studies pointing to repeated evidences of "government failure," received an increasingly respectful hearing in the 1970s.

The market liberals hardly could transform the Vital Center order, however, without control of the levers of political power. The Libertarian Party proved incapable of providing them that access, playing only a vanguard role. Although many market liberals did obtain government positions with Ronald Reagan's 1980 election, no serious reductions in government size occurred. For all his anti-Washington rhetoric, Reagan couldn't do serious damage to the New Deal–Great Society edifice.

The market liberal revival did help prejudice the climate of opinion against any further expansion of the state – witness the fate of President Clinton's health reform bill. This new skepticism toward government, a renewed, although wary, respect for the genius of the market, and a willingness to experiment with alternative delivery systems of government-financed services through privatization constituted the successes of the market liberals in America. For all of the recent influences of market liberal ideas within the more statist political economies of the social democracies and the old communist bloc, market liberals in the United States have not been able to build a coalition committed to dramatically rolling back the state. Instead Americans today exhibit an uncertainty about their expectations of government. This ambivalence is reflected in the disparity between the public's anti-government rhetoric and its support for what one recent critic has described as a "libertarian social welfare state." Similarly, intellectuals seem unable to agree upon a new public philosophy to supplant the much-abused Vital Center paradigm. This book is an attempt at describing how we arrived at the current impasse.

In writing this story I used the Libertarian Party Archives at the University of Virginian Library, Charlottesville, Virginia and various collections at the Hoover Institution Archives, Stanford, California. At the University of Virginia Library's Special Collections Department I should like to acknowledge the assistance of Laura A. Endicott. For assistance in locating relevant collections at the Hoover Institution Archives and for help in obtaining copyright clearances I am grateful to Pruda Lood and Carol A. Leadenham. At the Shawnee State University Library a special thanks is due Connie Salyers Stoner and Mary Cummings for cheerfully and expertly helping me locate sources.

The author also would like to express his sincere appreciation to the following who very kindly gave their permission to use their letters or unpublished writings: James M. Buchanan, David Boaz, Edward M. Crane, Milton Friedman, David A. Keene, Irving Kristol, Leonard P. Liggio, Ronald W. Reagan, William E. Simon and Ernest van den Haag. Michael Plunkett, Director of Special Collections at the University of Virginia Library, permitted me to quote from the Libertarian Party Archives. Stephen Stigler authorized the use of George J. Stigler's 1978 Mont Pelerin Society Presidential Address. Joan Kennedy Taylor granted permission to use several of Roy A. Childs, Jr.'s letters. Linda Whetstone, the daughter of Sir Antony Fisher, generously permitted me to quote from several of her father's letters to F. A. Hayek.

This book began as a doctoral dissertation within the Department of History, Ohio University. I shall always be very grateful to my advisor, Professor Alonzo L. Hamby, who encouraged me to take on a large topic, provided encouragement and incisive commentary throughout the writing process, and provided wise counsel on publication. At Shawnee State University, President Clive Veri, Provost A. L. Addington, and the Shawnee Development Fund respectively offered support, released time from teaching responsibilities, and a generous travel grant. My departmental colleague, Dr Robert A. Lawson, read portions of the manuscript and offered valuable advice on economics. Finally, I thank Professor Robert H. Ferrell for his kind interest in a former student.

John L. Kelley

List of Abbreviations

AEI	American Enterprise Institute for Public Policy Research
AFDC	Aid to Families with Dependent Children
AFL	American Federation of Labor
ALA	Alliance of Libertarian Activists
CBS	Columbia Broadcasting System
CEA	Council of Economic Advisors
CED	Committee for Economic Development
CETA	Comprehensive Employment and Training Act
CIO	Congress of Industrial Organizations
CLA	California Libertarian Alliance
CLS	Center for Libertarian Studies
CPB	Central Planning Board
EPA	Environmental Protection Agency
FEE	Foundation for Economic Education
FTC	Federal Trade Commission
GMU	George Mason University
IHS	Institute for Humane Studies
IEA	Institute for Economic Affairs
IRA	Independent Retirement Accounts
ISI	Intercollegiate Society of Individualists (renamed the Intercollegiate Studies Institute in the 1960s)
JLS	*Journal of Libertarian Studies*
LP	Libertarian Party
MPS	Mont Pelerin Society
NBI	Nathaniel Branden Institute
NICB	National Industrial Conference Board
NRA	National Recovery Administration
NYU	New York University
OIRA	Office of Information and Regulatory Affairs
OMB	Office of Management and Budget
OSHA	Occupational Safety and Health Administration
RLA	Radical Libertarian Alliance

SDS   Students for a Democratic Society
SIL   Society for Individual Liberty
SRI   Society for Rational Individualism
YAF   Young Americans for Freedom

1 The Triumph and Crisis of Vital-Center Liberalism

A significant aspect of the history of the United States in the twentieth century has been the expanding power of the state and the eroding autonomy of the private economy and civil society. Although the transition from an essentially unregulated capitalism to a mixed economy began even before the turn of the century – witness the enactment of the Interstate Commerce Act in 1887 – and gathered pace through years of Progressive reform, "war collectivism", and the twenties' corporatist experiments, quite arguably the true watershed came with the triumph of reform liberalism in the thirties. With the Great Depression acting as a catalyst, New Deal liberals established what the political scientist Michael D. Reagan has called the "halfway house of American political economy" – residing "somewhere in the middle, between pure capitalism and pure socialism."[1]

A new political economy, New Deal liberalism, now supplanted the old order of nineteenth-century liberalism. The basic tenets of this now "classical" liberalism had included the following propositions: trade between individuals had both "efficiency and freedom-enhancing properties;" the market was a "spontaneous order for the allocation of resources;" trade between nations would maximize wealth and reduce the likelihood of war; and "public policy should be limited to the few common concerns of individuals," principally protection of life, liberty and property.[2]

New Deal liberalism did not so much repudiate these principles as modify them and balance them off against other considerations prompted by the experiences of war and depression. Indeed, much to the annoyance of classical liberals, the New Dealers appropriated the word "liberal" and insisted that they were merely reconfiguring liberalism to accommodate it to the

1

exigencies of the age.[3] The historian Alonzo L. Hamby has described this transforming effect:

> The New Deal made collectivist democratic liberalism the norm in American politics. Without explicitly repudiating the hallowed values of individualism and competition, it established a mixed, welfarist economy, accepted large-scale bureaucratic organization, and created an economic–political situation of countervailing powers.[4]

Much of the New Deal's agenda assumed that *laissez-faire* capitalism was defective. It was thought to suffer from a tendency toward monopoly, inequitable distribution of wealth, market failure, and cyclical instability. The efforts to overcome the depression would give capitalism's critics an opportunity to design a new political economy; out of these efforts came regulated capitalism, the mixed economy and the social welfare state.

Memories of World War One's business–government cooperation suggested some sort of economic planning to win the "war" against the depression. Alternative recovery strategies were proffered at the time but each had its disadvantages. The classic response to depression had been for the government to restrain its expenditures, encourage business to invest, and speak of nothing but sunshine while waiting for confidence to rebuild. Hoover's policies had expanded beyond this traditional approach by increasing government expenditures on public works projects, lending money to major banks and insurance companies, and urging businessmen to maintain wages – but to little avail.[5]

Other purgatives for the economy had their advocates. Monetary inflation to stimulate the economy appealed to the agrarian wing of the Democratic Party but was anathema to the Eastern wing. Anti-trust activity had its supporters but whatever its possible effect on the future health of the economy, it would take far too long to use as a remedy for the immediate economic illness. Although by 1938 certain Roosevelt appointees were advocating a Keynesian approach, Keynes's ideas were exotic in 1933.[6]

This left the example of what wartime government–business cooperation had accomplished. Unfortunately, there was considerable confusion about the meaning of the war experience.[7] When General Electric's Gerard Swope spoke of planning it was government-sanctioned single-industry trade association-determined production levels and prices – in effect, legalized cartels. What liberal planners had in mind was quite different, thinking of businesses "not as private property but as public utilities;" although liberals also stressed cooperation, "they meant cooperation between business and labor, agriculture, and consumer, with government both as mediator and special friend of the non-business group."[8]

The ineffective National Recovery Administration (NRA) was the result of these cross-pressures. By restricting output, its production codes encouraged higher prices that probably offset any stimulative effect of mandated higher wages. Dominated by big business, the code authorities soon came under attack from organized labor, small businessmen, and liberals. When the Supreme Court declared the NRA unconstitutional in 1935 few mourned. The experience with NRA greatly discredited the "very idea of national planning."[9]

Despite its failure, the NRA offered a precedent for other forms of interest-group politics, where the goal was government assistance in escaping market discipline. During the 1930s various sectors of the economy organized, lobbied, and achieved government-sanctioned cartelization, subsidization, or protection through such legislation as the Agricultural Adjustment Act, the Guffey-Snyder Act, the Motor Carrier Act or the Connally "Hot Oil" Act.

The experience of the NRA got many businessmen accustomed to working together and thinking along the lines of cartelization (where that tendency was not already present). Three ingredients were necessary for a successful effort to obtain congressional support: a desire, an effective lobbying organization, and an "plausible" justification. The latter often was an intellectual fig-leaf but was often resorted to all the same. Thus the maritime industries justified government regulation and subsidies as serving the national interest. The oil and coal industries argued for cartelization on the grounds of conservation. The trucking and air carriers insisted that they were quasi-public utilities. Labor benefitted from the image of the "little guy" at a time when the animus towards business was rather strong. Farmers played on the American nostalgia for the "agrarian way."

Not all sectors of the economy were cartelized in the 1930s as the New Deal's attitude toward business concentration was confused and contradictory.[10] Within the Democratic Party there were at least four different economic traditions: the agrarian interest in inflation dating to William Jennings Bryan, the small government philosophy of devotees of Grover Cleveland; the trust-busting tradition of Louis Brandeis and the New Freedom; and the New Nationalism of Theodore Roosevelt and Herbert Croly. Layered over these philosophical positions were the special interests of agriculture and labor and business, each seeking security against the economic storm.[11] As for the public, it was charmed by smallness and decentralization, but feared to give up the efficiencies of large-scale mass production. Although alarmed by sensational charges of corporate malfeasance, they were reluctant to endorse the kind of government economic planning advocated by Rexford Tugwell or Mordecai Ezekiel. The interplay of these factors produced the modern mixed economy with what Ellis Hawley has described as its "impairment of the efficiency of the competitive system without the compensating benefits of rationalized collective action."[12]

The Supreme Court initially resisted this expansion of national authority over the economy, striking down the first Agricultural Adjustment Act and the NRA. But in 1937 the Court surrendered, upholding the constitutionality of the National Labor Relations Act and the Social Security Act. A new national police power via a generous interpretation of the commerce clause now assured, as Robert Higgs has noted, that "virtually any federal economic regulation whatsoever would be free of constitutional restraint." A recent reviewer of this episode concluded that what happened in 1937 was revolutionary: the "United States made a fundamental change in its system of government without formally amending the Constitution." As a result the "Constitution [was] no longer, in consequence, an instrument by which the people [bound] their legislatures, their judges and themselves."[13]

Variously called the "broker state," "New Deal liberalism," or "interest group-liberalism," the new system pleased no one fully. Like most results of political compromise it lacked intellectual elegance. Arthur M. Schlesinger, Jr. characterized it as the work of a man, Franklin D. Roosevelt, who

> transcended systems for the sake of a more complex vision of America, which included elements of coordination and of decentralization, of nationalism and of internationalism, and thus also included means of preventing any system from being pushed to logical – and possibly destructive – extremes.[14]

Other writers have been less generous. Thomas K. McGraw, for example, has suggested that "it is possible to trace a line from the politics of the thirties to the present-day demands of an endless roster of interest groups: industries, labor unions, ethnic groups, feminists, farmers and so forth."[15]

Roosevelt early in the New Deal came about as close as anyone to defending the approach in economic terms, noting that "What we seek is balance – balance between agriculture and industry and balance between the wage earner, the employer and the consumer."[16] Perhaps the best justification for the broker state was a political one. Roosevelt suggested this in a 1936 commencement speech at Rollins College:

> It is the problem of Government to harmonize the interests of these groups which are often divergent and opposing, to harmonize them in order to guarantee security and good for as many of their individual members as may be possible. The science of politics, indeed, may properly be said to be in large part the science of the adjustment of conflicting group interests.[17]

The New Deal political economy provided a certain degree of security for its beneficiaries while inevitably generating some economic inefficiencies – inefficiencies that were deemed tolerable when they were recognized at such. Once the system was institutionalized "regulators traded innovation for stability."[18]

What is striking is how reluctant FDR's opponents to the left *and* the right were to accept the long-term viability of such a hybrid position. The socialist Harold Laski rejected the idea that one could build a "via media between capitalism and socialism." Editors of *The New Republic* agreed, insisting that "either the nation must put up with the confusions and miseries of an essentially unregulated capitalism or it must prepare to supersede capitalism with socialism."

For some conservatives Roosevelt was America's Kerensky, an interim figure destined like his 1917 Russian counterpart to be swept away by an even more radical revolution. Speaking in terms of a stark dichotomy, Hoover rejected any Kerensky-like compromise. "Either we shall have a society based upon ordered liberty and the initiative of the individual, or we shall have a planned society that means dictation no matter what you call it or who does it. There is no half-way ground." Even the usually moderate Alf Landon joined the naysayers in the heat of his 1936 failing effort to win the presidency, offering the nation a forced choice between a "planned economy" or a "democratic form of government."[19]

In retrospect these predictions of calamity seem a bit paradoxical in a nation that had a constitutional order premised on balance. Why was it so hard for some Americans to imagine a stable mixed economic order? Perhaps it was because some liberals advocated more radical changes. "Roosevelt and many of the New Deal policymakers had feelings about commerce that ranged from simple disinterest to positive revulsion."[20] Perhaps it was because in the 1936 presidential campaign Roosevelt down played the rhetoric of cooperation and spoke the language of class politics.[21] Perhaps it was because many Americans genuinely feared the potential for an American dictatorship in the thirties. Although America did not emulate Mussolini's corporatism or establish any of Stalin's gulags, the seeming opportunities alarmed many perfectly normal Americans.[22] Those who feared that the *via media* was unstable surely were not reassured by Friedrich Von Hayek's *The Road to Serfdom*, published in the US in 1944. Hayek warned that centralized planning led to dictatorship; the phrase "democratic socialism" was oxymoronic.[23]

If the transformation from a mixed economy to a totalitarian system was going to take place, many feared, as did Hayek, that war would provide the opportunity. Both liberal and conservative isolationists warned that American entrance into World War Two would bring dictatorship, either fascist or communist.[24] Yet in fact, American experience in World War Two belied these fears. Although the war encouraged Americans to look to Washington for succor, the feared dictatorship failed to materialize. Countervailing powers defeated any temptations to "rationalize" America in the interest of the Leviathan. When Roosevelt gave his support to legislation requiring national service it produced one of those curious political alignments characteristic of a pluralistic society. Arrayed against the bill were the National Association of Manufacturers, the Chamber of Commerce, the AFL and the CIO. Supporters included the War and Navy Departments, the American Legion and the Communist Party![25]

Paradoxically, the war effort may have assured that this *via media* would not edge over into some form of authoritarianism. For it was, according to the Keynesians, the massive deficit financing of the war that provided the stimulus to end the depression. The war's expansion of employment – seemingly a consequence of forced massive deficits – was an early and unplanned form of "military Keynesianism."[26]

Of all the essential features of modern liberalism, attempted management of the economy through Keynesian techniques was the latest to develop. Although Keynes met with Roosevelt in 1934, the President seems to not have understood him. Advocates of the Keynesian macroeconomics managed to persuade the President in the wake of the 1937 depression to call for a $3 billion deficit-financed recovery program.[27] How committed Roosevelt was to the Keynesian approach remains uncertain. In 1939 he privately urged his cabinet to speak publicly in favor of what he called "compensatory fiscal policy," but as late as 1945 he apparently had not fully comprehended the Keynesian message, as he then indicated his hope that the national war debt could be quickly extinguished.[28]

Two broad views of the proper role for the state competed for favor in the late New Deal. Some members of the Roosevelt administration argued that as a naturally harmonious economy was impossible, a permanently active government would be needed to supervise the behavior of corporations and defend consumers. Others placed more emphasis on the new Keynesian fiscal techniques to stimulate growth and solve social problems.

Both schools could draw support from the writings of Alvin Hansen of Harvard, the premier interpreter of Keynes to America in those days. Hansen claimed that the American economy had reached maturity, with few new frontiers to exploit. This interpretation seemed to offer support for both the regulatory and Keynesian views of the role of the state. As most industries were mature, businessmen would seek profits through collusion, thus necessitating a strong regulatory state. Keynesian fiscal stimulus would be necessitated to substitute for lost business investment opportunities. As wise federal spending would require planning, this suggested a substantial role for the National Resources Planning Board in targeting public works and formulating an intelligent fiscal policy.[29]

II

Enthusiasm for planning and the regulatory state faded even among New Dealers during World War Two as they encountered difficulties with planning, as anti-planning Republicans gained strength in Congress, and as the connection between planning and the very totalitarian nations they were fighting became evident. Simultaneously, the wartime prosperity gave new credibility to the business class and raised serious doubts, as Hansen admitted, about the "mature economy" thesis. As a result, argues Alan Brinkley, by war's end liberals had come to terms with capitalism. "They praised the New Deal for having solved the problems of capitalism;" they had used the state to save the economy without intruding the state too far into the economy." Reaching an accommodation with capitalism they now believed that "economic growth was the surest route to social progress." Rather than further reshape capitalist institutions, reformers "would reshape the economic and social environment in which those institutions worked." Government should play a balancing role, to "permit it to compensate for capitalism's inevitable flaws and omissions without interfering very much with its internal workings."[30]

Brinkley may somewhat predate the reconciliation between liberalism and capitalism that Schlesinger was to identify in 1949 as the Vital Center.[31] Nelson Lichtenstein, writing from a labor-left perspective, argues that a labor-capital accord (cost of living adjustments, productivity-based wage increases, privatized social welfare benefits, acquiescence in managements's rights to determine production goals) was not reached until the late forties. Until that time there was an opportunity for the triumph of a "social Keynesianism" rather than the "commercial Keynesianism" incorporated into the Vital Center. This "social Keynesianism" would have been a continuation of the wartime cooperation between management and labor espoused by certain liberal capitalists (Eric Johnston, Paul Hoffman, and Henry Kaiser) and the CIO's Phil Murray.

The result would have been a social welfare state similar to those of Northern Europe and the conversion of the Democratic Party into a labor party. Lichtenstein's own evidence shows just how improbable was such an outcome. President Harry S. Truman never was sympathetic to this approach. Indeed, Roosevelt's successor was an instinctive "big tent" pluralist who wanted the Democratic Party to be a broad-based coalition in which labor would have to get along with farmers, small business men, Southern segregationists and Northern blacks.

Other factors worked against the possibility of a Scandinavian-style comprehensive social welfare state. The American Federation of Labor rejected it, preferring voluntarism. Furthermore, the public's support for labor unions was in steep decline. Republicans triumphed in the 1946 congressional elections and enacted Taft–Hartley the following year. The Second Red Scare ultimately forced the CIO to expel eleven member unions to counter charges that the labor movement was heavily influenced by communists.[32]

The tempering of the utopian elements in the liberal credo probably was a reasonable and necessary accommodation if liberalism was to remain an important force in American politics. In

1945 liberalism faced the questions of whether it could survive the death of its greatest leader and develop roots in the American soil. If the reform movement had not rejected its popular front mentality and restrained its eschatological impulses by incorporating the insights of Reinhold Niebhur and Arthur Schlesinger, then liberalism might have failed by 1948. The New Deal wasn't destroyed by the Cold War. New Deal liberalism's impulse had been slowed if not stopped by 1938. Post-war polls showed most Americans apathetic about reform.[33]

Truman and his Chairman of the Council of Economic Advisers, Leon Keyserling, even hesitated to endorse commercial Keynesianism. They did, however, advocate the "economics of growth." Rejecting the proposition that social welfare policies should be financed by redistribution of wealth, Keyserling announced that social programs could be financed through increased federal revenues generated by an expanding private economy. Federal economic policies might facilitate that growth but the dynamo producing that "social dividend" would be the private sector.[34]

This growing respect for capitalism, albeit regulated capitalism, was a hallmark of Vital Center liberalism in the fifties and early sixties. In 1949 Schlesinger wrote *The Vital Center*, chastising the "doughface progressive" for his "sentimental belief in progress" and his conviction that the elimination of private property would produce heaven on earth.[35] In 1952 John Kenneth Galbraith published *American Capitalism: The Concept of Countervailing Power* in which he argued that big labor, big agriculture, big distribution and big government now restrained the power of big business; together they provided a substitute for the competition that had "regulated" small-scale capitalism in a now bygone era.[36]

Twelve years later, as this "Age of Consensus" entered its twilight years, Richard Hofstadter asked "What Happened to the Antitrust Movement?" and marveled at the transformation that had overcome old New Dealers like David Lilienthal and A. A. Berle, both of whom had published books in the fifties praising the social responsibility of big business.[37] This reconciliation between liberals and big business reflected a larger "celebration of America" to which many intellectuals succumbed in the fifties.[38] If this encomium for the capitalist order sounded similar to the rhetoric of the twenties, there were differences. These new cheerleaders for capitalism insisted on an "'umpire state' to promote, police, and mediate between economic interests."[39] Clearly this "New Liberalism" was no celebration of classical liberalism. What it was, as Lynn Hanrahan has shown, was an effort to reassure Cold War-era Americans that "the new capitalism was considerably more stable than its predecessor." Americans thus could cast off any lingering "depression psychosis" and focus on the prosecution of the Cold War, confident that a properly constrained capitalism was a progressive force.[40]

III

When the party of Vital Center liberalism returned to the White House with the election of John F. Kennedy in 1960, it brought with it a skeptical but confident technocratic style of liberalism. Bruce Miroff has characterized Kennedy as an exemplar of "pragmatic liberalism" – a form of liberalism which disguised its own ideological qualities by insisting that America was a land of shared values, leaving only the search for the most technically efficient means to implement those shared values. Those instrumental questions were "complicated and technical, and best left to the expertise of the political elite – or else explosive and divisive, and best left to the sobriety of the political elite."[41]

Stripped of its critical tone, this is a good description of Vital Center liberalism prior to the mid-sixties, when that consensus began to unravel. Unlike the old capitalism, the new version was "democratic" and had a "revolutionary potential for social justice." The key to this potential was economic growth, which would produce a "natural harmony of interests," with the workers "becoming members of the middle-class." Those social problems that remained could be solved by technocratic knowledge.[42]

If economic abundance was to be the source of "capital" for domestic reforms, then the first task for the Kennedy liberals was to stimulate the economy. All three members of Kennedy's

Council of Economic Advisors – Walter Heller of the University of Minnesota, James Tobin of Yale, and Kermit Gordon of Williams College – were Keynesians. Heller urged Kennedy to seek a tax cut to energize the economy. This proposal to deliberately engineer a deficit at a time when the economy was not in depression but only expanding more slowly than preferred was an example of advanced Keynesian thinking: economists could micro-manage or "fine-tune" the economy to achieve a higher GNP than absent government ministrations might occasion.

The incorporation of this theory in the 1964 "Kennedy" tax cut would be the final stage in the political legitimization of Keynesian economics. Most economists had already accepted the Keynesian paradigm as a result of the apparent stimulative effects of the 1938 tax cut and of the massive World War Two deficits. After the war the debate within the profession centered on how to apply Keynesian techniques in more normal times and whether additional interventions were necessary to produce social justice. Herbert Stein has identified four "schools of thought" in the late forties and early fifties:

1. "Strict and exclusive Keynesians" who relied almost exclusively on fiscal policy to maintain full employment, dismissed the risks of inflation, and generally were unenthusiastic about government economic planning or additional regulation of the economy.

2. "Reformers and planners" who endorsed Keynesian techniques but also argued for an advanced liberal agenda of government economic coordination and major expansion of the social welfare state.

3. "Conservative macroeconomists" who accepted the general thrust of Keynesian ideas but insisted that monetary policy played a role in determining demand, worried about inflation because of the likely inflationary bias of political management, and doubted the practical feasibility of making the timely economic measurements necessary for fine-tuning the economy.

4. "Conventional Conservatives" who rejected Keynes and all his works and cast "anathemas" on the New Deal.[43]

The Keynesianism of the "conservative macroeconomists" prevailed as *de-facto* government policy until the 1960s. The approach was given the imprimatur of the "enlightened" business community when endorsed by the Committee on Economic Development (CED) in its 1947 policy statement, *Taxes and the Budget: A Program for Prosperity in a Free Economy*. The CED document called for a budget and tax rates calculated to produce a modest surplus at high employment. This would provide an "automatic stabilizer" for the economy: during prosperity the budget surplus would dampen inflation and during recession, the deficit produced by lowered revenues would stimulate the depressed economy.

During the Eisenhower years, the automatic stabilizer system was employed in 1953–54 and 1958 when the government declined to raise taxes in the middle of recessions.[44] This passive form of Keynesianism was as far as the administration would go and it never publicly acknowledged its Keynesian nature, but as Eisenhower confided to Secretary of the Treasury Robert Anderson, the concept of an annually balanced budget was "by way of being a great cliché, anyway."[45]

To admit to a Keynesian approach would have opened Eisenhower to attacks from the conservative, Chamber of Commerce, National Association of Manufacturers small-business wing of the party, for whom "Keynes" was a symbol for a positive activist government that was only one step removed from socialism.

When Kennedy took office in 1961 his political advisors were keenly aware of political opposition to Keynesian ideas among conservatives, including Southern Democrats. When Harvard Economist Paul Samuelson chaired a pre-inaugural task force on economic policy, Ted Sorensen and Richard Goodwin sat in and were horrified that the panel was considering a tax cut. They saw to it that the idea was quickly shelved.[46]

Only after Kennedy had been thoroughly tutored by Walter Heller in the advantages of the new economics did the President make his famous 1962 Yale Commencement address in which he rejected ideological rhetoric and advocated a technocratic liberalism. Kennedy boldly proclaimed that "[w]hat is at stake in our economic decisions today is not some grand warfare of rival ideological passions which will sweep the country with passion but the practical management of the modern economy."[47] Although the Keynesians were jubilant about the speech, Kennedy hesitated until late 1962 to propose a tax cut. Kennedy delayed until he had evidence that much of the business class would support him.

In fact the climate of opinion had been changing within the business class for some time. As far back as the mid-fifties the Committee for Economic Development – representing more "progressive" business sentiment – had endorsed the idea of tax cuts in a non-depression situation. In the summer of 1962 the more conservative Chamber of Commerce endorsed tax cuts to overcome stagnation and prevent a possible recession. When Kennedy spoke to the Economic Club of New York that December he preached the gospel of the new economics to a receptive audience. The president of the National Association of Manufacturers responded enthusiastically to Kennedy's message. The same day as the speech the CED issued a policy statement calling for immediate tax reduction to stimulate growth. Heller summed up the growing consensus in a December 16, 1962 memo to Kennedy:

> When the Chicago Board of Commerce, the AFL-CIO, the CED, and the U.S. Chamber of Commerce are on the same side – when repeated editorials in Business week are indistinguishable from those appearing in the *Washington Post* – the prospect for action cannot be wholly dim. Can 3000 members of the N.Y. Economic Club be wrong?[48]

Although passage of the tax cut was delayed until 1964, its enactment was viewed at the time as the great political triumph of the Keynesian paradigm. It provided confirmation of certain attitudinal changes among educated elites that had been under way for some time. An indication of the change was the 1964 response of the Harvard Class of 1939 to the survey question: "Are you in favor of or opposed to the ideas of John Maynard Keynes?" More than four out of seven responded favorably towards Keynes.[49]

No one did more to form the economic views of post-World War Two collegiates than Paul Samuelson, himself a Hansen student. In 1948 Samuelson published *Economics: An Introductory Analysis,* which quickly became the primary pedagogical dispenser of Keynesian macro-economics, selling tens of millions of copies in more than 25 languages by 1985.[50] In a 1985 lecture, Samuelson wittily reflected on the impact of his text:

> Soon the smoke of burning mortgages could be sniffed in Belmont, Massachusetts. More than this, J. K. Galbraith's prophesy in a *Fortune* review, that a new generation would receive its economics from *Economics*, turned out to be right on the mark. PAS was heard to mutter complacently, "Let those who will write the nation's laws if I can write its text-books." Being denounced by William Buckley for blaspheming God and man at Yale, the textbook took on a new aura of respectability and sales soared all over the world.[51]

Samuelson accurately characterized the influence of his text. The generation of university students who studied Samuelson (and his imitators) were predisposed to believe that demand-management might enhance economic growth; the performance of the economy in the mid-1960s seemed to provide confirmation.

Delighted by this boom, *Time* put Keynes on its December 31, 1965 cover and declared his theories "a prime influence on the world's free economies." The news weekly was confident that a prudent application of Keynesian principles had permitted the nation to "avoid violent [business] cycles" while achieving "phenomenal economic growth" with "remarkably stable prices."[52]

Social reformers were equally enthusiastic about the 1964 tax cut's implications: reform projects could be financed without challenging the social covenant between the broad middle class and the government. As Heller put it in 1966: "When the cost of fulfilling a people's aspirations can be met out of a growing horn of plenty – instead of robbing Peter to pay Paul – ideological roadblocks melt away, and consensus replaces conflict."[53]

IV

The Vital Center consensus was beginning its collapse at the very time that Heller was publishing its celebration in 1966.

Committed to exceeding Roosevelt's record, Lyndon Baines Johnson had launched nearly simultaneous wars against domestic poverty and communist insurgency in South East Asia. But as Doris Kearns has noted, there was a crucial difference between the two presidents' timing: "Roosevelt did not attempt the New Deal and World War II at the same time. Only Johnson among the Presidents sought to be simultaneously first in peace and first in war".[54]

Worse yet, although Roosevelt's overseas enemies, the Axis powers, were credible threats to American national security, such could not readily be concluded about North Vietnam. Whatever the plausibility of the Johnson Administration argument that North Vietnam was a junior partner of a threatening "Peking–Jakarta axis," the argument collapsed after 1965, when the Indonesian army crushed the attempted PKI coup and China, enveloped by the Cultural Revolution, turned inward."[55]

Johnson pressed on with his dual wars, resisting counsel from his Keynesian economic advisors in December 1965 that a tax increase was necessary to contain inflationary pressures produced by the stimulative effect of defense spending. Fearful that a call for tax increases would spell doom for funding of his domestic programs, the President produced a budget projection for fiscal 1968 that relied on the hidden assumption that the Vietnam War would end by the summer of 1967. Johnson did not finally ask Congress for a 10 percent surtax until August 1967. The Revenue and Expenditure Control Act did not become law until June 28, 1968, too late to prevent an inflation rate of 4.7 percent in December 1968.[56]

Reflecting in 1970 on this unhappy episode, Arthur M. Okun, Johnson's last Chairman of the Council of Economic Advisors, suggested that Congress "must face up to the challenge either by improving their record or by delegating authority to the President."[57] But this observation only confirmed the points made by critics of the "New Economics." Milton Friedman, Professor of Economics at the University Chicago and a leading monetarist, had repeatedly warned against using fiscal policy as a "balance wheel" for the economy. Not only would such correctives likely come too late to have the desired effects but politics would likely make it difficult to raise taxes to cut off an inflation. An "asymmetry" would develop regarding the manipulation of tax rates, "making the declines politically more palatable than the rises."[58] Delegating authority to the President to make fiscal policy, as Okun suggested, would only confirm the warning by anti-Keynesians that Keynesian techniques were biased towards authoritarian rule.

Friedman's attack on Keynesian macro-economic policy during the Johnson years went beyond pointing out the technical and political impediments to its timely application. He insisted that Keynesian assumptions were wrong. There was no Keynesian "multiplier" capable of stimulating a lagging economy. The fiscal stimulus provided by government deficit spending would be canceled out by the government borrowing necessary to finance the deficit. Furthermore, raising taxes to soak up inflation when an economy was over-heated wouldn't stop inflation. Although increased taxes would withdraw dollars from the economy, there would be a compensating increase in availability of dollars because the government's borrowing needs would drop.[59]

The late sixties gave an opportunity to test Friedman's proposition that "money mattered" against the Keynesian predictions of first Gardner Ackley and then Okun at the CEA. In September of 1966 Ackley looked at the increasing deficit and predicted accelerating inflation. Friedman looked at the credit crunch engineered by the Federal Reserve that spring and predicted a recession. Although the economy never went into actual contraction there was no growth in the first quarter of 1967 and only modest growth in the second. Friedman's forecast had been the more accurate of the two.

A second test came in the second half of 1968. In the light of the adoption of the Revenue and Expenditure Control Act providing for a 10 percent surtax and a $6 billion reduction in planned expenditure, Okun, now Chair of the CEA, predicted GNP would grow only 1 percent for the last six months of 1968 and not at all for the subsequent six months. Friedman looked at evidence that the Fed was pumping up the money supply and predicted inflation. *Contra* Okun, in December 1968 the GNP was growing by 4 percent, unemployment stood at 3.3 percent and inflation was nearing 5 percent. Keynesians were forced to admit that money mattered, that the multiplier was no ways near as large as previously thought, and that crowding-out did occur.[60]

Friedman was already launching additional assaults on the Keynesian edifice. In his 1967 Presidential Address to the American Economic Association he argued that the Phillips Curve – which suggested a trade-off between inflation and unemployment – was not a permanent relationship. Once employees began anticipating inflation they would raise their wage demands sufficiently to curtail any stimulative effects of the inflation. Only an accelerating inflation rate, Friedman warned, could produce a reduction in unemployment beyond the short term. "The temporary trade-off comes not from inflation per se, but from unanticipated inflation, which generally means, from a rising rate of inflation."[61]

Friedman insisted that there was a "natural rate of unemployment" to which unemployment rates would tend absent government monetary interventions. If Friedman was correct then this meant that another purpose for an activist government macroeconomic policy was weakened. There was no case for viewing relatively high rates of inflation as an acceptable trade-off for keeping unemployment low. The full implications of Friedman's critique came with the stagflation of the seventies when "[w]hat looked like a stable Phillips curve from 1960 to 1969, as the economy went through a long phase of expansion, fell apart as inflationary expectations got built into the economy."[62]

Disillusioning experiences with trying to fine-tune an economy and the theoretical and empirical assaults from the monetarists and the rational expectations schools combined to produce a crisis of confidence for many Keynesians by the mid-seventies. In a "Statement of Purposes" in the 1978 inaugural issue of the *Journal of Post Keynesian Economics* the editors acknowledged the problems with Keynesianism. The débâcle of stagflation had demonstrated "its policy ineptitude."[63] The same year the economist James W. Dean interviewed 15 prominent older economists at the annual convention of the American Economic Association. Dean found that they had "retreated from activism, crediting their latterly wisdom to an inextricable mix of old age, events inconsistent with Keynesianism, and even the immutable advance of logic."[64]

V

The crisis of Vital Center liberalism extended far beyond problems with macro-economic management. Attempts of the Kennedy and Johnson administrations to eliminate poverty confronted a vastly different and more complicated situation than Roosevelt had faced in the thirties. The poverty of the thirties was palpable and widespread. Although the poverty of the sixties was substantial, the Administration thought it was isolated and receding. There was no sense that pressures from the poor or their spokespersons required a dramatic initiative. As Daniel Patrick Moynihan noted in 1969, "the war on poverty was not declared at the behest of the poor: it was declared in their interest by persons confident of their judgement in such matters."[65]

Walter Heller began lobbying Kennedy for a coordinated antipoverty program in 1962. Although Kennedy did approve Heller's establishment of a poverty task force, there was little sense at the time of Kennedy's death that the national was facing any social crisis.[66]

Johnson proceeded to make the poverty issue his own, portraying it as Kennedy's last wish, although there is little evidence for this proposition.[67] When the War on Poverty turned sour, it tarnished the Vital Center. The stories of corrupted community action programs, violent Job Corps camps, and burning innercities contributed to the increasing public skepticism of government's competency and its public disinterestedness. According to public opinion surveys the percentage of the public that trusted government to do what is right "Only some/None of the time" increased from 22 percent in 1964 to 31 percent in 1966 and 37 percent in 1968. The percentages who thought government was run for a "Few big interests" expanded similarly: 1964 (18 percent), 1966 (38 percent) and 1968 (44 percent).[68]

The disillusionment extended to many within the intellectual class. The failures of the Johnson programs produced "a crisis of the spirit for American liberalism" with the more radical elements concluding that "the United States was a more malign nation at the end of Johnson's administration" while those who were to become the neoconservatives "began to question the whole complex of assumptions that lay beneath American liberalism."[69]

The sixties had begun with considerable confidence among the intelligentsia that government intervention informed by social science could solve social and economic problems. Testifying before a congressional committee in the late fifties, Paul Samuelson assured the members that "a community can have full employment, can at the same time have a rate of capital formation it wants, and can accomplish all of this compatibility [*sic*] with the degree of income distribution it ethically desires."[70]

Galbraith was equally confident of the therapeutic powers of the state:

> Much can be done to treat those characteristics which cause people to reject or be rejected by the modern industrial society. Educational deficiencies can be overcome. Mental deficiencies can be treated. Physical handicaps can be remedied. The limiting factor is not knowledge of what can be done. Overwhelmingly it is our failure to invest in people.[71]

As political scientist Robert C. Wood, a member of Kennedy's Academic Advisory Committee and later Johnson's Secretary of HUD, has noted, social scientists were increasingly confident of their capacities by 1960: "The conviction that 'our time had come' rang through professional journals, scholarly press books, and the public pronouncements of academic experts."[72]

Operating within the Vital Center paradigm, the Kennedy and Johnson administrations sought primarily technocratic knowledge from the academy. Systems analysis, cost-benefit calculations, econometric studies, behavior modification – these were the terms of the "action-intellectuals" of the sixties. A 1965 memo from John H. Rubel to Sargent Shriver illustrates their assumption of humanity's essential plasticity. Analyzing the Job Corps program Rubel told Shriver that it was a complex machine designed to mold people. "The input – the raw material – that is fed into this machine is people. The output is people. It is the function of this machine to transform people."[73] Despite Rubel's air of confidence, experience with War on Poverty programs suggested that transforming people was more difficult than anticipated. A raft of studies, many of them commissioned by government agencies presiding over aspects of the reform agenda, challenged the expectations of the action-intellectuals.

Education researchers, for example, found results that dashed liberal hopes. The Office of Education commissioned James S. Coleman to determine what quantifiable measures best correlated with student performance so that federal compensatory monies might be most effectively targeted. The 1966 Coleman Report concluded that there was no credible evidence that such factors as classroom size, expenditures per pupil, teachers' salaries or quality of the curriculum had any significant affect on learning.[74]

Coleman's data were reanalyzed for the US Commission on Civil Rights by Thomas pettigrew of Harvard who discovered in it evidence that black students attending predominantly white schools had better grades than those in segregated schools. Although the Commission did not call for busing to achieve integration, it did suggest that the federal government should set a uniform standard for racial balance, perhaps no more than 50 percent black student population per school, and then provide financial assistance to achieve this balance.[75] Given the nature of residential patterns in most cities, such a standard could only be achieved through busing. In 1972 the Harvard sociologist David Armor reviewed the evidence on busing's effects on black achievement. He concluded that "none of the studies were able to demonstrate conclusively that integration has had an effect on academic achievement as measured by standardized tests."[76]

Similarly discouraging evaluations of job training programs were available by the late sixties. A 1968 report on the 1962 Manpower Development and Training Act concluded that it at best trained its participants for low-skill jobs for which there already was a large supply of labor. Reports on the Job Corps were equally depressing. Throughout the first decade of its existence, two-thirds of the participants quit before completing the program. Graduates did no better in the job market than "no shows" (applicants for the program who had not appeared).[77]

Whatever chance there was for many Great Society programs to succeed was vitiated by Johnson's own actions. Determined to be loved, to establish his own record separate from Kennedy's, and to exceed Roosevelt's record of legislative achievements, Johnson was often incautious in the extreme.[78] Disgusted with conservative critics, he told Richard Goodwin that "I'm sick of all the people who talk about the things we can't do. Hell, we're the richest country in the world, the most powerful. We can do it all".[79]

He expanded an urban pilot program, adding projects in as many congressional's districts as thought necessary to insure legislative passage. Thus the Model Cities Program, intended by Robert Wood's Task Force to fund five or six demonstration projects, was increased to 66. White House officials promised more than one hundred legislators that they would not be overlooked when the time came to select the winning cities. When the choices were made the winners were selected primarily on political criteria. The Model Cities Program proved a failure: monies were too small for the number of cities involved and the federal bureaucracies that were supposed to cooperate refused, protecting their turfs. In his evaluation of this episode, Thomas S. Langston concluded that the planners and intellectuals were hopelessly naive:

> Mainstream liberal ideologists were generally ill-prepared for the trench warfare of bureaucratic politics. They failed to foresee that their plan's assumptions regarding the coordinating and planning capacities of government were in fact assumptions, not statements of fact. They also, in part because of the absence in their ideology of an ascriptive component, underestimated the popular and political resistance their plans would face.[80]

The New Deal coalition had always been an amalgam of interest groups whose loyalty to liberalism had been greatly dependent upon their protected position within the mixed economy. Even admirers of the pluralist, Madisonian model of the

American system, such as Robert Dahl, had to admit that inter-est-group liberalism accommodated primarily those who were politically active. "Hence if a group is inactive, whether by free choice, violence, intimidation, or law, the normal American system does not provide it with a checkpoint anywhere in the process." Dahl had suggested that the "excluded" could gain "entry" by threatening violence, threatening to deprive other groups of their legitimacy, or by acquiring legitimacy and "hence motivating the in-groups to incorporate the outgroup."[81]

These War on Poverty efforts to expand opportunities for minorities and the poor threatened the power of the Democratic Party's traditional interest-groups. The idea that the poor might be organized so they could assert themselves like other better-positioned groups prompted activists/social scientists Lloyd Ohlin and Richard Cloward to endorse the Johnson administra-tion's establishment of community action programs. Expectations varied, however, as to how community action programs would operate to "empower" the poor; moderate reformers assumed that the local agencies would coordinate the delivery of services and job training so that the poor could ultimately leave the ranks of the impoverished. They hoped to "get the poverty out of the people – and afterward the people out of the poverty."[82] Radicals like Cloward anticipated using the tactics of confrontation such as rent strikes and school boycotts as part of a strategy whose ultimate goal was redistribution of income.[83]

The War on Poverty had assumed that economic growth pro-duced by Keynesian demand-management would create more jobs, civil rights laws would break down racial barriers to those jobs, and various social and educational programs would combat the culture of poverty and prepare the poor for job opportunities. The Council of Economic Advisors (CEA), however, suggested that some poverty was structural and would not be eliminated by such strategies. To the extent that poverty was structural, the CEA advised that it could only be eliminated by government job creation and income transfers.[84]

By 1965 a growing segment of expert opinion was becoming skeptical of the ability of rehabilitation to move people from poverty; support was growing for some sort of guaranteed annual income.[85] In 1966 Sargent Shriver, head of the Office of Economic Opportunity, told CBS that some sort of income-maintenance program was necessary.[86] The following year, Frances Fox Piven and Richard Cloward, with assistance from the Legal Aid Office – created by the War on Poverty itself – helped George Wiley establish the National Welfare Rights Organization.

This welfare lobby tried to facilitate access to welfare benefits and demanded a guaranteed annual income of $6500 for a family of four. The message of the National Welfare Rights Organization was that in America practically every interest group received welfare, most of it more bountiful and less legitimate than that received by the poor. "It's called 'farm subsidies' or 'defense contracts' or 'guaranteed loans' or 'oil depletion allowances' or 'tax-free capital gains' – in short socialism for the rich and free enterprise for the poor."[87] Thus in a matter of several years agents of liberalism had gone from designing a program to aid the poor in escaping welfare to institutionalizing welfare recipients as an interest group.

Rejecting the "culture of poverty" argument, some liberal intellectuals offered justifications for the new scheme. Poverty was the result of forces external to the poor and welfare should be viewed as a right.

> This view, or something very much like it, lay behind the drive that began in the mid-1960s and reached its apogee in the early 1970s, to deliver welfare payments ... without any coercion or requirements that recipients of aid do anything in return for it.[88]

An example of this reasoning was Yale Law Professor Charles A. Reich's argument that new forms of property rights were developing as a result of the growth of the state. Governments provided citizens with various boons: income and benefits, jobs, occupational licenses, franchises, contracts, subsidies, and services. For Reich, benefits like unemployment compensation, Social Security, or public assistance should be construed as property. They represented an individual's rightful claim on the public-interest state. As it was impossible to return to the old *laissez-faire* capitalist order, the state must guarantee the autonomy of the individual by vesting him with these new property rights. "Only by making such benefits into rights can the welfare state achieve its goal of providing a secure minimum basis for individual well-being and dignity in a society where each man cannot be wholly the master of his own destiny."[89]

If the National Welfare Rights Organization never achieved its goal of a $6500 guaranteed annual income, it did participate in the defeat of President Richard M. Nixon's proposed guaranteed annual income bill. Attacking the $1600 figure for a family of four as totally inadequate, it characterized the bill's work requirement as "genocide." Advanced liberal Senators denounced the Nixon proposal as miserly. Perhaps most generous was Senator Eugene McCarthy, who called for a minimum grant of $5000 with a marginal tax rate so low that the program would have cost $100 billion per year.[90]

If advanced liberalism's views on welfare rights challenged American values about self-reliance and the responsibility to work, affirmative action as it developed by the late sixties proved hard to reconcile with the American vaunted rhetorical support for individualism. But in truth, the New Deal had done much that contradicted that ideal. The cartelization of favored industry, subsidization of farmers, and regulation of labor markets could not readily be squared with the older doctrine of equality before the law. Just the same, although New Deal liberalism had endorsed special rights for privileged groups, it had never promised equality of outcome. Even with the Wagner Act backing them, labor unions still had to rely on their own bargaining skills. "Any equalizing of results that might follow, however – and the act did anticipate that the 'purchasing power of wage earners in industry' would be increased – was up to individual and group effort."[91]

The War on Poverty did become a vehicle for black social mobility. In 1970, 57 percent of all black male college graduates and 72 percent of black female college graduates worked for government, many of them in programs that had their origins in the sixties. Black employed in the private sector were disproportionately found in companies that came under the affirmative action strictures of the Equal Employment Opportunities Commission established by the 1964 Civil Rights Act.[92] But these affirmative action achievements produced "a social cleavage that fractured the American consensus on the meaning of justice itself."[93]

Stymied in 1968 by the old-style politics of the New Deal's traditional interest groups, Senator George McGovern's 1972 presidential bid was the vehicle chosen by the new elements (environmentalists, feminists, gays, welfare rights activists) seeking to expand the range of players in Democratic Party interest-group politics. Also supporting McGovern in 1972 was the old-line liberal reform group, Americans for Democratic Action, which had been transformed in 1968 by "socialists who had repudiated the limited welfare state, independent Democrats who had lost faith in the Democratic Party."[94]

Elected under the "McGovern Rules," the demographics of the 1972 delegates differed markedly from those of previous nominating conventions. Between the 1968 and 1972 conventions the number of women delegates increased from 13 percent to 40 percent, blacks and other non-whites from 6 percent to 15 percent, those under age 30 from 3 percent to 22 percent. Elements of the New Class (primarily professionals such as lawyers, teachers, journalists or information managers who worked for the government or were employed in post-industrial sectors of the private economy) increased in number while the proportions of businessmen, workers, and farmers decreased. Iowa's delegation, for example, had no farmers, while New York's, representing the most unionized state in the country, had three union members and nine representatives of gay liberation organizations.[95]

The gap between the attitudes of the delegates to the national convention and of rank-and-file Democrats could hardly have been starker. For 57 percent of the delegates the major consideration in social welfare policy should be to abolish poverty; only 22 percent of the rank and file agreed, some 69 percent of them indicating that the obligation to work was the prime consideration. On busing the gap was even more glaring, with 66 percent of the delegates favoring it while 82 percent of the rank and file opposed it. While 78 percent of the delegates thought the prime consideration in dealing with crime was protection of the rights of the accused, only 36 percent of the rank and file agreed.[96]

The 26 000-word platform only confirmed these delegate preferences, with its call for immediate withdrawal from Vietnam and its endorsement of busing, increased progressivity in the income tax, a guaranteed annual income above the poverty line, abolition of capital punishment, amnesty for draft resisters and gender equity in the allocation of top government positions.[97] Unfortunately for the new interest groups, McGovern's defeat proved so devastating, winning the electoral votes only of Massachusetts and the District of Columbia, that Presidential liberalism proved incapable of resurrection for at least 20 years.

VI

By the early seventies paradigmatic Vital-Center liberalism had demonstrated unanticipated weaknesses. Its reliance on Keynesian macro-economics had proved excessive as it proved impossible to fine-tune an economy with the blunt tools of fiscal and monetary policy. Similarly the Keynesians were at a loss to explain "stagflation." Unable to maintain the high growth rates of the sixties or to contain inflation, liberalism's unindexed progressive tax rates were driving middle-class taxpayers into brackets previously reserved for the affluent.[98]

Vital Center liberalism had defaulted on its promise to end poverty and dependency. The 1968–69 report of the Social Science Research Council pointed to the hubris of such a venture: "We want to eliminate poverty, crime, drug addiction and abuse; we want to improve education and strengthen family life, but we do not know how."[99] Efforts to acquire the knowledge that would permit the elimination of poverty through the meliorative techniques of technocratic liberalism proved unavailing. Systematic experiments with a negative tax, for example, demonstrated considerable work disincentive and family break-up, prompting social science researchers Gary Burtless and

Robert H. Havemen to conclude that "if you advocate a particular policy reform of innovation, do not press to have it tested."[100]

Liberals also had increasing doubts about the wisdom of their commitment to interest-group liberalism. A particularly influential critic was Theodore J. Lowi, recognized in an American Political Science Association survey as the most significant political scientist of the seventies.[101] In *The End of Liberalism*, first published in 1968, Lowi had indicted interest-group liberalism for producing a bloated government. He warned that "[g]overnment that is unlimited in scope but formless in action is government that cannot plan." Lowi faulted the basic assumptions of the pluralist model and rejected the idea that a system of bargaining interest groups was self-correcting. He called into question the assumption that all "groups have other groups to confront in some kind of competition" and declared it a myth that "when competition between or among groups takes place the results yield a public interest or some other ideal result."[102]

Lowi's critique of interest-group liberalism was widely assigned in political science classes in the seventies. One of Lowi's readers was David A. Stockman, future Director of President Ronald W. Reagan's Office of Management and Budget (OMB). Re-reading *The End of Liberalism* during the 1972 McGovern campaign, Stockman found that Lowi's message "rang out with decisive lucidity." Here was a political Rosetta Stone for the future OMB Director, explaining public policy "not [as] a high-minded nor even an ideological endeavour, but simply a potpourri of parochial claims, proffered by private interests parading in government dress."[103]

Although a Democrat was elected President in 1976, Jimmy Carter came to office not as an advocate of expanded government but rather as a self-avowed fiscal conservative. Although he claimed to be quite liberal regarding the environment, civil rights, and helping people rise from poverty, he failed to demonstrate how these agendas could be advanced without large new expenditures and regulations.[104] Eventually frustrated in his efforts, Carter seemed to all but give up on liberalism in his 1978 State of the Union Address: "Government cannot solve our problems. It can't set our goals. It can't define our vision.

Government cannot eliminate poverty, or provide a bountiful economy, or reduce inflation or save our cities."[105]

This presidential abdication illustrated the depressed condition of the party of liberalism in the late seventies. No longer the proponent of new ideas, liberalism found itself in a debilitated state as for the first time in its history it was now forced to confront a serious intellectual and political challenge from the right.

With a nearly 50-year record available for inspection by 1980, New Deal liberalism and its rococo embellishments of the sixties had been targeted for more than a decade by a re-born classical liberalism. Although lying long in the womb, this vigorous new champion of the spontaneous order now threatened to drive an enervated reform liberalism from the field, perhaps heralding the long-awaited political realignment.

2 The Revitalization of Market Liberalism

Writing in 1950, Lionel Trilling lamented that New Deal liberalism so dominated American political thought. Conservatism, he observed, offered only "irritable mental gestures" rather than sustained rigorous thought. Liberalism risked becoming "stale, habitual and inert." To avoid this condition liberals would need to be their own critics.[1]

This "Age of Consensus" dominated the academy and the national media in the fifties and sixties and formed what William C. Berman has called an "informal liberal establishment." Within its intellectual ranks were

> economists from the Brookings Institution, policy planners at the Ford Foundation, social scientists and law professors from Harvard University and other elite institutions, journalists from the *New York Times* and the *Washington Post* ... and powerful public interest law firms in Washington.[2]

As it was a broad consensus there was room for argument but clearly the center of gravity shifted leftward in the sixties, producing policy advocacy by "advanced liberals" that could hardly be distinguished from socialist ideas.[3]

However broad the liberal spectrum by the mid-sixties, all these variants inherited from New Deal liberalism certain views regarding capitalism that clearly distinguished them from classical, or market, liberalism. They all rejected the proposition that spontaneous economic forces could maintain full employment and efficient utilization of factors of production. This deficiency of capitalism necessitated an active and flexible macroeconomic policy. Additionally, following an indictment as old as the Progressive Era, they charged that capitalism had a tendency towards monopoly and suffered serious market failures – producing negative externalities, an inadequate supply of public goods, and an inequitable income distribution. Furthermore, the consumer in a *laissez-faire* regime found himself unprotected against errors of judgement caused by insufficient information or his preference for present consumption over future well-being. Clearly, the New Deal liberal concluded, an activist government had to protect the citizen by using the national police power.[4]

How activist and with what instruments would vary with the individual reformers. Some preferred a social democracy similar to the Scandinavian model; others opted for a vigorous application of "commercial Keynesianism," regulated industries, and a restrained welfare state. But in no cases were there calls for a substantial reduction in the government's obligations.

I

Challenging this broad consensus in 1965 was a reviving but as yet little-noticed defense of market liberalism that was to mount a remarkably strong public critique of reform liberalism's assumptions. This almost moribund classical liberal stream had begun to revive at the end of World War Two with the 1944 publication of Friedrich von Hayek's *The Road to Serfdom*. Hayek had warned that centralized planning would doom both democracy and capitalism, leading to one form of totalitarianism or another:

> It is now often said that democracy will not tolerate "capitalism". If "capitalism" means here a competitive system based on free disposal over private property, it is far more important to realize that only within this system is democracy possible. When it becomes dominated by a collectivist creed, democracy will inevitably destroy itself.[5]

As Peter J. Boettke has recently noted, Hayek anticipated the arguments of the Public Choice school of economists "in pointing out the organizational logic implied in the substitution of community decision making by its representatives to form a collective plan for the private decisions of individuals in the market place." As the decision-makers will not have the information available to rationally plan the economy, that information being decentralized and often tacit, those persons who have a "comparative advantage in exercising discretionary power will survive."[6] Not good men but rather the cynical and thuggish would rise to the top.

The book received considerable attention in England where Hayek held a Chair at the London School of Economics, but its reception in the United States was quite beyond anything the author could have anticipated. Henry Hazlitt and John Davenport reviewed it favorably in *The New York Times Book Review* and *Fortune* respectively. The Reader's Digest distributed a condensed version and various business organizations purchased bulk quantities of the book for distribution to members.[7]

Predictably, liberal journals such as the *New Republic* dismissed the book as over-wrought and hackneyed while Herbert Finer rushed out a response, *The Road to Reaction*, that called Hayek's little book the "most sinister offensive against democracy to emerge from a democratic country for many decades." Government planning was not antithetical to democracy, Finer asserted, because in the elective process voters would be "judging the purposes of the plan, and the merits of the men and the measures to carry it out." Plans in a democracy would not be imposed from the top down but rather, responsive to the demands of the people. "Hayek's Assumption is that political power is neither limited in scope, restricted in authority, responsible in operation, nor co-operative and decentralized in execution. This assumption," warned Finer, "is stupid."[8]

The vigorous reaction to *The Road to Serfdom* may have been attributable in good part to Hayek's insistence on identifying Nazism and communism as equal offenders against the liberty of the individual.[9] In 1944 "popular frontism" was still acceptable to a majority of American liberals. Whether Hayek's emphasis on the similarity of Nazism and communism was spontaneous is uncertain. He may have been influenced by the ideas of his mentor, Ludwig von Mises, who published *Omnipotent Government* in the same year as *Serfdom*. Mises, another Austrian economist in exile from the tyrannies of Nazism, warned in *Omnipotent Government* that American liberals had to purge themselves of their support for restrictions on economic liberties if they were to defeat the forces of totalitarianism. Mises's message that New Deal Liberalism's economic policies were just a pale version of Hitler's policies garnered him little popularity at a time when the reputation of *laissez-faire* capitalism was perhaps at its nadir.[10] Later, when the Cold War developed, Vital-Center liberals were more open to his suggestion of similarities between fascism and communism.[11] Undoubtedly the Mises and Hayek tracts exaggerated the danger that the American mixed economy might fall prey to totalitarian temptations. Perhaps this is explained by the fact that both of them were central Europeans who had little experience with the strengths of a pluralistic democracy. James Madison had argued in Federalist Papers Ten and Fifty-One that a multiplicity of factions would be a bulwark against tyranny. Vital Center liberals were to find Madison's thought reassuring as they re-examined modern democracy's susceptibility to manipulation by totalitarian movements.[12]

The long-term survivability of a regulated capitalism seemed less probable to many intellectuals in 1945 than it was to become with time. The Austrian economic historian Karl Polyani in *The Great Transformation*, published the same year as Hayek's *Serfdom*, anticipated the passing of a capitalist order. Polyani insisted that the nineteenth-century market system was an artificial contraption imposed upon society by the state. It had proved so destructive of social bonds that even in the 19th century certain controls – factory laws and agrarian tariffs – were imposed to restrain it. With the Great Depression market capitalism had been destroyed and the "Great Transformation" commenced: "Within the nations we are witnessing a development under which the economic system ceases to lay down the law to society and the primacy of society over that system is secured."[13] Another great Austrian economist, Joseph Schumpeter, contemporaneously (1942) wrote in *Capitalism, Socialism and Democracy* of the inevitable passing of capitalism, destroyed by the collapse of traditional bourgeois values and the system's spawning of an intellectual class alienated from the system.[14]

It was to rally the supporters of classical liberalism against such dire forecasts that Hayek called together a conference in April

1947 at the Hotel du Parc on Switzerland's Mont Pelerin. Among the 39 participants from 10 countries, 17 were from the United States. Although most participants were economists (20) there was a sprinkling of political scientists, journalists and businessmen. Among those present who were to play a role in the political revitalization of market liberalism in the United States were Milton Friedman (University of Chicago), F. A. Harper (Foundation for Economic Education), Henry Hazlitt (*Newsweek*), Ludwig von Mises (New York University), Leonard E. Read (Foundation for Economic Education) and George Stigler (Brown University.)[15]

Hayek sought to create a kind of "International Academy of Political Philosophy" which would have the task of "purging traditional liberal theory of certain accidental accretions which have become attached to it in the course of time, and facing up to certain real problems which an over-simplified liberalism has shirked or which have become apparent only since it had become a somewhat stationary and rigid creed."[16] Hayek emphasized that a reflexive faith in old creeds would not suffice:

The old liberal who adheres to a traditional creed *merely* out of tradition, however admirable his views, is not of much use for our purposes. What we need are people who have faced the arguments from the other side, who have struggled with them and fought themselves through to a position from which they can both critically meet the objection against it and justify their views.[17]

Discussions went on for more than a week, reflecting the varying continental, British and American understanding of the requisites for a liberal order. Of special concern to the British and European delegates were the desperate circumstances of much of post-war Europe. Professor W. E. Rappard of the Graduate Institute of International Studies clearly stated the difficulties confronting those who would seek to revitalize classical liberalism: "Man, having become politically his own master by the rise of democracy, and being physically exhausted by the fatigues of the thirty years' war, is clamoring for social security and equality, much more than economic progress or freedom."[18]

This led to a discussion of how to deal with poverty in a liberal order. The diversity of answers (minimum wage laws, poor relief, better mobility and freer access to labor markets) suggested how nettlesome this problem would prove for market liberals. Interestingly, Milton Friedman argued for his negative income tax idea at this inaugural meeting of the Society:

> No democratic society is going to tolerate people starving to death, if there is food with which to feed them ... I want to propose that we maintain the kind of progressive income tax now in force, but also with progressive negative taxation below the exemption limit. ... This policy is suggested as a *substitute*, not an *addition*, to present social policy. Substitute for unemployment relief, old age pensions, etc.[19]

Already in 1947, Friedman was insisting that a negative income tax had to be a complete substitute for all other forms of public assistance, a position to which he still adhered in the early seventies during the discussion of the Family Assistance Plan.[20]

Hayek had hoped that the group would be able to agree on specific economic policies that would flow from a commitment to classical liberalism, but there was too wide a range of opinion. All agreed that there were some public goods that governments should provide but no agreement on what those goods were.

Opinions differed about how to stabilize an economy, with some advocating the use of fiscal measures while Friedman called for systems which were "automatically active in response to stimuli." Perhaps anticipating their later more visible disagreements on the proper role for government in controlling the money supply, Hayek asked Friedman, "How can monetary policy be automatic, and outside the ranges of politics?" George Stigler suggested that perhaps everyone could agree that government should control all money-making institutions. There was no consensus on this point either.[21]

Although unable to agree on a specific liberal program, the Society's members did agree to a "Statement of Aims" that reflected their broad consensus. The Statement warned that the "central values of civilization" already had been lost or destroyed "over large stretches of the earth's surface" while in other areas they were endangered "by current tendencies of policy." The Society attributed these development to the growth of a historical view which denied "all absolute standards" and questioned the "rule of law." These changes had been "fostered by a decline of belief in private property and the competitive market," institutions which were vital for the survival of liberty.[22]

The Statement called for a research program that would define the proper functions for the state, determine how to re-establish the rule of law, explore the "possibility of establishing minimum standards [of welfare] by means not inimical to initiative and the functioning of the market," devise "methods of combatting the misuse of history for the furtherance of creeds hostile to liberty, and promote the "creation of an international order conducive to the safeguards of peace and liberty."[23]

II

This "research program" produced an avalanche of studies over the next 40 years that called into question many of the premises of the political economy of New Deal liberalism. Although there were several centers of this activity, the University of Chicago was the vanguard through the seventies. Milton Friedman developed the monetarist challenge to Keynesian macro-economics, argued that the Great Depression was caused by errors of the Federal Reserve, and asserted that the Phillips curve was wrong, there being no permanent trade-off between unemployment and inflation.[24]

George Stigler conducted extensive investigations into the origin and efficacy of government regulation of business, concluding that in most cases the "regulation is acquired by the industry and is designed and operated primarily for its benefit."[25] His study of state regulation of electrical utilities found no evidence that such regulation produced electrical prices lower than those in states without regulation.[26]

Other studies on monopoly were done by Yale Brozen, of the University of Chicago's School of Business. He examined profitability under conditions of oligopoly and found a "lack of persistence of 'high' rates of return in highly concentrated industries."[27] Brozen argued that the real source of inefficiencies in the economy were the government-established and maintained ones. The agricultural and transport cartels sanctioned by the federal government raised prices above market clearing levels. State and local licensing barriers to entry for many trades added to the consumer's burdens. In all, Brozen estimated these "monopoly profits" in 1968 at perhaps $50 billion.[28]

The assumption that large corporations achieved their status by predatory pricing (selling below cost) was challenged by John McGee of the University of Chicago Law School. McGee examined the early twentieth-century case of the Standard Oil trust and concluded that there was no evidence in the 10 000+ pages of the trial record to support the conclusion that the court found Standard guilty of predatory pricing. Furthermore, McGee argued, it would have been irrational for Standard Oil to engage in such practices. Such price reductions hit large firms particularly hard because they had a disproportionate share of the business. Furthermore, competitors could just shut down and wait until prices return to a profitable level. Price wars inevitably spread to neighboring regions, escalating the costs to the "predator".[29]

Harold Demsetz argued that higher profits in concentrated industries reflected greater efficiencies, reputation and goodwill, however transitory those distinguishing qualities. If those profits reflected price-collusion, then even smaller firms should have been able to raise their prices. Demsetz's studies found no positive correlation between those rates of returns and levels of concentration in an industry. He reasonably concluded that an active anti-concentration policy by the Department of Justice might actually increase consumer prices.[30]

Members of the "Chicago School" also responded to the charge that "oligopolistic" corporations maintained high profits by deploying expensive advertising campaigns. These costly exercises, the traditional argument went, would act as "barriers to entry" for smaller firms seeking to compete in a market. Studies by Lester Telser conducted in the sixties, however, found that the correlation between advertising budgets and industrial concentration was very low and erratic.[31]

The Chicago economists reacted strongly to John Kenneth Galbraith's charge in *The Affluent Society* that advertising's purpose was "to bring into being wants that previously did not exist."[32] If Galbraith's premise were granted, not only would it violate one of the fundamental axioms of market liberalism – the rationality of the individual and his capacity to best assess his own utility – but it would lend support to Galbraith's argument that the private sector consumed resources better spent in the public sector.

At its 1960 meeting the Mont Pelerin Society devoted a panel to a discussion of Galbraith's book. Stigler found Galbraith guilty of anti-democratic attitudes. "If I can show you ... that people are essentially silly with their income ... I can also persuade you that people are stupid and careless in other departments of life." Indicting Galbraith for ignoring the advertising conducted by the public sector, Stigler estimated that in 1960 alone at least $100 million would be spent on radio and television ads devoted to the selling of political products.[33]

Hayek, also on the panel, found the Galbraith claim to be just a modern version of the old socialist assertion that the problem of production had already been solved; all that was left was the problem of distribution. He dismissed Galbraith's distinction between "absolute needs" and artificially-created ones:

How complete a 'non-sequitur' Professor Galbraith's conclusion represents is seen most clearly if we apply the argument to any product of the arts, be it music, painting, or literature ... Surely an individual's want for literature is not original with himself.[34]

Subsequently George Stigler and his Chicago students, especially Gary Becker, offered a new perspective on advertising. In a pioneering 1961 article Stigler argued that information for a consumer was a scarce commodity; as such he would invest only so much time and money in seeking information about products before making a purchase. Advertising thus reduced the consumer's "transaction costs."[35]

The term "transaction costs" came to be strongly identified with another branch of the Chicago school, the "Law and Economics Movement." The term was popularized in the 1960 Ronald Coase article, "The Problem of Social Costs," published in what became perhaps the premier journal of the movement, the University of Chicago's *Journal of Law and Economics*. Coase argued that in a world of perfect information, with clearly defined property rights, and no impediments to parties negotiating with each other, then the economic activities of one party could not impose external costs on others.

Where the costs of negotiating an agreement were zero, all affected parties would be included in a settlement and there would be no need for the state to regulate the economic activity. Coase went one step further with his argument. In a world of zero transaction costs, he argued, it wouldn't matter to which party government assigned property rights or the legal liability for damages caused, say, by pollution. Whether the right to pollute was granted to the factory or the right to be free from pollution was granted to local residents, in a world of zero transaction costs the same allocation of economic resources would result. If the right to pollute was assigned to the factory and the value of the damage done to local residents was less than the value of the pollution-producing production, then no bargain would be struck and the pollution would continue. If the right to be free from pollution was assigned to the residents of the area, then the factory would be willing to pay them for the right to pollute. Coase emphasized that the law did need to provide a clear assignment of property rights for such an analysis to be fruitful:

> It is necessary to know whether the damaging business is liable or not for damage caused since without the establishment of this initial delimitation of rights there can be no market transactions to transfer and recombine them. But the ultimate result (which maximizes the value of production) is independent of the legal position if the pricing system is assumed to work without cost.[36]

Coase's article, cited 661 times in scholarly journals between 1966 and 1980, "established the paradigm style" for the Law and Economics movement.[37] It assumed that economic actors were rational maximizers of their utility, who were quite capable of reaching efficient decisions where transaction costs were negligible and property rights were clearly assigned. The state should facilitate such private bargaining by seeking to lower the barriers to efficient bargaining and by clearly assigning property rights.

As Harold Demsetz pointed out in an important 1967 article, "Towards a Theory of Property Rights," transaction costs could be "large relative to gains because of 'natural' difficulties in trading or they [could] be large because of legal reasons." Anticipating Garrett Hardin's discussion of the "tragedy of the commons," Demsetz pointed out that if property rights were assigned to the community, the results were likely to be inefficient. Where a single person owned the resource, he would "attempt to maximize its present value by taking into account alternative future time streams of benefits and costs" but it would be very difficult for the multiple "owners" of a collective resource to reach such an agreement. Communally-owned property was thus likely to be over-used, with "future generations" being required to "speak for themselves." As Demsetz pointed out, the transaction costs of such an intergenerational conversation might be quite high. An assignment of property rights to individuals would both encourage efficient use of the resource and economize on the negotiating costs involved in internalizing all negative externalities.[38]

The domain of Law and Economics included economic analysis of the effects of the law, the determination of legal rules that would promote economic efficiency, and the explanation of why specific legal rules were adopted.[39] Economic analysis showed that regulatory laws frequently failed to achieve even their stated goals, whatever the cost to economic efficiency. Thus George Stigler's former student, Sam Peltzman, concluded in a 1974 study that the 1962 Amendments to the Food, Drug and Cosmetic Act failed to reduce the proportion of ineffective drugs reaching the market. This failure had come at a high cost: a halving of the number of new drugs on the market per year, doubling the cost of producing a new drug, and increased costs to consumers. Peltzman subsequently evaluated laws requiring safer automobiles, concluding that the laws didn't markedly lower fatality rates per accident. Drivers had responded to the lowered "costs" by driving faster and more recklessly; the results were increases in the rates of pedestrian deaths and greater property damage, that canceled out much of the beneficial effect the law had on passenger death rates.[40]

This interest in the economic effect of laws obviously didn't originate with the Law and Economics scholars. During the Progressive Era economists like Richard T. Ely called for regulation of business because he had concluded that the common law had become an ally of often predatory businesses. Other turn-of-the-century economists like Thomas Nixon Carver and Edwin R. A. Seligman advocated a graduated income tax. They reasoned that in as much as all individual's utility curves were essentially the same, wealth redistribution could promote utility maximization.[41]

These arguments for business regulation and a redistributionist state had not gone unchallenged. In the thirties, for example, Lionel Robbins of the London School of Economics suggested that the extension of marginal utility analysis to interpersonal comparisons rested on a false assumption:

> To state that A's preference stands above B's in order of importance is entirely different from stating that A prefers *n* to *m* and B prefers *n* and *m* in a different order. It involves an element of conventional valuation. Hence it is essentially normative. It has no place in pure science.[42]

Robbin's "ordinalist" argument did not prevent New Deal-era economists from continuing to advocate redistributionist measures but they were forced, as the economist James M. Buchanan has noted, to introduce an "externally defined social welfare function, which they admitted to be dependent on explicit ethical norms." The problem with this approach was that there were "as many social welfare function as there [were] people to define them."[43] Most Law and Economics practitioners of the sixties opted for a definitions of economic efficiency that avoided this problem of interpersonal utility comparisons. They concluded that most statutory law couldn't pass even the comparatively relaxed Kaldor-Hicks standard (which required that net benefits exceed costs), let alone those of Pareto-superiority or Pareto-optimality.

Richard Posner of the University of Chicago Law School, in his comprehensive treatise, *Economic Analysis of the Law* (1972), suggested that statutory law was the realm of special-interest legislation, whereas the common law (broadly interpreted to mean all forms of judge-made law) ought to be the realm which promoted economic efficiency or "wealth maximization." Posner insisted that the courts should seek to promote economic efficiency rather than any other goal.[44] Judges, appearances to the contrary, could do little to redistribute wealth. A rule, for example, that made it difficult to evict a noisy tenant would only result in the landlord raising rents to compensate for this higher cost. Indeed the cost of such a move, argued Posner, might be to simply redistribute wealth within the class of tenants, away from the responsible tenant to the "feckless" one.

> So an efficient division of labour between the legislative and judicial branches has the legislative branch concentrate on catering to interest-group demands for wealth distribution and the judicial branch on meeting the broad-based social demand for efficient rules governing safety, property, and transactions.[45]

Posner concluded that most common-law doctrines generally promoted wealth maximization.[46] In situations where transaction costs were low, the common-law doctrines encouraged individuals to conduct their business through markets by defining property rights and protecting them through legal remedies such as injunctions, restitution, punitive damages, and criminal punishment. Where the transaction costs were high the common law priced "behavior in such a way as to mimic the market."[47]

Although profoundly skeptical of the ability of statutory law to promote economic efficiency, Posner had to admit that there were some problems involving property rights for which common-law rules could not provide a wealth-maximizing solution. Widespread pollution was famously such a case because the "individual injury may be too slight to justify the expense of litigation to the victim."[48] Coase had anticipated this problem but he had warned that "the governmental administrative machine is not itself costless." Furthermore, there wasn't any reason to believe that government regulations "made by a fallible administration subject to political pressures and operating without any check, will necessarily always be those which increase the efficiency with which the economic system operates."[49] In this observation, Coase summed up a theme of the Public Choice school, just then aborning.

III

Coase's skepticism towards government efforts to correct "market failures" may have reflected his 1958–64 membership in the University of Virginia's Department of Economics, the birthplace of Public Choice economics. While the Chicago School devoted much research to defending capitalism against the charge of market failure, the "Virginia School" of Public Choice economics reversed the lens, and examined government performance, using the tools of economic analysis. The early leaders of this approach were James M. Buchanan and Gordon Tullock. Both were products of the University of Chicago, Tullock receiving a law degree in 1947 and Buchanan earning a Ph.D. in economics the following year. According to Buchanan's later reminiscences, when he entered Chicago in 1946 he was one of "a group of libertarian socialists who placed a high value on individual liberty but simply did not understand the principle of market coordination."[50] Under Frank Knight's influence at Chicago Buchanan quickly underwent a conversion experience, becoming a "born again" free-market economist.

Always something of a self-styled outsider and populist, Buchanan took appointments at various southern universities before accepting a post at the University of Virginia in 1956. The following year, with G. Warren Nutter, another young Chicago-trained economist, he established the Thomas Jefferson Center for Studies in Political Economy, committed to the preservation of a "social order based on individual liberty." During the next

10 years Virginia produced several graduates who were to make their own contributions to the Public Choice School, notably Robert Tollison and Richard Wagner, as well as two economists who were to have prominent positions in the Reagan administration, Paul Craig Roberts and James C. Miller III. Gordon Tullock arrived in 1958 as a post-doctoral student, joined the faculty, and with Buchanan founded in 1963 what was to become the Public Choice Society.[51]

Public Choice drew upon the insights of economists such as Kenneth Arrow, Anthony Downs and Mancur Olson, whose research raised serious doubts about how effectively democracy as a political system could formulate and reflect the public interest. In 1951 Kenneth Arrow mathematically demonstrated the "paradox of voting:" if three or more individuals use different criteria in classifying their preferences where more than two options are available, no voting procedure can produce a coherent collective choice.[52]

In 1957 Anthony Downs developed the idea that the well-documented voter ignorance was perfectly rational. The transaction costs for a voter to inform himself on the issues were in excess of any likely gain by his voting knowledgeably on the issues. And in an observation that was to see much elaboration by the public choice school, Downs suggested that "[c]itizens who are well-informed on issues that affect them as income-earners are probably not equally well-informed on issues that affect them as consumers."[53]

In 1965 Mancur Olson challenged the pluralist school of political science in its assumption that an interest group democracy could approximate the public interest. Olson argued that rather than being easy, it is hard for interest groups to be formed because the organized group's benefits – tariffs for farmers or higher wages for workers – would be received by all, regardless of whether they contributed. This is the classic problem of the "free rider" that all potential purveyors of public goods encounter. Olson argued that, consequently, small groups were much more likely to organize successfully to obtain government benefits. To prevent the occurrence of the "free rider" problem once an organization was established it would seek government assistance, such as recognition of the union or closed shop. Olson's message was that interest-group liberalism tended to favor the concentrated interest at the expense of the diffuse interest, the producer at the expense of the consumer.[54]

Buchanan was keenly interested in these examples of "government failure" and he sought to design a "constitutional order" that would minimize them. For Buchanan this was as much a ethical pursuit as a scientific one:

> Underneath its abstract analysis, the Virginia research program has always embodied a moral passion that our adversaries have fully appreciated. The program has advanced our scientific understanding of social interaction, but the science has been consistently applied to the normatively chosen question. How can individuals live in social order while preserving their own liberties?[55]

An early expression of his thinking is found in a paper "Economic Policy, Free Institutions, and Democratic Process," delivered at the 1959 Oxford meeting of the Mont Pelerin Society. In the paper Buchanan insisted that there was no such thing as a social welfare function, there being "no unitary or group 'mind' which orders various states of society and somehow chooses among them rationally." Rather, political choice in a democracy is the result of collective decision-making in which the individual "is motivated in the same way that the individual in the market place is motivated." This results in coalition-formations, or log-rolling, that produce expenditures that couldn't possibly garner a majority vote if voted on individually. Buchanan parried Galbraith's insistence that there was a "social imbalance" between public and private spending in favor of the private by insisting that "it may be shown quite readily that majority rule with log-rolling will lead to an overexpansion of the public sector."[56]

Buchanan and Tullock elaborated on this argument three years later in *The Calculus of Consent*. The authors brought the logic of economic analysis to bear on constitution-formation and legislative decision-making rules. The authors argued for a decision-rule of unanimity or near-unanimity for establishing a constitutional order, one which defined human or property rights. Such a unanimity decision-rule also could be applied to statutory legislation to insure an economically efficient outcome, but the cost of reaching such a consensus would prove prohibitively expensive:

> In small groups the attainment of general consensus or unanimity on issues thrown into the realm of collective choice may not involve overly large resource costs, but in groups of substantial size the costs of higgling [*sic*] and bargaining will amount to more than the individual is willing to pay.[57]

At the other pole would be a simple-majority decision rule. Although the authors did not endorse any specific supra-majority rule for enacting regular legislation, their analysis left little doubt that they deemed a simple majority rule as costly to the individual where the government activity "benefits specific individuals or groups in a discriminatory fashion and ... is financed from general taxation."

Rejecting the "naive" assumption that men sought the public interest when they engaged in collective decision-making, "man's reason [being] the slave of his passions," Buchanan and Tullock asked whether the pursuit of self-interest "could be turned to good account in politics as well as in economics?"[58] Unless the voters abided by the Kantian imperative to vote for the common good, then majority rule would, through log-rolling, inevitably produce government expenditures in excess of the optimum. This was especially likely as a result of Supreme Court decisions since the thirties which had interpreted the commerce clause so broadly that "legislative action may now produce severe capital losses or lucrative capital gains to separate individuals." This new constitutional permissiveness necessitated some "additional and renewed restraints" on simple majorities, such as super-majority decision rules.[59]

If simple-majority voting on government benefits permitted the advantaging of organized interest groups at the expense of the individual (and of the society), what had prevented such prior interest-group "exploitation" of the public? Although Buchanan and Tullock were to answer this question at great length in later works, they raised a cautionary note in the book's final chapter, "The Politics of the Good Society":

> For centuries the Judeo-Christian world has accepted certain ethical ideals, at least to some degree. Among those ideals has been the responsibility of the individual to make choices on the basis of an interest broader than that which is defined by his own selfish short-run gains.[60]

The implied doubt that religious restraint (absent constitutional restrictions) would suffice to restrain the "logic" of collective action seemed confirmed to Buchanan by the seventies. Noting the fortyfold increase in government expenditures between 1900 and 1970 he wrote of the "threat of Leviathan" and wondered if modern man could "impose constraints on his own government, constraints that will prevent the transformation into the genuine Hobbesian sovereign?"[61]

Whence came this seemingly irresistible expansion of government size? The Public Choice school offered a variety of answers. William A. Niskanen attributed it in part to the incentive structure of the bureaucrat, which he found strikingly similar to that of politicians and most people. Namely they valued "income, perquisites, power, prestige" and consequently "bureaucrats try to maximize the budget of their bureau."[62] More comprehensive was the explanation offered by Allan Meltzer that government grows more rapidly whenever the cost are diffused or hidden and the benefits are, relatively, concentrated. "The principal reason is that politicians can organize supporters at lower cost by offering new programs than by offering either tax reduction or elimination of existing programs."[63]

Gordon Tullock developed a powerful critique of such program expansion in his 1967 pioneering article, "The Welfare Costs of Tariffs, Monopolies, and Theft." After elaborating an argument that the welfare costs of monopolies or tariffs were substantial, he suggested that even simple government transfer programs had serious societal costs. Both those parties seeking the government payments and those trying to prevent them would expend substantial sums in seeking these transfers. As Tullock pointed out, "the problem with income transfers is not that they directly inflict welfare losses, but that they lead people to employ resources in attempting to obtain or prevent such transfers." The greater the number of seekers for such government-provided "rents," the greater the social or welfare costs to the society.[64] Developing this point in 1971 paper, Tullock noted that most such redistribution took place within the broad middle class (20th to 90th income percentiles). They were not the product of the poor using voting power to transfer income from the above-median incomes voters to those below the median. Rather, they were transfers from the unorganized to the politically influential.[65]

The potential for such transfers (or "profits" or "rents") inevitably led to "rent-seeking," the investment of large sums of money to acquire these transfers or "rents." Buchanan warned that

[a]s the expansion of modern government offers more opportunities for rents, we must expect that the utility-maximizing behavior of individuals will lead them to waste more and more resources in trying to secure the "rents" or "profits" promised by government.[66]

All of these explanations suffered from at least one deficiency: why hadn't these same forces worked to dramatically expand the size of the government prior to the thirties? In an impassioned 1977 volume Buchanan and Richard E. Wagner found the answer in "the political legacy of Lord Keynes." Keynesianism, they argued, stood on its head the Smithian analogy between financial prudence in a family and a kingdom. The Keynesian message could be summarized as "What is folly in the conduct of a private family may be prudence in the conduct of the affairs of a great nation."[67] This new dictum violated the old "fiscal constitution" axiom that "expenditures were ... to be financed from taxation." With such a requirement there would be "less temptation for dominant political coalitions to use the political process to implement direct income transfers among groups."[68]

The old fiscal constitution collapsed gradually. The first stage was the acceptance in 1938 of budget imbalances produced by depression and, after 1941, those necessitated by war. The second innovation was the acceptance in the fifties of a budget deficit itself as a contributor towards recovery. The Kennedy administration gave the old fiscal constitution the *coup de grâce* when it accepted such advanced Keynesian concepts as "fiscal drag" and "fine-tuning." Budgets now were deliberately planned to be in deficit or surplus at different points in the business cycle. The result, for Buchanan and Wagner, was an unmitigated disaster:

> After 1964, the United States embarked on a course of fiscal irresponsibility matched by no other period in its two-century history ... Who can look into our fiscal future without trepidation, regardless of his own political or ideological persuasion?[69]

In 1962 Buchanan and Tullock had spoken of the potential restraining influence of the Judeo-Christian tradition or the Kantian imperative on temptations to raid the Treasury. By 1978, Buchanan had cast off any hopes for a revival of those fellow-feelings, opting to focus on the possibilities of institutional reform. He had endorsed a balanced budget amendment in 1975 and now called for a revitalized federalism, arguing that self-sacrifice was more evident in small communities.

> Despite the flags and the tall ships of 1976, there is relatively little moral-ethical cement in the United States which might bring the internal moral-ethical limits more closely in accord with the external community defined inclusively by the national government. ... While I am not some agrarian utopian calling for a return to the scattered villages on the plains, I shall accept the label of a constitutional utopian who can still see visions of an American social order that would not discredit our Founding Fathers.[70]

Buchanan concluded with the warning that in the absence of a "constitutional revolution" the rent-seekers would continue to maximize their profits even though their activities were a negative-sum game for the society.

Caught in a prisoner's dilemma where any rent-seeker's self-denial would simply result in a reallocation of available rents to the other profiteers, supporters of government restraint faced a daunting challenge. They had either to produce a moral regeneration of the country, or persuade the mass of interest groups that interest-group pluralism in its rococo, baroque stage was so reducing the economy's efficiency that the rent-seekers were destroying their own rent-producer.

IV

Although perhaps the Chicago and Virginia schools' ideas received the most attention during the seventies resuscitation of market liberalism, important contributions also were made by the Austrian school. Marginalized in the post-war period by the economics profession because of its reputation for apriorism, skepticism towards mathematical models, and emphasis on microeconomics, the Austrian approach ultimately was to experience a revival of interest in the eighties.

Mises and Hayek were links with the older Austrian economics elaborated in the writings of Carl Menger, Eugen von Bohm-Bawerk (Mises's teacher) and Friedrich von Weiser. These late nineteenth-century Austrians had made important contributions to the marginalist revolution, replaced the labor theory of value with subjective value, and explained interest on capital as required because of the higher valuation of earlier to later possession of goods.[71]

Many of these ideas were incorporated into mainstream economics, prompting Mises to conclude in 1932 that there were now mostly only differences of terminology among the various neo-classical schools. Yet there remained unarticulated differences that became particularly manifest in the famous socialist calculation debate of the thirties.[72] In 1920 Mises had published an article challenging the feasibility of socialism. As elaborated in his subsequent treatise, *Socialism*, Mises argued that socialism was impracticable because it eliminated markets in factors of production and the prices that came with them. In the absence of such pricing information, no socialist decision-maker could intelligently choose "between the infinite number of alternate methods of production." Mises insisted that the gas and water municipal socialism was practical only because such institutions were embedded within an "otherwise capitalist system" which allowed them to mimic its performance and pricing practises.[73]

In response, the socialist economist Oscar Lange proposed a system that would allow prices for consumer goods and labor to fluctuate according to demand, but prices for capital goods would be set without relying on real markets or extensive data collection. A central planning board would designate prices for capital goods and managers of state-owned firms would be told to maximize profits. The Board would raise or lower their prices in response to the development of shortages or surpluses.

Although Lange admitted that no central planner could possibly solve the literally thousands of simultaneous equations needed for a rational (efficient) allocation of resources, Hayek found Lange's solution no better. It was, wrote Hayek,

> as if it were suggested that a system of equations, which was too complex to be solved by calculation within reasonable time and whose values were constantly changing, could be effectively tackled by arbitrarily inserting tentative values and then trying about until the proper solution was found.

Although Hayek admitted that there was "no *logical* impossibility" in such an approach, it would require a central authority that was not only all-knowing but omnipotent, able to "change without delay every price by just the amount that is required." Emphasizing a criticism that the Austrians made of neoclassical economics, Hayek suggested that Lange's proposal was premised on "the pure theory of stationary equilibrium." If in the real world, one encountered "approximately constant data" where consumer preferences weren't constantly changing, then Lange's proposal might not be "so entirely unreasonable." Hayek insisted that Lange's scheme was feasible only where there was "much more extensive agreement among members of the society" about economic goals "than will normally exist." Anticipating his argument in *The Road to Serfdom*, Hayek warned that such a consensus could only be obtained by "force and propaganda."[74]

Writing privately to Hayek in 1940, Lange admitted that Hayek had moved "'the weight of the argument from pure static aspects to the dynamic ones'" and promised a solution, but it was never forthcoming.[75] Despite Hayek's trenchant criticism of Lange's solution, most economists seemed to have thought at the time that Lange had refuted Mises's argument. Perhaps this was attributable to the essentially neoclassical nature of Lange's argument.

Undeterred by now being out of favor, Mises assembled his arguments into a monumental work, *Human Action*, published in 1949 – thanks to Henry Hazlitt's influence with the editor – by Yale University Press. *Human Action* was a systematic exposition of Mises's general theory of human action, or "praxeology", which he then applied to human choice among competing ends, or economics. There followed an exposition of the deductively derived understanding of choice under market conditions, the business cycle and its relation to money and credit policies, the impossibility of socialist calculation, and the folly of interventionism.

A paean to capitalism, the book was a deductive "summa" where all flowed from axiomatic first principles and right reason. For Mises, the laws of praxeology could not be refuted by empirical tests, because:

> They are, like those of logic and mathematics, a priori. They are not subject to verification or falsification on the ground of experience and facts. They are both logically and temporally antecedent to any comprehension of historical fact.[76]

Despite the author's disinclination to build an empirical case for market liberalism – something that would await the contributions of the Chicago School – Mises's work met with rhapsodic praise from classical liberal reviewers. Rose Wilder Lane characterized it as the "most powerful product of the human mind in our time," while Henry Hazlitt, reviewing the work in his weekly *Newsweek* column, suggested that *Human Action* might be the book that could "turn the tide" against statism. Murray Rothbard, then a graduate student in economics at Columbia University, later wrote that the book changed the course of his life. Mises had created, Rothbard said, "a system of economic thought that some of us had dreamed of and never thought could be attained: an economic science, whole and rational, an economics that should have been but never was."[77]

Despite the enthusiasm of old-style liberals, little praise was heard from mainstream economists. As far as supporters of the ruling Keynesian neoclassical paradigm were concerned, whatever contributions the Austrian tradition had to make already had been incorporated into mainstream economics by 1930. John Kenneth Galbraith dismissed the Austrians, suggesting that the Austro-Hungarian empire got its revenge for America's entry into World War One by exporting its free-market economists to the US.[78] In 1964 Paul Samuelson, soon to be a Nobel laureate in economics, rejoiced that "we have left behind us" the "exaggerated claims that used to be made in economics for the power of deduction and *a priori* reasoning by classical writers, by Carl Menger, by the 1932 Lionel Robbins, by disciples of Frank Knight, by Ludwig von Mises."[79]

When Mises died in 1973, the Austrian school seemed likely to be studied primarily by historians of economics. Hayek had mostly quit writing economics in the fifties and sixties, devoting himself to the study of political philosophy and social theory. Although there remained devotees of the Austrian approach, especially at the Foundation for Economic Education (FEE) and the Institute for Humane Studies (IHS), their influence did not penetrate very far into the upper reaches of the academy at the time. Probably the most common avenue for introduction to Austrian economics in the early 1970s was through the libertarian movement, where the economist Murray N. Rothbard, who had studied with Mises, kept the flame alive.[80]

Just as the Chicago and Virginia schools benefited from the crisis of the Vital-Center political economy, so too did the Austrians. By the mid-seventies the Austrian approach was experiencing something of a rebirth that has continued to the present.

Perhaps the decisive moment was the 1974 Royalton Conference where Israel M. Kirzner, Ludwig Lachmann and Rothbard came together to survey the fundamentals of Austrian economics for a interested group of students and academicians. In the introduction to the book, *The Foundations of Modern Austrian Economics*, that resulted from the Conference, Edwin G. Dolan characterized Austrian economics as "Extraordinary Science" – "work involved in the search for and establishment of a new paradigm" at a time when the old paradigm was "at a point of breakdown."[81]

Certainly, compared to mainstream economics, the Austrians were heterodox. They employed a different methodology, reasoning from a few basic axioms to deductive conclusions whose validity could not to be tested by empirical observations, there being no constant quantifiable relation between economic variables. They challenged basic assumptions of neoclassical economics, such as the usefulness of equilibrium analysis, given that what was really important was understanding how markets might even approach equilibrium. They argued that economic models that manipulated statistical aggregates to predict economic performance were worse than useless because of the incomparability of many of the aggregates and the lack of constancy in the relationship between variables. An honest economics, for an Austrian, could only make qualitative predictions, never quantitative ones. Dolan suggested that Austrian economics was simultaneously more and less ambitious than orthodox economics. More ambitious because it lays "bare the true causal relationships at work in the social world" but less ambitious because it did not "seek to establish quantitative relationships among economic magnitudes."[82]

Such an emphasis on questions of theory and methodology might seem to leave Austrian economics with relatively little to say about "applied" political economy, but such has not proved to be the case. For example, Israel Kirzner in his studies of the role of the entrepreneur argued the speciousness of arguments for government regulation of markets. Those regulations were justified by measuring the results of actual markets against a perfect market at equilibrium (where there were many buyers and sellers, buyers and sellers had perfect knowledge, and supply exactly equaled demand so that the market cleared).

Measured by these standards, most markets failed to be fully coordinated. Kirzner argued that these were totally unrealistic standards that reflected a failure to understand the market as a process of discovery. "An analytical world in which no entrepreneurship at all is permitted," noted Kirzner, "can explain nothing but the pattern of equilibrium; it completely lacks the power to explain how prices, quantities, and qualities of inputs and outputs are systematically changed during the market process."[83] Perfect coordination in markets, he argued, was impossible. The contribution of the entrepreneur was his success at driving the market towards equilibrium even though it never reached that point.

> Long before this corrective process can possibly lead to even approximate coordination, changes in the basic data of the market (individual preferences, the endowments of resources, and available technology) will have rendered the hypothesized state of full equilibrium (defined with respect to the initial state of the data) utterly irrelevant.[84]

That a government agency could possibly improve upon the "efficiency" of the entrepreneur, given the decentralized nature of information and the often rapid changes in the basic data of the market, seemed doubtful in the extreme. Thus what Hayek had argued was impossible for a socialist economy – better coordination than that provided by the market – was affirmed by Kirzner and the Neo-Austrians for a regulated market economy.

Although there were clear differences between the three schools of free-market economics (perhaps most famously, between the Austrians and the Chicagoans regarding money and banking), frequently, as Kirzner acknowledged, their arguments reinforced each other when it came to policy conclusions.[85] Thus in the field of economic regulation the Chicago studies empirically showed how consumers suffered from it, the Virginia school explained the search for cartelization as an effort at rent-seeking, and the Austrians deductively demonstrated that governments couldn't improve upon market coordination. The combined effect of these three schools' arguments was often compelling.

V

By 1980 the market liberals had been conducting a research and educational program for over 30 years. Hayek and those other classical liberals who joined to form the Mont Pelerin Society knew that market liberalism had been routed in the academy by mid-century. They were convinced that its restoration would depend upon influencing the academic economists, and then the general-interest intellectuals, Hayek's dealers in "second-hand ideas," who influence the ever-wider concentric circles of social thought. Determined to try to change a climate of opinion, Hayek foresaw an educational effort that would take decades to have its full effect. He acknowledged that the direct influence of economists or political philosophers was negligible. "But when the ideas have become common property, through the works of historians and publicists, teachers and writers, and intellectuals generally, they effectively guide developments."[86]

This wide dissemination of free-market ideas began with the activities of the members of the Mont Pelerin Society. A roster of the Society's members reads like a "who's who" of classical liberalism's devotees among academicians, intellectuals, journalists and businessmen.[87] Three of the founding members, F. A. Hayek, Milton Friedman, and George Stigler received the Nobel Prize in Economics (in 1974, 1976, and 1982 respectively). James Buchanan, President of the Society between 1984 and 1986, became a Nobel Laureate in economics in 1986. Receipt of the Prize gave a certain cachet to the laureates' pronouncements; a fact not lost on them, their supporters, or their opponents.[88]

Those triumphs for the Society's leaders came in the seventies and eighties. In the early years the organization's greatest achievement may have been to "save the books." Reflecting on this period from the vantage of 1985, James Buchanan concluded that

It is difficult to appreciate just how close to effective extinction the central idea of market order came in mid-century. ... After Mont Pelerin, the Society became the institutional embodiment of the central idea of market order. The "books were saved."[89]

Although this may overstate the enfeebled condition of market liberalism, the Society's early meetings did offer opportunities for the friends of the market order to reassure themselves that they were not alone and to hear and debate papers, many of which subsequently appeared in scholarly outlets.

By the time of Friedman's presidency of the Society in 1970, the time in the wilderness had passed and he lamented the very success of the organization. "Attendance at our meetings by members and guests has become so large that the organization of each general meeting is a major enterprise." He feared that some participants were viewing the meetings as social occasions "rather than exciting intellectual experiences."[90] Friedman was frustrated by the unwieldy size of the organization (there were 330 members by 1970). Calling a special meeting of the Board of Directors in September 1971, he proposed that the group seriously consider having a twenty-fifth anniversary meeting in 1972 and then disbanding.

The Directors demurred, arguing that the Society still performed important functions, such as

putting like-minded people in communication with one another; stimulating an exchange of ideas; promoting participatory learning; and encouraging members to foster, through scholarly activity and in other ways, a fuller understanding of the moral and institutional requisites of a free society.

Furthermore, the meetings were fun, providing, according to board member, Leonard Read, "'an intellectual picnic.'"[91]

Although the Board of Directors rejected Friedman's proposal for organizational euthanasia, they agreed to have more regional meetings and a General Meeting only every two or three years as financial and organizational resources permitted. An absolute limit of 25 new members per year would start in 1972 and continue for five years. Despite these efforts at gaining control over the organization, membership reached 461 by 1984.

Although it is difficult to precisely define the contribution of the Society to the revitalizing of market liberalism, its gatherings introduced like-minded people, permitted networking and provided something of an intellectual bazaar for those members who were not academics. Indeed by 1984 only 50 percent of the members were academics; the other half included businessmen, members of private research institutions, politicians, lawyers, and government officials.[92] The organization was an influence on numerous free-market think-tanks and research organizations including the Heritage Foundation in the United States, the Centre for Independent Studies in Australia, the Institute Economique de Paris, the Fraser Institute of Canada and the Escuela Superior de Economía y Administración de Empresas of Argentina.[93]

A particularly good example of how this process worked is the case of Antony Fisher who was responsible for the establishment of the Institute for Economic Affairs in London, and then helped incubate the Fraser Institute in Vancouver, British Columbia; the Pacific Institute of Public Policy Research in San Francisco; the Fisher Institute in Dallas and the International Center for Economic Policy Studies (subsequently renamed the Manhattan Institute) in New York. Fisher, a graduate of Eton and Cambridge, was a RAF fighter pilot during World War Two when he read the Reader's Digest condensed version of Hayek's *Road to Serfdom*. Fisher was so impressed that he sought out the author at the London School of Economics and asked what he could do to reverse the trend. Hayek discouraged him from going into politics. The Austrian economist encouraged Fisher to "join with others in forming a scholarly research organization" that could act as a transmission belt for market liberal ideas and their "application to practical affairs."[94]

Fisher remembered Hayek's advice. In the early fifties he developed a highly successful business, Buxted Chickens, without government subsidies. He was aided in his effort by Professor Karl Brandt, a professor of agricultural economics at Stanford University who happened to have been one of the charter founders of the Mont Pelerin Society. Brandt subsequently invited Fisher to address the Society's 1954 meeting on the topic of "The Government and Agriculture."

Inspired by meeting Ludwig Von Mises and seeing Hayek again, he commissioned a free-lance economic journalist to write a short monograph advocating *The Free Convertability of Sterling*. Sales took off when the American economic journalist Henry Hazlitt, who also was a founding member of the Mont Pelerin Society, gave it a favorable review in a *Newsweek* column.

Encouraged, Fisher took the plunge and established the Institute for Economic Affairs (IEA) in 1957, employing Ralph Harris (Lord Harris after 1979) and Arthur Seldon as fund-raiser and academician respectively. In 1959 Harris helped organize the 10th International Conference of the Mont Pelerin Society at Oxford and in 1960 the IEA began issuing a series of short monographs, the Hobart Papers, which received praise even from the Fabian Society for their rigor and quality. The IEA became the intellectual center of the revitalized liberal movement within the Conservative Party that brought Margaret Thatcher to power in 1979.[95]

In 1974 Fisher retired from his business and threw himself into efforts to replicate the IEA story elsewhere. He was invited to Vancouver to be a trustee of the newly-formed Fraser Institute, which he also served as temporary acting director. Corresponding regularly with Hayek, he reported his multiple evangelical efforts with enthusiasm in July 1975:

> I myself, have just paid a visit to Ed Prentice in Portland and then to San Francisco and on to Los Angeles where the International Institute for Economic Research is taking shape and has $75 000 in the bank. ... On Tuesday I visit Calgary and then on to Toronto, the object being to raise money for this [Fraser] Institute.
>
> ...
>
> I have a phone call from a rich businessman in Washington who has watched the IEA progress and has set up his own organization and has asked for some assistance from myself. You may know that a group has been set up in Amsterdam ... Arthur Shenfield has put me in touch with new friends of his in Australia and they have asked me if I would visit that country.[96]

A month later Fisher wrote Hayek enthusiastically that "I am more inclined than ever to think it timely to press every accelerator to get as many IEA-type operations going as quickly as possible."

In April 1976 Fisher reported to Hayek his enthusiasm for the progress of the Fraser Institute, with its monographs denouncing rent controls and wage and price controls selling briskly. By now Fisher was starting to develop in New York the International Center for Economic Policy Studies (the Manhattan Institute), funded by William J. Casey, former head of the Import/Export Bank and future Director of Central Intelligence during the Reagan administration. "I go to Australia in May and I have invitations and enquiries from France, Iran, Brazil and many other places." In June 1977 Fisher wrote Hayek to report that "Prof. Philip Gramm of Texas A & M has agreed to be the research director on a part-time basis of an organization to be called the 'Fisher Institute'." Fisher would serve as a trustee and promised to do his best to "ensure that this Institute lives up to the reputation of the IEA and the Fraser Institute."[97]

One year later, having taken up residence in the same San Francisco apartment block as Milton Friedman, Fisher now was a Director of the Pacific Institute for Public Policy Research, based in the same city. Hayek wrote to compliment him on his efforts and, with renewed optimism, predicted that "If the politicians do not destroy the world in the next 20 years, I am sure a new and less misguided generation will be able to take charge."[98]

By 1981 Fisher was associated with so many think-tanks that he decided to set up an umbrella organization, the Atlas Economic Research Foundation, to assist them and promote further proliferation. In 1987 Atlas joined with the Institute for Humane Studies, by now based at George Mason University, to provide guidance, educational programs, and financial help for a growing family of offspring. When Sir Antony died in 1988 (only weeks after he had been knighted by Queen Elizabeth II for public service) the worldwide network consisted of 40 institutes in 20 countries.[99]

Although Fisher's hyperactive evangelicalism was unusual, he exemplified one of the fundamental reasons for the increased prominence of classical liberal ideas in the seventies and eighties: the increasingly generous financial support of business-men and foundations. In the forties and fifties classical liberal scholarship had had to rely on a few small foundations, often run by the donor or a first- or second-generation family member. Among these were the William Volker Fund and the Earhart Foundation.

Initially established as a charitable organization in 1932 by William Volker, a millionaire Kansas City, Missouri wholesale furniture dealer, the Volker Fund increasingly devoted itself to promoting classical liberalism. Under its President, H. W. Luhnow, it financed the travel of American participants to the 1947 organizing meeting of the Mont Pelerin Society. In the fifties it supported Hayek's and Mises's research, published volumes in the William Volker Fund Series in the Humane Studies, and sponsored conferences at Claremont Men's College and Wabash College. Bruno Leoni's *Freedom and the Law*, Friedman's *Capitalism and Freedom* and Hayek's *The Constitution of Liberty* were all incubated at Volker conferences.[100]

The Earhart Foundation, created by the founder of the White Star Refining Company, promoted classical liberalism by establishing the "Earhart Fellowships." By 1957 these one-year non-recurring grants of $3000 had gone to 75 graduate students in economics. Among its recipients were Anthony Downs, Hans F. Sennholz (sponsored by Mises), Ben A. Rogge, and Gary Becker. Friedman, in nominating Becker in 1953, noted that "there is no other student that I have know in my six years at Chicago who seems as good as Becker or as likely to become an important and outstanding economist." Friedman was prescient; in 1992 Becker won the Nobel Prize in Economics for his studies in human capital.[101]

If Hayek's "less misguided generation" was to develop, it would be in part as a result of the educational efforts directed at college students, from whose ranks would come the next generation's elite. In a 1949 article in *The University of Chicago Law Review* Hayek had emphasized that the Left had always focused its message on the intellectual elite "while the more conservative groups have acted, as regularly but unsuccessfully, on a more naive view of mass democracy and have vainly tried directly to reach and persuade the individual voter."[102]

Anticipating this call for a protracted educational campaign, Leonard Read had established in 1946 the Foundation for Economic Education (FEE), to promote the Hayekian counter-revolution. Read, a self-taught student of economics and the "freedom philosophy," had been General Manager of the Los Angeles Chamber of Commerce from 1939 to 1945. In that post he campaigned against all forms of statism in speeches and pamphlets, even inviting Mises to give a series of lectures in 1944 on "free, competitive enterprise."

By 1945 Read had concluded that he needed to devote all his time to the educational campaign. He went east to work as Executive Vice President of the National Industrial Conference Board (NICB), an educational organization founded in 1916 to educate teachers on "the basic laws of economics and the operation of the American economy." Read found the job frustrating. The NICB was supported by contributions from business, unions, educational institutions, and government agencies. As a result, the organization's public forums had to be "balanced," with "both sides" of an issue being presented. Read felt that "statism" was so dominant in the corridors of government, education, the media, and even amongst many businessmen, that in a "balanced" presentation free-market ideas would lose.[103]

After eight frustrating months with the NICB, Read decided, with the support of friends in academia and the business world, to establish an educational organization that would devote itself entirely to promoting the principles of market liberalism. The Foundation for Economic Education commenced its work in 1946, operating first out of New York City office space provided by the Equitable Life Assurance Company but quickly moving to its present location just north of the city at Irvington-on-Hudson. Three Cornell University economists, F. A. Harper, Paul Poirot and W. Marshall Curtiss joined the staff, providing the organization with a vital intellectual reserve. In 1947 Read travelled to Switzerland for the founding of the Mont Pelerin Society, where he must have heard with satisfaction Hayek's call for an extended educational campaign, guided not by "what is practicable at the moment" but by what decades of what intellectual combat would make practicable.[104]

From its beginning, Read's organization sympathized with the approach of the Austrian economists, and both Hayek and Mises presented lectures at the Irvington headquarters, the latter until the year before his death in 1973. Indeed it was through Leonard Reed's influence that the Volker Fund agreed to pay Mises's salary at New York University after 1948. Similarly, it was due to the influence of Henry Hazlitt, a founding member of the FEE's Board of Directors, that Yale University Press published Mises's *Omnipotent Government, Bureaucracy*, and *Human Action*.[105]

Much of the FEE's educational campaign consisted of the distribution of short "homiletics" and essays, published in *Notes from FEE* and *Essays on Liberty*. By 1952 the organization had a mailing list of over 28 000 to whom it could offer such items as Bastiat's *The Law* or Henry Hazlitt's *Economics in One Lesson* (both selling over 500 000 copies by 1971).[106] In 1954 the FEE had the opportunity to significantly broaden its influence when it came to the rescue of the financially failing classical liberal bi-weekly journal, *The Freeman*. Through its subsidiary, Irvington Press, the FEE purchased the *Freeman*, to keep it afloat.

Founded in 1950, this third version of *The Freeman* (preceded by Albert Jay Nock's original in the twenties and Frank Chodorov's brief revival in the late thirties) had been edited by John Chamberlain, Henry Hazlitt and Suzanne LaFollette. Mises saw it as the best hope for a serious libertarian journal, but it had accumulated a debt of almost $360 000 by 1954. Although the FEE brought back Frank Chodorov as editor and he doubled its previous circulation of 12 000, the market for old-style liberalism proved too small for solvency. In 1956 Read redesigned it as a 64-page monthly anthology of short articles, *The Freeman: Ideas on Liberty*. In that format, and available free to all who requested it, *The Freeman* survived.

The FEE did not limit itself to its publishing enterprises. In 1947 Reed established a college-business exchange program that over the next 24 years provided fellowships for more than 1600 teachers from 189 colleges and universities to study the actual operations of a firm during the faculty member's summer vacations. The FEE also targeted high-school debate programs; starting in 1951 the organization annually provided debate packets to more than 1000 debate coaches. Beginning in the early fifties, Read and his staff travelled throughout the United States to provide weekend seminars, often to business groups. Courses were also taught at Irvington throughout the year and, beginning in 1959, the FEE offered week-long summer courses.

The FEE was a pioneering organization and its influence came not only through its own activities but through the lives of those it touched. Anthony Fisher took inspiration from the FEE when he founded the Institute for Economic Affairs in 1957. Various foreign alumni of FEE courses or summer schools were inspired to start their own institutions. Perhaps the most unusual of these was Universidad Francisco Marroquín, founded in 1972 by the Guatemalan businessman and FEE alumnus, Dr Manuel F. Ayau. All graduates of the university, regardless of the curriculum they studied, had to take courses on the teachings of Hayek and Mises. In 1980 Dr Ayau became the twelfth President of the Mont Pelerin Society.[107]

The FEE sought to appeal to a variety of audiences: businessmen, professionals, and students. Its senior staff economist, F. A. Harper, however, wanted to establish a research and education organization that would be an "informal graduate school ... combining learning and work on problems of liberty without the impediment of the 'licensing process'." Harper envisaged an interdisciplinary center similar to the University of Chicago's Committee on Social Thought, which Hayek had joined in 1950 as a professor of moral and social philosophy. Unable to commit the FEE to such a project, Harper moved to the San Francisco area in 1958 and joined the Volker Fund as a Senior Research Economist.

In 1961 Harper persuaded the Volker Fund to finance a modest version of Harper's dream, the Institute for Humane Studies (IHS). The Fund transferred to the IHS all its educational programs. Although the Volker Fund gave the new Institute nearly $120 000 before the philanthropy dissolved itself in 1962, the loss inevitably slowed the full realization of Harper's vision. By 1966, however, the IHS was recovering and that year granted nine fellowships for independent study in Menlo Park, near the resources of Stanford University and the Hoover Institution. Conferences and symposia expanded in number, reaching sixteen in 1970. Reflecting Harper's commitment to exploring all aspects of human liberty, the IHS by the early seventies was sponsoring research and conducting conferences on property rights, legal and political theory, international economics, state control of education, and revisionist history.[108]

Another market liberal organization, the "Intercollegiate Society of Individualists" (later the "Intercollegiate Studies Institute" in the sixties), focused more narrowly on college students. This quiet but remarkably effective organization was inspired by Frank Chodorov. A libertarian friend of Albert Jay Nock, Chodorov was publisher, and then both editor of *The Freeman* (1937–42) and Director of the Henry George School of Social Science.

Dismissed from his posts in 1942 because of his staunch anti-war sentiments, Chodorov launched his own personal journal, analysis [*sic*], in 1944 and eventually attracted the readership of such young libertarians as William F. Buckley, Jr., and Murray N. Rothbard. Chodorov began writing for *Human Events* where he published an article in 1950, "A Fifty Year Project," which led three years later to the establishment of the Intercollegiate Society of Individualists.[109]

In "A Fifty Year Project" Chodorov reflected on the changes in America since 1900 and concluded that the most startling change had been the "transmutation of the American character from individualist to collectivist." The socialists had accomplished this by organizing campus political societies whose "graduates" often went into the ideas fields: publishing, teaching, the law and politics. When the Depression came, Roosevelt had turned to the professors for advice. Chodorov wondered how many of those professors had been associated with socialist groups in college, suggesting that "that would throw light on the transmutation of the American character."[110]

What the socialists had done could be reversed by focusing on the campuses, the incubators of future leaders. Classical liberals should establish "Individualistic Clubs" linked through a national organization that would distribute literature and provide lecturers. Chodorov warned that such an educational effort would be a long struggle. "Nobody living now will see a free society in America. But, in fighting for it one can have a lot of fun."[111]

The Intercollegiate Society of Individualists (ISI) modeled itself on the Intercollegiate Society of Socialists. Buckley agreed to be its first President, but because of the young author's many speaking engagements Chodorov quickly assumed the post, demoting Buckley to Vice President. In its early years ISI primarily provided materials given to it by others, distributing by 1956 over 500 000 pieces of literature to 10 000 interested students and faculties.[112]

One of the more significant contributions of ISI was its inspiration for University of Chicago graduate students to establish *The New Individualist Review* in 1961. Although edited by students and including student contributions, the *Review* also was an outlet for criticisms of Vital Center liberalism by some of the reigning paradigm's most staunch adversaries, including Milton Friedman, F. A. Hayek, Richard B. Weaver, George Stigler (who all at various times served as Editorial Advisors), Yale Brozen, Gordon Tullock, Israel Kirzner, Ludwig Von Mises, Murray Rothbard, and G. Warren Nutter. The *Review* was distributed on over 40 campuses and was one more signpost of the quickening classical liberal revival spurred on by the ISI.

In the sixties the ISI expanded its mission significantly. In 1963 it established the *Intercollegiate Review* as a venue for conservative academicians to present accessible articles on political theory, economics, religion, history, and literature. The ISI offered this "journal of scholarship and opinion" free to all faculties and students who requested it.

Perhaps more significantly, in 1964 it launched the Richard B. Weaver fellowship program; by 1993 Weaver fellowships had financed the graduate training of over 400 recipients. As its creator E. Victor Milione noted with satisfaction in 1993, most ISI fellows went into teaching or writing careers, producing "a formidable conservative bloc in the academy, as well as in politics and public policy institutions." Although the program had a narrowly-focused audience, "it probably has the highest multiplier effect and the greatest impact."[113] Among the successful recipients of Weaver fellowships had been James Gwartney, Professor of Economics at Florida State University, whose *Economics: Public and Private Choice*, with its strong public choice emphasis, was in the early nineties the third best-selling economics textbook in the country.[114]

A good example of the long-term influence of the ISI was the career of Edwin J. Feulner. After gaining a MBA from the Wharton School of Finance in 1964 he won a Weaver fellowship and attended the London School of Economics. When he returned to Georgetown University for graduate work between 1965 and 1968, his roommate was another ISI member and Weaver Fellow, John F. Lehman, who was to be Secretary of the Navy during the Reagan administration. While at Georgetown, Feulner received a fellowship controlled by a another ISI member, Richard V. Allen, who became Reagan's first National Security Advisor. After working as a policy analyst for Melvin Laird, Feulner joined the staff of Congressman Phil Crane who was a ISI member, lecturer, and member of the *Intercollegiate Review's* Editorial Advisory Board. By the time Feulner received his Ph.D. from Edinburgh University (1981) he was President of the Heritage Foundation and Treasurer of the Mont Pelerin Society. Had Frank Chodorov survived to the eighties – he died in 1966 – surely he would have cited Feulner's career as an example of what he sought to promote through his "fifty year project."[115] Looking back from the perspective of the early eighties, Milton Friedman concluded that the Chodorov's Intercollegiate Society of Individualists and the Mont Pelerin Society were the "two organizations in particular [which] served to channel and direct" the revitalized "interest in the philosophy of classical liberalism."[116]

If the classical liberals had secured a beach-head by 1970, the next decade saw the "breakout." For example, Henry Manne, a graduate of the University of Chicago's Law School, became an evangelist of the Law and Economics gospel. While a Professor of Law at the University of Rochester, he launched in 1971 a three-week Economics Institute for Law Professors. In 1976, after moving to the University of Miami Law School, he established a parallel program for federal judges. Through these intense sessions in microeconomics (humorously described as "Pareto in the Pines" and then "Pareto in the Palms" after their first two locations), free-market economists like Friedman, Demsetz, and Armen Alchian had instructed by 1979 some

15 per cent of the federal circuit and district court judges and 100 law professors, many from leading law schools. Concurrently the Law and Economics movement penetrated the leading law schools, where it became *de rigueur* to have at least one economist on the faculty; economists with law degrees (or vice versa) became increasingly common, and after 1975 there was explosive growth in the number of journal citations to the movement's founders.[117]

Students of Friedman and Stigler at Chicago, Buchanan and Tullock at Virginia, Armen Alchian and William Allen at UCLA, and Douglas North and Steven Cheung at the University of Washington fanned out, taking the market liberal gospel to other schools. Institutes and centers with free-market sympathies began to pop up at universities: the Center for the Study of Public Choice established by Tullock and Buchanan (1969); the Law and Economics Center at the University of Miami, directed by Henry Manne with Roger Leroy Miller as Associate Director (1974); the Center for the Study of American Business at Washington University created by Murray Weidenbaum (1975); the Center for Political Economy and Natural Resources organized by John Baden and Richard Stroup (1978); and the Social Philosophy and Policy Center at Bowling Green State University, developed by Ellen Paul (1981).[118]

The venerable Hoover Institution took on a new vitality with the 1960 arrival of D. W. Glenn Campbell as Director. A prodigious fund-raiser, Campbell produced a 600 percent increase in the Institution's income between 1959 and 1970. In the seventies numerous prominent market liberal scholars and political intellectuals affiliated with the Hoover as Senior Fellows, including Martin Anderson (1971), Seymour Martin Lipset (1975), Milton Friedman (1976), and Robert Conquest (1977).

In 1971 the Hoover initiated a Domestic Studies Program with an initial $1.2 million contribution from Mr and Mrs David Packard; followed in the late seventies by a contribution of over $7.5 million from a philanthropy. The program conducted major conferences on such topics as inflation, income redistribution, national health policy, monetary economics, anti-trust laws, political economy and macro-economics.

One product of those conferences was the 1980 Hoover volume *The United States in the 1980s* which provided policy guidance for the new administration of Ronald W. Reagan, himself an Honorary Fellow at the Hoover. Of the 37 individuals who contributed to the authorship or production of this volume, nine served as full-time members of the Reagan administration. Subsequently, Mikhail Gorbachev hailed the book as the Bible for the Reagan administration.

With at least four Nobel laureates in economics associated with the Hoover by 1983, and with 50 of the Hoover's scholars or former fellows having served in some capacity in the Reagan administration by 1985, this west-coast think-tank's intellectual prominence and political influence could not be denied. When *The Economist* subsequently ranked the world's leading think-tanks, it placed the Hoover as number one, noting that it was "hard to match for sheer intellectual firepower."[119]

Robert Poole, editor of the libertarian monthly *Reason*, reviewed with amazement from the perspective of the mid-eighties the progress made by market liberals in the academy:

> The best selling textbook when I was in school was Samuelson's – a Keynesian interventionist book, but it was year after year the top choice. It's not even in the top three any longer, and books that are much more favorable to free markets and skeptical of government intervention and control are now among the top sellers. ... All over the country there are schools where the Chicago or other offshoots of the basically free-market anti-intervention viewpoint is a dominant view. University of Washington, Washington University in St. Louis, Emory, Miami, VPI, George Mason – you just keep counting them up. It's really amazing what's happened.[120]

Arguably, even more impressive had been the proliferation in the seventies of market-liberal think-tanks operating outside the university orbit. Among them were the Institute for Contemporary Studies (A. Lawrence Chickering, Executive Director, 1972); the Heritage Foundation (Paul Weyrich, President, 1973); the Fraser Institute (Michael Walker, Director, 1975); the International

Institute for Economic Research (William R. Allen, President, 1975); the Cato Institute (Ed Crane, President, 1977) and the aforementioned Pacific Institute and Manhattan Institute in 1978.[121]

These think-tanks espoused the doctrines of the Chicago or Public Choice schools (with the partial early exception of Cato) and tended to focus on policy analysis. Inevitably, business executives and business-oriented foundations could more easily be persuaded to fund their efforts than those research centers committed to Austrian economics or to historical, legal, and philosophical studies. The Center for Libertarian Studies (CLS) and the Institute for Humane Studies suffered under both fund-raising liabilities. Where the IHS ultimately thrived, the CLS, after a promising start, withered.

The Center for Libertarian Studies (CLS) was the outgrowth of a series of Libertarian Scholars Conferences held in the New York City area from 1972. Organized in 1976, the CLS's officers included Walter Grinder as Secretary and Executive Director, Walter Block as Treasurer, and Murray Rothbard as editor of the *Journal of Libertarian Studies: An Interdisciplinary Review* *(JLS)*. The Board of Advisors was certainly impressive enough, including Hayek, Yale Brozen, and Henry Hazlitt plus a raft of other readily recognizable members of the market liberal community of scholars.

True to its title, the *JLS* was an interdisciplinary journal. In addition to articles on Nozick's defense of the minimal state, Leonard Liggio on French classical liberalism, and Hayek on a free-market monetary system, early issues contained numerous articles on historical topics from a libertarian perspective. Joseph R. Stromberg wrote on "The War for Southern Independence: A Radical Libertarian Perspective;" Terry Anderson and P. J. Hill recounted "An American Experiment in Anarcho-Capitalism: The Not So Wild West;" Murray Rothbard related "The Foreign Policy of the Old Right."

This promising start, plus a continuing series of successful Libertarian Scholars Conferences, suggested a bright future for the CLS. Unfortunately, by the late seventies/early eighties the Center was suffering from unprofessional management, wrangling among board members, and disagreements about the organization's mission. Additionally, fund-raising became increasingly difficult as the number of free-market think-tanks exploded. Murray Rothbard's feud with one of the organization's backers, the Wichita, Kansas billionaire Charles Koch, may have complicated the organization's financial problems. By the end of 1981 Board members were openly discussing the possibility of dissolution.[122]

As the Center for Libertarian Studies' progress slowed, the Institute for Humane Studies' accelerated. Although the IHS had suffered a blow with F. A. Harper's death in 1973, Charles Koch, acting now as both Chairman of the Board and President, took it in hand and expanded programs. The Institute took over the Center for Independent Education and conducted summer seminars and conferences on broad issues like compulsory attendance and private versus public control of education. In other activities historian Leonard Liggio conducted summer seminars in revisionist history, intending to overcome the "modern anti-capitalist bias in historical studies and the traditional tendency to politicize history." One of Liggio's most significant accomplishments was his editing of the *Literature of Liberty: A Review of Contemporary Liberal Thought*, which he brought with him from the Cato Institute when he joined the IHS full-time as vice president of academic programs in 1978.

Committed to promoting Austrian economics, the IHS funded the 1974 South Royalton conference and hosted Hayek as a Distinguished Visiting Scholar for two months in 1975. The Law and Liberty project Summer Fellows explored how constitutional, statutory and administrative law had increasingly restrained the individual's liberty.

Seeking to reinvigorate the common-law tradition as a bulwark for liberty, the Institute sponsored in 1979 a symposium on "Change in the Common Law: Legal and Economic Perspectives" at the University of Chicago Law School. Although sympathetic to many of the insights of the utilitarian school of the Law and Economics movement, the Institute promoted a natural law basis for rights.[123] IHS scholars like Randy E. Barnett pointed the danger of a utilitarian approach: "This is the view that changing circumstances require a 'flexible' interpretation of constitutional prohibitions; that if we need an economic policy bad enough, it must be constitutional."[124]

Although the IHS was doing good work, by the end of the decade its leaders concluded that they should focus their efforts on identifying and nurturing young academic talent. Liggio particularly welcomed the refocus.[125] He was fascinated by Thomas Kuhn's argument in *The Structure of Scientific Revolutions* that a competing scientific paradigm came to supplant an older one when numerous observed anomalies overload the "carrying power" of the older system.[126] Liggio noted that Harper had read and liked Kuhn's book, recognizing that "in the crisis emerging in America and the world, libertarian theory was a prime candidate to replace the dominant political and economic thought." Liggio was much encouraged by Kuhn's suggestion that a new scientific paradigm does not so much convince the defenders of the old, as attract the young scientists – those too young to be firmly committed to the old explanatory system.[127]

IHS leaders hearkened to Liggio's arguments, appointing him President in 1980. A reinvigorated fund-raising campaign generated more than $600 000 in 1979. In soliciting money from corporate executives, the Institute acknowledged that contributions would not immediately return profits. The IHS was making long-term investments in human capital where the payoff might be ten years in the future. As with Hayek and the Mont Pelerin Society and Chodorov and the Intercollegiate Studies Institute, Liggio and the Institute were preparing for a protracted struggle.

V

The classical liberals' think-tanks and educational institutions in the seventies could draw on a much wider range of business and foundation support than in the sixties. The sixties had been a time of general business prosperity, with after-tax rates of return on non-financial institutions averaging 9 percent, the highest since World War Two. The situation reversed in the seventies. Suffering from waves of inflation, declining productivity growth, increased international competition, and growing dependency on imported oil, corporate profits averaged only 5.9 percent between 1975 and 1978 – the lowest since World War Two.

These economic setbacks for American business were duplicated in the political arena where business found itself increasingly on the defensive. Critical attitudes towards business visible on college campuses in the late sixties also were evidenced in the anti-business public interest movement and the "social regulation" enacted by Congress between 1969 and 1972. The growing prominence of the generally anti-business "New Class" was suggested by the fact that in 1972, for the first time in American history, college-educated citizens voted more heavily for the Democratic Party than did those with less education.[128]

The noted neoconservative Irving Kristol acted as a catalyst in persuading businessmen that the threat of the New Class was real and that coordinated responses were necessary. Kristol had a long history of intellectual combat dating back to his student days as a Trotskyite in Alcove No. 1 at City College of New York in the late thirties. Involved in combative political journalism after World War Two successively at *Commentary*, *Encounter*, and *The Reporter*, Kristol became Senior Editor of Basic Books in 1960; in 1965 he joined with Daniel Bell to launch *The Public Interest*. Named Henry B. Luce Professor of Urban Values at New York University in 1968, Kristol became a columnist for the *Wall Street Journal* in 1972 and joined the American Enterprise Institute in 1978 as a Senior Fellow.[129]

Kristol had a latitudinarian definition of the New Class, including within it "scientists, lawyers, city planners, social workers, educators, criminologists, [and] public health doctors," especially those serving in the public sector, and warned that they sought power in order "to propel the nation from that modified version of capitalism we call the 'welfare state' toward an economic system so stridently regulated in detail as to fulfill many of the anti-capitalist aspirations of the Left."[130] In his *Wall Street Journal* columns during the mid-seventies he characterized intellectuals as a power-seeking adversary culture that businessmen could ignore only at their peril:

> You can only beat an idea with another idea, and the war of ideas and ideologies will be won or lost within the "new class",

not against it. Business certainly has a stake in this war, but for the most part seems blithely unaware of it.[131]

Seconding Kristol in his call for a modern *Kulturkampf* was William E. Simon, Secretary of the Treasury during the Ford Administration. In a widely read 1978 volume, *A Time for Truth*, Simon called for the development of a "powerful counterintelligentsia" that would "launch a broad challenge of the assumptions and goals presently underlying our political life." As President of the John M. Olin Foundation, Simon supported the establishment of a series of endowed university chairs held by market liberals while he tried to alert the business classes to the dangers of losing the battle of ideas.[132]

Actually, the business class had begun to respond by the early 1970. One indication was the increased prominence of the American Enterprise Institute for Public Policy Research (AEI). Founded in 1943 with the purpose of educating the public about business and providing Congress with evaluations of pending legislation from a business perspective, it remained so ineffective that its founders considered abolishing it in the early fifties. Its ultimate salvation came through William J. Baroody who joined the organization in 1954 as Executive Vice- President.

Baroody may have been the first "policy entrepreneur." Neither a businessman nor an intellectual, he saw his responsibility as bringing the two together in fruitful collaboration. Hammering home the theme that the liberals had a monopoly on ideas in Washington, DC, via the Brookings Institution, he warned that such a lack of intellectual competition threatened the health of a free society. The Institute expanded rapidly in the seventies, developing from a budget of $1 million and a staff of 18 at the beginning of the decade to a staff of 150 and a $10 million budget by the early eighties. It elevated its visibility by establishing four journals in the late seventies: *Regulation*, *Public Opinion*, *Foreign and Defense Policy Review*, and *The AEI Economist*. Thus while the Brookings Institution continued with its publication of scholarly books, the AEI was targeting a wider audience as well as policy-makers.[133]

Even more focused on policy-makers was the Heritage Foundation. Established in 1973 by two congressional staffers, Edwin J. Feulner and Paul M. Weyrich, with the financial assistance of brewing tycoon Joseph Coors and the Scaife Foundation, Heritage initially emphasized "New Right" social issues. With the departure of Weyrich in 1977 to establish the Committee for the Survival of a Free Congress, Feulner became President and moved the Foundation toward more intellectual respectability, establishing in 1977 the quarterly *Policy Review*, an outlet for semi-scholarly articles by conservative, neoconservative, and libertarian intellectuals.

What set Heritage apart from the AEI was its emphasis on direct policy advocacy rather than analysis, as exemplified by its "backgrounders" – 20 to 30-page critiques from a conservative perspective of current policy proposals. These were distributed gratis to congressional staffers and journalists. Rather than investing large sums of money in a staff of senior scholars like AEI, Heritage employed mostly young scholars and activists and relied on a "resource bank" of over 1600 conservative scholars (published as its *Annual Guide to Public Policy Experts*) that it could call upon for more detailed studies. Thus the AEI and Heritage reflected a time-honored principle of market liberalism: the benefits of division of labor and comparative advantage.[134]

The AEI and Heritage were able to call on the contributions of a variety of conservative foundations in the seventies. Among the largest contributors were (with their major sources of wealth): the Bechtel Foundation (construction); the Adolph Coors Foundation (brewing); the Fred C. Koch Foundation (energy, real estate); the Lilly Foundation (pharmaceuticals); the John M. Olin Foundation (agricultural chemicals); the J. Howard Pew Freedom Trust (Sun Oil); the Smith Richardson Foundation (Vicks Vaporub); and the Sarah Mellon Scaife Foundation (Gulf Oil).[135] Many of the centers, institutes and think-tanks had depended on seed-money from these foundations for their start-up costs. Murray Weidenbaum's Center for the Study of American Business received start-up assistance from the Olin Foundation; Heritage was established with grants of $250 000 from Coors and approximately $900 000 from Scaife; Scaife contributed $75 000 to establish the Institute for Contemporary Studies; the Cato Institute was dependent upon Koch funding for its creation.[136]

Of all the conservative benefactors, perhaps Richard Mellon Scaife was the most influential. His philanthrophy began in the early sixties; by the mid-nineties he had given more than $200 million to conservative and libertarian organizations such as the Hoover Institution, the Committee on the Present Danger, *The American Spectator*, the American Enterprise Institute and the Law and Economics Center. Scaife's contributions went to both the high-profile institutions and to the more modest shops.[137]

An instance of the latter was the World Research Institute (WRI) to which Scaife gave $1 million between 1973 and 1981. Founded in 1969 by Theodore B. Loeffler to promote free-market ideas on college and university campuses, WRI mailed in 1972–73 a survey on "attitudes toward government" to over 32 000 college students and over 11 000 faculty members throughout the United States. The average student respondent provided answers consistent with the "free-market philosophy" on less than a fifth of the question.[138]

To combat these perceived deficiencies WRI produced short films, a series of pamphlets and a free newsletter, *World Research INK* (containing interviews with Hayek, Friedman, Robert Nozick, Bernard H. Siegan and other free-market scholars) that it mailed to 50 000 students, professors, media outlets, government officials and trade associations in the United States and 41 other countries. Perhaps its most influential "product" was *The Incredible Bread Machine*, an argument for maximizing personal and economic liberty, produced as both a film and a book. By 1979 there were more than 200 000 copies of the book in print and sales of the film had topped 1100. Hayek saw the film in 1977 while visiting the Institute for Humane Studies and was rhapsodic: "I think the effort is admirable. The framework is marvelous. ... I am sure that it will be tremendously effective." When Hayek expressed interest in meeting the young authors, the result was another half-hour film – showcasing Hayek.[139]

Friends of Hayek called upon Scaife again in 1975 to underwrite a regional meeting of the Mont Pelerin Society at Hillsdale College, devoted entirely to a celebration of the Laureate's contributions to economics and social science. Scaife funded a testimonial dinner in Chicago, a media conference prior to the Society's meeting, the meeting itself, and the publication by New York University Press of a book derived from the papers delivered at the conference. To ensure that the book received adequate attention, the market liberal promotional efforts went into high gear. Don Lipsett, a former regional director of the ISI, now working as Director of Foundation Relations at Hillsdale, reported to Hayek that he had sent out 200 review copies and an additional 150 copies to economists. Hillsdale's mailing list generated 1200 sales, ISI purchased 2000 copies to sell (at discounted prices) to its members, and Kenneth Templeton of the Liberty Fund promoted the book to about 6000 names on its mailing list.[140]

The conservative foundations were responsible for the publication of two of the most successful books promoting supply-side economics. On a recommendation from Kristol, the Smith Richardson Foundation provided Jude Wanniski with $40 000 to write *The Way the World Works*. The same foundation financially supported the writing of George Gilder's *Wealth and Poverty*, a supply-side paean to the entrepreneur as gift-giver.[141]

The foundations were responsible for underwriting one of the most successful vehicles produced in the seventies to promote market liberalism, Milton Friedman's 1980 *Free to Choose* 10-hour public television series. Robert Chitester, President of the Erie, Pennsylvania, PBS station and originator of the idea, obtained grants from the Scaife and Olin foundations, plus the Reader's Digest Association, Getty Oil, General Motors, and Bechtel.[142]

Friedman was a free-market evangelical who was quite prepared to take to the road to promote the gospel of liberty. He had learned of his 1976 Nobel Prize in Economics while barnstorming Michigan for a state constitutional amendment requiring a balanced budget.[143] His classic *Capitalism and Freedom*, first published in 1962, had advocated a host of reforms that either subsequently were tried or actually adopted as policy (floating exchange rates, a monetary rule to guide the Federal Reserve, a voluntary army, educational vouchers, the negative income tax, and deregulation of the transportation industries).[144] The econ-

omist Robert H. Nelson has characterized the book as "one of
the most influential in the history of American social thought."[145]
Writing from the vantage point of 1982 the economists William
Breit and Roger L. Ransom attributed Friedman's successes to
his remarkable combination of talents, including his debating
skills:

> With the exception of Keynes, no economist of his time can
> match his power of persuasion in the black art of debate. What
> Mencken once said of Nietzsche can appropriately be said as
> well as of Friedman: "When he took the floor to argue it was
> time to send for the ambulances."[146]

Friedman's television series proved a surprising success with
an estimated 10 million viewers on PBS alone. Subsequently it
was broadcast in 10 other countries. The book accompanying the
series appeared on *The New York Times* best-seller list, eventually selling over 400 000 hardback copies in the US and even
more in Japan.[147]

In it Friedman declared that the "tide is turning." Throughout
the world free-market forces were advancing and statists were
retreating. In Sweden the Social Democrats lost control in 1976
for the first time in 40 years, while in England Margaret
Thatcher's Conservative government came to power in 1979
pledged to reversing more than 30 years of social democracy. In
America Friedman found encouraging signs: California's adoption of Proposition Thirteen, the passage of tax-limitation measures in various states, the reaction against the hidden taxes
produced by double-digit inflation, and the growing awareness
of government failure. The contrast between what government
had promised and what it had provided was "so pervasive,
so widespread, that even many of strongest supporters of big
government have had to acknowledge government failure."[148]

Although Friedman acknowledged the importance of events for
changing public attitudes, he insisted that the "climate of opinion"
had a substantial effect on popular attitudes, "determin[ing] the
unthinking preconceptions of most people and their leaders, their
conditioned reflexes to one course of action or another."[149]

Unquestionably, the juice had gone out of Vital Center liberalism by 1980.[150] Faith in old-style liberalism had been declining for years. The election of Reagan illustrated the infirmity of a Rooseveltian economic order that had been "losing ground for almost fifteen years – almost from the moment of its greatest glory."[151] As early as 1969 Arthur M. Schlesinger, Jr. – the keeper of the Vital Center's flame – had written of a crisis of confidence. "Events seem to have slipped beyond our control ... until recently we have always felt that our leadership and our resources – moral and psychological as well as economic – were equal to any conceivable challenge. Are we so sure now?"[152] Writing in the same year, Peter Drucker reached perhaps a more jaundiced assessment of government's capacities to deliver. Because government no longer delivered on its promises, the nation was "rapidly moving to doubt and distrust" government's good intentions. What had once been a "torrid romance between the people and government," Drucker noted, now was just a "tired middle-age liaison" which no one knew how to end but "only becomes exacerbated by being dragged out."[153]

The government's economic failures of the seventies, most particularly, spiraling inflation and stagnant wages after 1973, only added to the growing public cynicism. Surveys showed that trust in government reached its lowest point in 1980 when 77 percent, up from 31 percent in 1964, indicated that government was run to favor a few big interests. Those who trusted the government to do what's right only some or none of the time increased from 22 percent in 1964 to 66 percent in 1980.[154] Reviewing this record in 1980, James L. Sundquist, a Senior Fellow at the Brookings Institution, acknowledged the profound public skepticism of government: "There is the judgement that government does not deliver on its promises, that after all the talk about cleaning up the 'welfare mess', closing tax loopholes, streamlining the bureaucracy, and cutting red tape, things always remain the same."[155]

Did this mean that the American public was ready for a radical reorientation toward its government? Were Americans prepared to act on the critique of statism developed by the market liberal intellectuals and their publicists? The libertarians hoped the answer would be in the affirmative.

3 Market Liberal Visions: The Libertarian Movement

Libertarianism developed in the sixties as a movement committed to defining and building the utopia implicit in the writings of the market liberal scholars. Although the movement included some graybeards, its membership came overwhelmingly from those under the age of 40. The movement had its center on the nation's college campuses then experiencing dramatic growths in enrollment. This expansion reflected the post-war "baby-boom" which added 13 800 000 members to the 14–24 age-cohort between 1960 and 1970.[1] Liberals wanted to give this bumper crop much wider access to higher education. This would promote social mobility for members of the New Deal coalition, educate a workforce to meet the challenges of international competition, and, promote Vital Center liberalism's vision of a "politically centrist, classless society."[2]

Ironically, the arrival of millions of new students on college and university campuses in the mid-sixties helped spark libertarian and New Left challenges to liberalism's political complacency. Although both movements could agree on their opposition to liberalism's Vietnam War, their visions of the good community prevented them from ever becoming allies. Where the New Left indicted liberalism for accommodating itself to capitalism and failing to build participatory democracy and a sense of community, libertarianism indicted liberalism for hamstringing capitalism and infringing the liberty of the individual. The New Left revolted against the accommodationist liberalism of the Vital Center. The libertarians revolted against accommodationist conservatism, best exemplified by the *National Review*, which had accepted a dramatic expansion of state power to ward off the perceived Soviet threat.[3]

81

The challenges for the libertarian movement in the sixties were multiple. It had to resolve tensions between the movement's anarcho-capitalists and minimal statists, define its relationships with traditional conservatism and the New Left, and develop appropriate organizational vehicles to promote its vision. In seeking answers to these questions libertarians were influenced by the ideas of certain market liberals. Included on the short list were the Austrian economists Ludwig von Mises, Friedrich von Hayek and Murray N. Rothbard, the Chicago school economist, Milton Friedman, and the novelist Ayn Rand, author of *Atlas Shrugged* and founder of the objectivist movement. As these writers' defenses of liberty were differently grounded, their understanding of a proper methodology for the science of economics discordant, and their attitude towards the legitimacy of the state varied, not surprisingly libertarianism was from the beginning a many-splintered thing, loosely held together by a common enemy – statism in all its manifestations.

The elder in this competitive pantheon was von Mises who arrived in America in 1940 from Switzerland seeking sanctuary from a Nazi-dominated Europe. In Europe, Mises's reputation as the pre-eminent theoretician of Austrian economics was well-established, but he was little known in the United States. Something of a mandarin who excoriated New Deal liberals for their trust in the state, Mises never became a member of the American intellectual establishment. Although he held a teaching position at New York University, with his salary ultimately paid for by the Volker Fund and the Foundation for Economic Education, he remained an outsider.[4]

His greatest influence on the libertarian movement came through his economics treatise, *Human Action*, and through his NYU students' subsequent contributions. In the 1950s a group of young disciples attended Mises's seminars. Included within the group were Rothbard, Leonard Liggio, Ralph Raico, Hans Sennholz, Louis Spadaro, Israel Kirzner, and George Reisman – the later four completing doctoral dissertations under Mises's guidance. All committed themselves to propagating the Austrian faith. Rothbard emulated Mises by producing in 1962 his own voluminous work on economics in the Austrian tradition, *Man,*

Economy and the State. Other Rothbard books analyzed the causes of the Panic of 1819 and the Great Depression from an Austrian perspective, explored deductively the damage done by government economic intervention, and portrayed American colonial history as a effort to throw off the shackles of mercantilism. Perhaps his most widely-read and influential book among libertarians was *For a New Liberty: The Libertarian Manifesto*, an attempt to portray almost all economic and social problems as by-products of state action. An advocate of anarcho-capitalism, he urged the young libertarian movement to eschew gradualism, asking "who ... will go to the barricades for a two percent tax reduction?"[5]

Leonard Liggio, an historian by training, found his opportunity to promote Mises's vision of classical liberalism when F. A. "Baldy" Harper, aided by the Volker Fund, in 1961 established the Institute for Humane Studies in Menlo Park, California. Liggio had met Harper in the early fifties when the former Cornell economist was working for the FEE and now he began lecturing frequently at IHS seminars, especially on historical topics.

When the IHS board named him Vice-President of Academic Programs in 1978 and then President, Liggio had an opportunity to build a permanent libertarian academic center. Liggio had made this argument in a 1978 memo "Toward a more Effective *IHS*," where he pointed out that the "original model for IHS was the Institute for Advanced Study at Princeton." Because "scholarship occurs not in isolation but in a community of scholars" and because "there would be no seminal research in libertarian thought without at least one institution to focus support and encouragement," the IHS had to develop a more substantial institutional base.

Convinced that "[n]ations are ultimately ruled by ideas, not men or groups", Liggio argued that libertarians had to get "academic positions at the key universities. ... One post at Harvard, Princeton, Chicago or Stanford is worth a hundred elsewhere." Although there were libertarian sympathizers like Friedman, Brozen, Stigler and Becker holding positions at elite schools, Austrian economists were almost completely excluded. Liggio attributed this absence to the fact that there were "no libertarian academics in graduate faculties to turn out enough libertarian graduates to make a big enough impact on the liberal establishment."

The situation began to change in the 1980s as the IHS, armed with an expanding budget, increased its program of summer schools, scholarships and post-doctoral fellowships for residencies at the IHS. Perhaps most effective was the Claude R. Lambe Fellowship Program for graduate study, consciously modeled after the ISI's Weaver program. Recipients of the Lambe Fellowships attended primarily elite schools; by 1986 Harvard was first with 20 percent of participants, followed by the University of Chicago, Oxford, Yale and New York University. Celebrating the program's tenth anniversary in 1993, Charles Koch reported that it had awarded $2 million to 300 students; 100 had graduated and half of them held faculty appointments, many of them at first-rank institutions. Liggio's mission to replicate the success of the Fabian Society in influencing elite attitudes was making headway.[6]

Although of all those who attended Mises's NYU seminars Rothbard and Liggio perhaps had the most direct influence on the libertarian movement, many of the others made contributions, including four who wrote dissertations with him: Israel Kirzner, Hans Sennholz, Louis Spadaro and George Reisman. Israel Kirzner joined the NYU economics department in 1957 and proceeded to develop the first graduate program in Austrian economics in the United States while leading the seventies Austrian revival. He was a frequent speaker at IHS seminars and Summer Schools of the Cato Institute. Thanks to Mises's influence, Hans Sennholz joined the economic faculty at Grove City College, which quickly became a center of Austrian economics. Upon retirement from Grove City, Sennholz became the Chairman of the Board of the FEE.[7] Another Mises student, Louis Spadaro, became Dean of Fordham University's Graduate School of Business Administration and was President of the Institute for Humane Studies in the late seventies. George Reisman taught at St John's University and then Pepperdine University where he authored *The Government Against the Economy*, an incisive critique of government price-controls that won praise from Hayek.[8]

Ralph Raico, who was only a student at the Bronx High School of Science when he started attending the Mises seminars, graduated from City College of New York in 1959 and then went to the University of Chicago where he studied with the Committee on Social Thought. While at Chicago he edited *The New Individualist Review*. He became a member of the Mont Pelerin Society and taught European history at SUNY-Buffalo. Active in the Libertarian Party in the seventies, he was a regular speaker at the Cato Institute's summer seminars. Reflecting on Mises's greatness as a teacher, Raico concluded that he was "what an ideal intellectual should be."[9]

II

Clearly Mises embodied the "summa" of deductive defenses of classical liberalism, but for every Mises acolyte there were 1000 who read Ayn Rand.[10] Surveying its readership in 1977, *Individual Liberty* found that 70 percent named Rand "as most influential in initially causing our readers to adopt libertarianism."[11] When *Liberty* magazine surveyed its readers ten years later Rand was placed first in influence, scoring an average rating of 4.02 (on a 1–5-point scale), closely followed by Rothbard at 3.93. Other stalwarts followed somewhat more distantly: Mises (3.65), Thomas Jefferson (3.10), Hayek (3.02) and Friedman (2.95).[12]

Rand's great work, the product of 13 years of effort, was *Atlas Shrugged*, an oversized novel set in a near-term future when the men of intellect go on strike against a socialist America. As much a polemic as a novel, the narrative was interlaced with long, repetitive, philosophical monologues which explicated Rand's philosophy of rational egoism. Rand preached that a man's own happiness was "man's only moral value;" self-abnegation or self-sacrifice for others was life-denying and destructive of self-esteem:

the proof of an achieved self-esteem is your soul's shudder of contempt and rebellion against the role of a sacrificial animal, against the vile impertinence of any creed that proposes to immolate the irreplaceable value which is your consciousness and the incomparable glory which is your existence to the blind evasion and the stagnant decay of others.[13]

Reminiscent of William Graham Sumner's *What Social Classes Owe to Each Other*, she announced that the only moral obligation one person owed another was rationality and fair-dealing. "Just as I support my life, neither by robbery nor alms, so I do not seek to derive my happiness from the injury or the favor of others." The initiation of physical coercion by another was expressly forbidden; what was forbidden for the individual was also forbidden for the state. Men of goodwill would live by being "traders," voluntarily exchanging goods and receiving mutual profit by the exchange.

Where Mises had provided a utilitarian justification of capitalism, freedom and private property, Rand insisted on grounding her defense of capitalism in a natural rights argument. For Mises a capitalist system was superior to a socialist system, because the latter "leads to a reduction in the productivity of labor" and had the "effect of diminishing wealth" rather than increasing it. Freedom was valued by liberals not because they were "instructed in the designs of God and Nature" but because free labor was the most productive form of labor and "therefore in the interest of all ... including the 'masters'." The Austrian defended private property not because it was the "privilege of the property owner, but a social institution for the good and benefit of all."[14]

Rand rejected such utilitarianism, instead defending capitalism as the institutional arrangements necessary for man's existence "qua man". She characterized the utilitarian argument for capitalism as a "collectivist claim," insisting that the "moral justification of capitalism lies in the fact that it is the only system consonant with man's rational nature, that it protects man's survival *qua* man, and that its ruling principle is: *justice*." Like Mises, Rand was a methodological individualist and she denied that the phrase "common good" had any meaning unless it meant merely the "sum of *all* the individual men involved." Allow the good of the majority to prevail at the expense of the minority, and then, she warned, all the individuals who make up the minority are "consigned to the status of sacrificial animals."[15]

After *Atlas Shrugged* came out in 1957 Rand published no more fiction, devoting herself to propagating her "objectivist" philosophy and offering social and political criticism to her disciples. Her intellectual major-domo and lover, Nathaniel Branden, prepared a 20-part series of lectures explicating Rand's ideas and established in 1958 the Nathaniel Branden Institute (NBI) in New York City. The lectures were so popular that Branden began offering them via tape transcription in other cities. By 1967 there were 25 000 "graduates" of the program, many of whom were young college students who proceeded to establish "Ayn Rand Societies" and "Students of Objectivism" groups on college campuses. For those wishing further access to Rand's social commentary and exegesis of her philosophy she began publishing in 1962 the *Objectivist Newsletter*, which became the *Objectivist* in 1966, and simply the *Ayn Rand Letter* after 1971. Lectures on university campuses began in the late fifties. Starting in 1961, she gave an annual lecture at Boston's Ford Hall Forum until the year before her death in 1982.[16]

What was Rand's appeal? Why were thousands of bright young men and women attracted to her?[17] Jerome Tuccille, who went on to be the 1974 gubernatorial candidate of the Free Libertarian Party of New York, suggested that Rand's appeal was especially strong to those young Roman Catholics or Jews who had lost their faith and sought some alternative certitude.

> Your protective shell is cracking. You're gradually becoming more and more exposed to the great agnostic world out there that the priests and brothers and rabbis have been warning you about ... And then you discover Galt's Gulch at the end of *Atlas Shrugged* and you know everything is going to be all right forevermore.[18]

Tibor Machan, another young libertarian influenced by Rand, related a similar story. Machan, who later became a professor of philosophy, teaching at Auburn University in 1989, recounted his struggle with growing doubts about his Catholic faith. Reading

Rand's *The Fountainhead* he came upon the passage where Howard Roark declared that a belief in God insulted his intelligence. After further reflection and an unsatisfactory conversation with his priest, Machan concluded that his mind gave him no grounds for believing in a deity, "so I disbelieve in God. I am an atheist."[19]

Roy Childs, an *enfant terrible* of the libertarian movement, first read *The Fountainhead* when he was sixteen. Planning to become a Christian minister, he was so disturbed by the novel's secularist message that he "literally burned the book, putting the ashes in a little box which I marked with a cross, and buri[ed] it in my backyard." Unable to dismiss Rand's message, he next read *Atlas Shrugged* and it shook him to his core. "My mind reeled, my thoughts erupted like a raging volcano – I broke down and cried."[20]

Rand was an active opponent of religion, viewing it as deadening to the intellect and requiring one to sacrifice one's own values for another's. When she met William F. Buckley, Jr. for the first time, she told him "You are too intelligent to believe in God!"[21] Rand's atheism, with its justification in "rational egoism", undoubtedly had its appeal to young people undergoing a crisis of faith. When Sharon Presley, herself a young libertarian, administered a series of psychological tests to conservative and libertarian activists for her master's thesis, she found that those who identified themselves as Objectivists were overwhelmingly atheists (91 percent) while only a few (9.7 percent) of the self-identified conservatives rejected theism.[22]

The appeal of Rand's message went beyond its glorification of unbridled reason; it offered the promise of a utopia, the "Utopia of Greed", as Rand called one of her chapters in *Atlas Shrugged*. Roy Childs retrospectively likened *Atlas Shrugged* to a bolt out of the blue. "It was if God had opened up the heavens and thrown down a few lightning bolts."[23] For most readers it was the first time they had read a moral, as opposed to a utilitarian, defense of capitalism. Rand's novel could be viewed as a response to Hayek's 1949 plea for a liberal vision to compete with the socialist vision: "What we lack is a liberal Utopia, a programme which seems neither a mere defence of things as they are nor a diluted kind of socialism but a truly liberal radicalism."[24]

Although Rand sketched out one possible libertarian utopia, she did not develop a movement committed to its construction. Many of those within her inner circle were ultimately excommunicated and those who simply came in contact with her often committed some "offense" warranting their exclusion. Nathaniel Branden, in his memoirs, admitted his share of the responsibility for creating the cult-like atmosphere around Rand.[25]

Rand and Branden insisted that Objectivism was intellectual property. Threatening legal action, they forbade groups to call themselves "John Galt Clubs" or "Objectivists." Many followers resisted and ultimately began to examine critically some fundamental Randian propositions. Warren H. Carroll, producer of an activist newsletter, *Freedom's Way*, between 1964 and 1968, responded to Rand's proprietary attitude by declaring that he would employ the term "rational libertarianism" rather than "objectivism." He protested against those "neutralizers" among

> libertarian teachers whose demand for total ideological conformity is so rigorous ... and whose awareness of our immediate political crisis is so defective that they actually attempt to *prevent* their students from taking any action for freedom other than recruiting more students for their courses.[26]

In the late sixties Jarret Wollstein formed the Society for Rational Individualism, committed to propagating Randian thought. As a student at the University of Maryland in 1966 he taught a course on Objectivism as part of the "Free University" movement, but he met resistance from the Nathaniel Branden Institute's representatives. Rand denounced Wollstein in the April 1967 *Objectivist* for his presumptuousness. That summer Wollstein attended the "National Conference on Forced Service" in New York City, sponsored by the Young Republican Club of New York City. Among the speakers was Dr Leonard Peikoff, a Randian disciple (and after Rand's 1968 break with Branden, her official spokesperson). Peikoff announced that he would not speak until Wollstein was expelled from the session. Subsequently Branden notified Wollstein that he was banned from all NBI lectures.[27]

Repeated experiences like Woollstein and Carroll's probably disposed many followers to reconsider their affiliation even before Rand abruptly denounced Branden and his Institute in 1968. When Rand broke with Branden, then the structure maintaining control of the Randian movement, the Nathaniel Branden Institute quickly folded as well.

III

The abrupt termination of the Rand–Branden liaison gave advocates of a more radical libertarianism – anarcho-liberarians – an opportunity to make inroads among Rand's followers. One such advocate was Roy A. Childs, Jr., whose "An Open Letter to Ayn Rand: Objectivism and the State" appeared in the August 1969 *Rational Individualist*. Although later the editor of *Libertarian Review* (1977–81), at the age of 18 Childs already was a veteran of the libertarian movement, having taught at Robert LeFevre's Ramparts College.[28]

In his "Open Letter" Child criticized Rand for being inconsistent. In her essay "The Nature of the State" she had denounced anarchism as a "naive floating anachronism" impossible of realization because "a society without an organized government would be at the mercy of the first criminal who came along and who would precipitate it into the chaos of gang warfare."[29] Yet Randian principles proscribed the initiation of force. Childs insisted that a government had to initiate force to maintain its monopoly on the use of force or else it wasn't a true government. If a competing enforcement agency sought to provide its services, the state could do one of two things. It could initiate force to maintain its monopoly status or it could allow competing enforcement agencies. If it did the latter, "then the Objectivist 'government' would become a truly market-place institution, and not a government at all." If it did the former, argued Childs, then Rand's government would partake of statism. "Once the *principle* of the initiation of force has been accepted, we have granted the premise of statists of all breeds, and the rest … is just a matter of time."[30]

Childs's argument prompted Jarret Wollstein to announce in his preface to Childs's "Open Letter" that a year's correspondence had persuaded him and the "National Office" of the Society of Rational Individualism of the validity of the "anarcho-capitalist" position. Henceforth the SRI would be an anarchist institution.[31] Subsequently the SRI merged with the National Libertarian Caucus to form the Society for Individual Liberty (SIL). With about 1000 members (estimates vary) nationwide in 1970 SIL proved to be an important building-block for the Libertarian Party. The founder of the Party, David Nolan, was a SIL campus leader. Ed Clark, the 1980 Libertarian Party presidential candidate, came into the movement at a SIL conference in New York City. Neither Nolan nor Clark were anarchists but the SIL included many who were.[32]

Childs's endorsement of anarchism was a reflection of a tension within the libertarian movement that it never resolved. Of the contemporary major writers influencing the libertarian movement in the late sixties – Rand, Mises, Hayek, Friedman, and Rothbard – only Rothbard was an anarchist. Rand believed that a constitutional republic committed exclusively to protecting men's lives and property was a vital part of an Objectivist utopia. Competing defense agencies such as Childs proposed would lead to civil war.[33] As the use of coercive force to enforce objective law was a natural monopoly, it followed that a government was simultaneously a necessity and also a potentially grave threat to liberty: "its actions have to be rigidly defined, delimited and circumscribed; no touch of whim or caprice should be permitted in its performance; it should be an impersonal robot, with the laws as its only motive power."[34] Although appalled by the growth of government in the twentieth century, Rand saw no alternative to the properly delimited state.

Mises agreed, describing the state as "essentially an institution for the preservation of peaceful interhuman relations." Beyond this function he would not go, even opposing government responsibility for charity because it ignored the link between production and distribution; governments assumed, he warned, that they could change the distribution of wealth without having an influence (negative) on production. Production and distribution were not separate processes. Government "confiscation" for social welfare purposes inevitably reduced production incentives and thus diminished the very wealth that previously had allowed private charity to provide relief. Government taxation for redistributionist purposes was just a special case of a more general problem. Government intervention in economic activity, even for avowedly limited purposes, was always counter-productive, lowering productivity and, through the intervention's failures or unanticipated deleterious side-effects, producing a demand for more intervention.[35]

For all his sanctions against government, Mises could not fathom how a society could survive without government. He believed that anarchists were naive in their assumptions about humanity, noting that "there will always be individuals and groups of individuals whose intellect is so narrow that they cannot grasp the benefits which social cooperation brings." Some were creatures of impulse and would not recognize that the immediate sacrifices that social cooperation requires produce future benefits.[36]

Hayek also rejected anarchism as chimerical. He argued that the goal of a true liberal was to support a system that maximized liberty and minimized coercion, but that coercion would always exist because "to prevent people from coercing others is to coerce them. This means that coercion can only be reduced or made less harmful but not entirely eliminated." Hayek even suggested that there might be a legitimate role for government in the provision of aid to the indigent and in financing of health care and education. His concern was "not so much with the aims as with the methods of government action."[37]

Despite the fact that his son wrote a book favoring it, Milton Friedman rejected anarcho-capitalism, concluding that although it was desirable it was technically impossible.[38] Governments had to "determine, arbitrate, and enforce the ground rules." Additionally, Friedman envisioned a role for government action in the provisions of "collective goods" such as national defense and in the preventing (or reduction) of negative externalities ("neighborhood effects") such as pollution.[39]

Against all of these proponents of a minimal government stood Murray N. Rothbard, an advocate of a stateless libertarianism.

Rothbard converted to the anarchist position shortly after he began attending Mises's seminar at NYU in the fall of 1949. Perhaps it was the rigorously logical Misesian approach that caused Rothbard to explore his unexamined premises. As he relates it, he had a conversation with some "left-liberal" fellow graduate students one night in the winter of 1949–50 and found himself caught by one of his interrogators in a seeming contradiction: Rothbard favored completely free private enterprise yet favored government police. Upon reflection Rothbard concluded that

> my whole position was inconsistent, and that there were only two logical possibilities: socialism, or anarchism. Since it was out of the question for me to become a socialist, I found myself pushed by the irresistible logic of the case, a private property anarchist, or, as I would later dub it, an 'anarcho-capitalist.'[40]

Rothbard began reading the nineteenth-century anarchists who favored capitalism (Lysander Spooner, Benjamin Tucker, Auberon Herbert) and perfecting arguments for anarcho-capitalism. Rothbard insisted that there weren't any truly collective goods, those for which non-payers could not be excluded and for whom one person's consumption did not restrict another's capacity to consume it. Even if there were quasi-collective goods, Rothbard wanted to know why governments had to provide them.[41]

Rothbard denied that a police force met the requirements of a public good. A police force need not defend every inhabitant of an area, nor did it have to give the same degree of protection. Similarly, a national defense system need not defend everyone equally; some areas would receive heavy protection, others might be nearly ignored. As for the argument that "collective goods" must be provided collectively because of the "free rider" problem, Rothbard dismissed this merely as a case where an individual's protection of his own self-interest just happened to benefit someone else. Rather than deploring this, we should be delighted. Rothbard concluded that the arguments for the existence of state-provided collective goods were the "smuggling of *unanalyzed,* undefended ethical judgments into a supposedly *wertfrei* system of economics."[42]

He insisted that there could be no monopolies that were not government-sanctioned ones. Whereas Mises perceived government provision of defense and legal services as merely the codification of a natural monopoly ultimately responsible to the people through the electorate, for Rothbard a government-sanctioned monopoly was everywhere and always an evil because it came into existence and was sustained by force or the threat of force.

Rothbard characterized a natural monopoly (or "limited-space monopoly" as he termed it) as just a situation "in which only one firm in a field is profitable." Whether multiple firms could compete in the delivery of services commonly thought to be natural monopolies (police, courts, national defense) were ultimately empirical questions for Rothbard.[43] Even if experience showed that defense services were limited-space monopolies and if the single "firm" subsequently used force to prevent any entry into the market for defense services, then we would be no worse off than before the libertarian experiment: "the worst that could possibly happen would be for the State to be reestablished. And since the state is what we have *now*, any experimentation with a stateless society would have nothing to lose and everything to gain."[44]

For Rothbard the state was so obviously odious that an experiment in anarchy held little peril for him. But who would join him in making the move to anarchism? He thought he found his answer in the youth rebellion of the mid-sixties. In 1965 Rothbard, joined by Leonard Liggio and H. George Resch, established the journal *Left and Right: A Journal of Libertarian Thought*. The trio sought to promote collaboration and possible union between libertarians of the right and those left-libertarians that Rothbard detected in the New Left.

> Our title ... reflects our concerns in several ways. It reveals our editorial concern with the ideological; and it highlights our conviction that the present-day categories of "left" and "right" have become misleading and obsolete, and that the doctrine of liberty contains elements corresponding with both contemporary left and right.[45]

According to Rothbard (classical) liberalism, not socialism, was the true party of the left; it had led the great eighteenth-century revolutions against the "society of status," introducing a partially achieved "society of contract" in the nineteenth century. Classical liberalism, Rothbard argued, subsequently lost its dynamism when it assimilated Social Darwinism's gospel of gradualism and substituted a utilitarian for a natural rights defence of liberty. Into the gap produced by liberalism's declining fervor stepped socialism. But socialism was not really to the left of liberalism, it was a "confused, middle-of-the-road movement. ... because it tries to achieve Liberal ends by the use of Conservative means," that is, via state power.[46]

Because socialism relied on the state to achieve liberty, it could be co-opted by conservatism, ultimately producing a hybrid ideology of social fascism. For Rothbard, American social fascism was codified in the New Deal but its roots could be found in the Progressive Era and World War One.

> Every element in the New Deal program; central planning, creation of a network of compulsory cartels for industry and agriculture, inflation and credit expansion, artificial raising of wage rates and promotion of unions within the overall monopoly structure, government regulation and ownership, all this had been anticipated and adumbrated during the previous two decades.[47]

Rothbard acknowledged his indebtedness to Gabriel Kolko's revisionist history of the Progressive Era, *The Triumph of Conservatism*, declaring that this "brilliant work" established that the reforms of that era "were not only uniformly hailed, but conceived and brought about by big businessmen." Far from monopoly being a natural tendency in an unregulated market economy, Kolko's book demonstrated to Rothbard's satisfaction that businessmen at the turn of the century had sought and achieved shelter from the rigors of a competitive market.[48] Rothbard and Liggio would give prominent play in *Left and Right* (and in its post-1968 successor, *Libertarian Forum*) to New Left historiography. The policy prescriptions of a Gabriel Kolko or Gar Alpervitz hardly accorded with libertarian preferences. Their writings, however, were useful against the reigning Vital Center paradigm.

Through a similar eclecticism Rothbard chose to ignore the progressive sympathies of the Pearl Harbor revisionist Harry Elmer Barnes and published his last article, "Pearl Harbor after a Quarter of Century." For Rothbard, America's entry into World War Two was the "crucial act in expanding the United States from a republic into an Empire." It imposed a permanent militarization upon the society, cemented the mixed economy, and raised Presidential power in foreign policy to despotic levels. If publishing Barnes's article would discredit American entry into World War Two, then it might help destroy the "last war-myth left ... the myth that here at least was a *good* war, here was a war in which America was in the right."[49]

Rothbard insisted on tactical flexibility. Inspired by the New Left's role in opposition to the Vietnam War and its support of several other positions favored by libertarians (opposition to the draft and support for drug legalization), Rothbard and other fusionist-minded libertarians downplayed the chasm separating the two groups' political economies. Reviewing New Left thought in the fall of 1965, Rothbard announced that "[i]n the broadest sense, the idea of 'participatory democracy' is profoundly individualist and libertarian." In the student enthusiasm for Paul Goodman's communitarian anarchism, Rothbard saw evidence that students would be receptive to the writings of the Old Right author, Albert Jay Nock. Claiming Thoreau as an intellectual ancestor of anarcho-capitalism, Rothbard argued that the use of civil disobedience by the early Student Non-Violent Coordinating Committee and the New Left indicated their libertarian spirit. Although he admitted that the New Left had not yet developed a schematic of its ideal society, he was convinced that they were working towards a "vision of the future that is the fullest possible extension of the ideals of freedom, independence, and participatory democracy: a free market in a free society."[50]

Another libertarian who shared Rothbard's hopeful view of the New Left was the young intellectual historian Ronald Hamowy. A young member of the "Circle Bastiat" in the fifties, editor of the increasingly libertarian *New Individualist Review* while a graduate student at Chicago in the early sixties, and subsequently a faculty member at Stanford, in 1966 Hamowy published an article in *The New Republic* calling for closer cooperation between libertarians and the New Left. To his welcome surprise he now found the New Left standing "emotionally as the heir of what is left of the 19th-Century liberal thought, classically the intellectual background of the American Right." He acknowledged that such a characterization did require him to overlook the New Left's disdain for the private sector and its demand for increased public expenditure, but there were hopeful signs.

> The New Left is beginning to realize what the old Left never managed to understand: that increasing the power of government rarely operates to the benefit of the poor. ... Rather it benefits the plutocrats ... trade union officials and other dignitaries of the power structure.[51]

In retrospect Rothbard and Hamowy's judgements look wide of the mark. Although the 1962 credal declaration of the Students for a Democratic Society (SDS), the Port Huron Statement, certainly included bits of "libertarian" rhetoric, its economic statements fundamentally clashed with the principles of *laissez-faire* economics, for example:

> Corporations must be made publicly responsible. ... The allocation of resources must be based on social needs. ... The main *private* forces of economic expansion cannot guarantee a steady state rate of growth, nor acceptable recovery from recession – especially in a demilitarized world. ... All these tendencies suggest that not only solutions to our present social needs but our future expansion rests upon our willingness to enlarge the "public sector" greatly.[52]

When a Young Americans for Freedom activist, Marick Payton attended a 1966 SDS convention as an interested observer, he was appalled by what he heard. Although he did acknowledge that some SDS members had a "psychological view consistent with aspirations for an individualistically oriented society," he found their economic ideas incompatible with this end:

> No derogative – ignorant, primitive, naive or grotesque – would be excessive in describing the economic "beliefs" characteristic of the New Left. ... That the SDS'ers are completely backward in their economic analysis was clearly shown by their expressed desire for "research to determine the causes of poverty." As is implicitly revealed by this suggestion for inquiry, wealth is presumed to be the state of nature and poverty a man-made phenomenon.[53]

Rothbard alluded to the problem in a 1967 essay, noting that the Port Huron Statement included the "mistaken notion that government is *essentially* a people's instrument for checking big business, but business has been able to keep that control weak – the nub of the Old Left position." He saw a hopeful sign in the Clear Lake, Iowa, SDS national convention in August 1966 where he detected a rejection of "social democrats" in the slate of new national officers selected. He offered as support for this interpretation the fact that the SDS National Council in its December 1966 meeting voted to concentrate its activities on an attack on the draft! Rothbard had become so fixated on the possibility for a left–right coalition that he was prepared to see any attack on the state as confirming the possibility for joint-efforts.[54]

Rothbard tried to make libertarianism attractive to the New Left in a piece he published in *Ramparts* in 1968. Noting that 20 years before he had been perceived as an extreme right-wing Republican who thought that Senator Robert A. Taft had sold out to socialism, he now was characterized as an "extreme leftist, since I favor immediate withdrawal from Vietnam, denounce U.S. imperialism, advocate Black Power and have just joined the new Peace and Freedom Party." Rothbard, rather like Ronald Reagan at a later date, insisted that he had not changed but rather the "Old Right" in the early fifties had changed its attitude toward the state to accommodate McCarthyism and the anti-communist crusade. William F. Buckley, Jr. and *National Review's* stable of "ex-fellow travelers and ex-Trotskyite" writers had turned their back on the Old Right's heroes – Mencken, Nock, Thoreau, Jefferson, Paine – and had adopted reactionaries such as Burke, Metternich and Hamilton as their new guides. The New Right's foreign policy was atomization of Russia and suppression of people's revolutions seeking to throw off feudal orders.

> On the domestic front, virtually the only conservative interests are to suppress Negroes ("shoot looters," "crush those riots"), to call for more power for the police so as to not "shield the criminal" (i.e., not to protect his libertarian rights), to enforce prayer in the public schools, to put Reds and other subversives and "seditionists" in jail and to carry on the crusade for war abroad.[55]

One person who read Rothbard's *Rampart* manifesto with enthusiasm was Karl Hess, Barry M. Goldwater's chief speech-writer in the 1964 presidential campaign. Never one to take an idea half-way, Hess had concluded after Goldwater's defeat that there was an inconsistency between his love of liberty and support for a large military. He joined the SDS and the Industrial Workers of the World, where he received their criticisms of mainstream liberalism with enthusiasm, recognizing in them many of the same critiques made by the right, except that they were more penetrating.[56]

Hess began a collaboration in March 1969 with Rothbard on a new journal, *The Libertarian Forum*. Two months later they formed the Radical Libertarian Alliance (RLA), with Hess as North American Coordinator, Roy Childs as Treasurer, and Walter Block as Corresponding Secretary.[57] The RLA was to be a rallying point for anarcho-capitalist libertarians prepared to work with the left against their common enemy, the state. Rothbard cautioned that libertarians working with other anti-statist forces in a united front must not hide their own beliefs but should "not be so sectarian as to insist that all of our working allies have theories of economics or political philosophy which agree with ours."[58]

RLA members from New York and Virginia attended the June 1969 SDS national convention in Chicago, hoping to attract allies from the left. Unfortunately, they arrived just when the SDS was imploding in fratricidal combat between its Revolutionary Youth Movement and the Progressive Labor Party elements. In the chaos of that climactic convention the RLA did, however, manage to attract several SDS chapters, including Lysander Spooner SDS chapter. These groups joined with dissident Young Americans for Freedom (YAF) chapters to form an Anarchist Caucus.[59]

V

By the time of the 1969 national convention in St Louis, YAF was experiencing conflict between its traditional conservative elements (the "trads") and an increasingly large and vocal libertarian element (the "rads"). The organization had been founded to channel the stirrings of student right-wing political activism exemplified by the 1960 Youth for Goldwater. More than 100 young conservatives from over 44 colleges had assembled at Buckley's Sharon, Connecticut, home in September 1960 to draft the "Sharon Statement." The Statement characterized the times as one of "moral and political crisis" when liberty was threatened internally by an overweening central government exceeding its Constitutionally-sanctioned functions and threatened externally by the "forces of international Communism [which] are, at present, the greatest threat to these liberties."[60]

In its early years YAF's campus organizations concentrated on attacking the National Student Association, working for Goldwater's 1964 presidential campaign and seeking to undermine trade between the United States and Soviet bloc countries. By the mid-sixties conflicts were developing within the organization. Tensions were implicit in the Sharon Statement which tried to "weld together the propertarian-anarchic-'objectivism' concepts of Ayn Rand with the laissez faire economic theories of Ludwig Von Mises and the foreign policy ideas of Barry Goldwater."[61] The Vietnam War and the youth rebellion made manifest what previously had been latent.

The National Office, thoroughly dominated by "trads," began purging state and local organizations guilty of various New Left-style deviations. A case in point was the 1966 revocation of the charter of the Moise Tshombe Chapter in Santa Clara, California. Organized in 1965 as a home for "Libertarians, Objectivists and Classical Liberals," the Tshombe chapter sought to "reach to the heart of the problem confronting the American Right, by reaching into the core of left-wing radical dissent Among [*sic*] American young people" and gaining "both respect and converts." What apparently raised the ire of the National Office was a chapter resolution calling for the repeal of legal restrictions on prostitution and the group's willingness to explore a host of topics from a strictly freedom perspective:

> the immoral restraint of the Selective Service System; the denial of constitutional rights to American indians; trading by America's "allies" with North Vietnam; the immoral compulsoryness of the Social Security System; and the unconstitutional restraints on individual use of such substances as LSD and Marijuana.[62]

One consequence of the dissolution of the Tshombe chapter was the formation in April 1966 of the Alliance of Libertarian Activists (ALA), active in the San Francisco Bay Area, particularly on the Berkeley campus. The ALA was formed by former members of the Tshombe YAF chapter and the Cal Conservatives for Political Action, itself a continuation of Cal Students for Goldwater – both started by Daniel Rosenthal, a mathematics graduate student at Berkeley. To protest the draft, which he called the "Selective Slavery System," Rosenthal went on a 10-day hunger strike in front of the Berkeley draft board office. In early 1966 the Cal Conservatives and the SDS cosponsored an antidraft rally at Sproul Hall. The ALA sought to continue cooperative efforts by forming an anti-draft organization, Students Opposed to Conscription, and picketing the Oakland induction center.[63] Invited to contribute articles to the campus paper, the *Daily Californian*, the ALA tried to persuade the campus leftists that they shared many common goals, including "psychedelic and sexual freedom, an uncensored press, freedom of travel, and a non-aggressive foreign policy." In the Fall of 1966 they sponsored well-attended lectures at Berkeley by Timothy Leary's colleague, Dr Richard Alpert. The ALA attempted to merge left and right.

> On the Right we appeal to limited-government libertarians, Students of Objectivism, individualist anarchists, autarchists, and neo-classical liberals, among others; on the Left, we appeal to voluntary communalists, voluntary syndicalists, psychedelic libertarians, etc. The conventional labels of leftist and rightist are all but obsolete; the real issue is this: will economic, social and political arrangements of whatever form be made by *voluntary* or coercive means?[64]

The ALA expressed attitudes that were increasingly heard among college conservative groups, including YAF. At its 1967 National Convention in Pittsburgh, the YAF libertarians first became aware of their number. Dave Walter and Don Ernsberger of the Pennsylvania delegation called a meeting to discuss common concerns with about 100 like-minded "libertarians and neo-objectivists." After the convention, with three libertarians including Walter now on YAF's National Board, the insurgents made plans for moving YAF towards a more libertarian position at the 1969 St Louis Convention or, failing that, bolting to form a new organization.[65]

While the new Libertarian Caucus prepared for the 1969 convention, Rothbard launched his own effort to split off the libertarians from the conservatives in YAF. A month before the convention, Rothbard published in *Libertarian Forum* his indictment, "LISTEN YAF," denouncing YAF as a fascist organization and urging libertarians to

> get out, form your own organization, breathe the clean air of freedom, and then take your stand proudly and squarely, not with the despotism of the power elite and the government of the United States, but with the rising movement in opposition to that government.

Ernsberger, leader of the new Libertarian Caucus, did not appreciate Rothbard's efforts and fired off a letter telling him that his meddling only made the problems of converting YAF to the libertarian cause more difficult.[66]

Notwithstanding Ernsberger's discouraging words, Karl Hess, Jr. led an "Anarchist Caucus" of perhaps fifty members to the St Louis convention, prepared to press Rothbard's indictment of YAF. Ernsberger's Libertarian Caucus arrived prepared to push a series of rather modest goals designed to move YAF towards a libertarian position.

All these Caucus proposals were defeated, as were all libertarian candidates for the National Board. Also rejected by the convention were proposals calling for legalization of marijuana and an immediate pull-out from Vietnam. Reflecting the convention's dominance by the "trads," it passed a resolution calling for an end to the Vietnam War within one year or else escalation to an invasion of the North, the closing of Haiphong Harbor, and the destruction of the dikes along the Red River.

Judging from the vote for the National Board, the libertarian strength, including the anarchists, did not exceed 250 out of about 1000 delegates.[67] David Walter, who already had been dismissed as Pennsylvania State Chairman because of his libertarian sentiments, charged that the "trads" used their control of the National Office and the Convention to distort the outcome. Not only could they dismiss dissidents like Walter under the hierarchial structure authorized by the National By-laws, but the trads apparently magically created delegates and chapters at will.[68]

Even in the absence of this old-style political manipulation the "trads" almost certainly would have carried the day, but their tactics galvanized the libertarians and won them new recruits. At the end of the convention they gathered to arrange for the establishment of a network to link all libertarian groups; out of those discussions came the Society for Individual Liberty, established in October 1969 by the merger of the Libertarian Caucus with the Society for Rational Individualism.[69]

Media attention to this internecine squabble within the Right provided the libertarians welcome free coverage. For the conservatives it was an embarrassment. William Buckley had delivered the opening address at the St Louis convention but declined to debate Karl Hess when he unexpectedly appeared at the convention. Buckley's *National Review* subsequently cast "anathemas" on the renegades for failing to recognize that all liberty must be exercised within the bounds of a tradition. Ronald Reagan, now widely viewed as the heir-apparent to Goldwater conservatism, was alarmed by what he read about the convention, prompting him to write David A. Keene, YAF National Chairman, for reassurance. Reagan worried that the goals of preserving the principles of a free society were under attack from "a faction within YAF [that] would seek to thwart those goals under the guise of 'libertarianism'." Keene sought to reassure Reagan that all was in hand as a result of expelling twelve California members who had deviated from the conservative consensus reflected in the Sharon Statement.

> Traditionally, YAF has united the "Traditionalists" such as Russell Kirk and the "Libertarians" such as Stan Evans. ... In an organization which allows some diversity, there always is the possibility that some will join who do *not* share the consensus, and we have recently found that there is a very small group of pseudo-anarchists in YAF who are not in accord with our organization's beliefs.[70]

Clearly Keene was putting the best face on a problem of more substantial dimensions than he admitted, but Reagan seemed to be satisfied. Writing in December to the new California YAF State Chair Reagan was philosophical: "It was inevitable that YAF would be infiltrated and an attempt made from the inside. But you've handled it quickly and correctly. ... We're with you."[71]

VI

In retrospect, 1969 was a breakthrough year for the libertarian movement. Two new influential and remarkably long-lived movement publications, *Reason* and *The Libertarian Forum*, were now active. Rothbard and Hess organized the Radical Libertarian Alliance to trawl for allies among the New Left. Don

Ernsberger formally created the Libertarian Caucus within YAF. The subsequent confrontation between Trads and Libertarians at the YAF national convention prompted the departure of several thousand libertarians, many of whom joined the newly created Society for Individual Liberty, which by 1970 had over 1000 members on the nation's college campuses. In California the deposed and disaffected libertarian YAFites created the California Libertarian Alliance (CLA), centered in the Los Angeles area with perhaps 1000 members. In February 1970 the CLA sponsored the "Left/Right Festival of Liberation" at the University of Southern California where over 500 listed to representatives of Left and Right including Carl Oglesby, SDS President in 1965–66, and John Hospers, who two years later was to be the Libertarian Party's first presidential candidate.[72]

Despite such outreach efforts the burgeoning libertarian movement was to remain overwhelmingly a deviation of the Right. Rothbard's dream of making common cause with the New Left proved abortive. In the previous October Rothbard and the Radical Libertarian Alliance had held a New York Libertarian Conference with over 200 in attendance, some coming from as far as the west coast. The delivery of papers by academics and activists on the merits of an anarcho-capitalist society and the evils of the state was apparently too structured for many of the Left anarchists in attendance, who demanded rap sessions and immediate action against the state. In a Saturday night speech Karl Hess called for direct action; the unintended result was a decision by a majority to join the following morning a New Left March on Fort Dix, New Jersey. An exasperated Rothbard remained behind with the rump, trying to conduct business as usual.[73]

Shortly thereafter Rothbard broke with Hess and denounced any dalliance with a left which he described as becoming "largely Stalinoid" and now "rapidly disintegrating." He blamed the New Left for the counter-culture, its one residue that seemed likely to be permanent. Rothbard was distressed by what he saw as the counter-culture's "contempt for reason, logic, clarity, systematic thought" and its exaltation of "immediate, momentary sensory awareness, aggravated by hallucinatory drugs."[74]

In retrospect it apparently was easier for a Rightist to develop a principled hatred for the state and all its works than for a Leftist to learn to celebrate bourgeois striving and capital accumulation. Although the two groups could support draft resistance or opposition to the Vietnam War, their ultimate goals divided them.[75] Despite the libertarian movement's failure to incorporate a sizeable leftist element in its coalition against the state, many of the Left's passions – anti-imperialism bordering on anti-Americanism, sympathy for Third-World revolutions, support for decriminalization of victimless crimes, opposition to gradualism and compromise – became identified with the anarcho-capitalist wing of the movement.

Libertarianism in the early seventies was a diverse group.[76] On the extreme left were anarcho-syndicalist and anarcho-communist sects briefly linked together in 1969–70 with some anarcho-capitalists through the Radical Libertarian Alliance. When their respective appraisals of the virtues of private versus communal property systems proved incompatible, most of the fraternizing anarcho-capitalists joined the Society for Individual Liberty, which increasingly became an anarcho-capitalist organization, adopting a black flag with a dollar sign as its official symbol.[77] Anarcho-libertarians denounced any form of statism, treated much of the history of the American republic – from the sanctioning of slavery and theft of Indian land to the growth of the corporate state – as one long litany of abuses of liberty, and revelled in the findings of revisionist historiography on the Cold War and the origins of the American empire.

To the Right of the anarcho-capitalists were the Objectivists and conservative libertarians, many of them former Goldwater Republicans. These two groups made up a clear majority of those who formed the Libertarian Party in 1971. Both supported a limited, constitutional republic, were unsympathetic to hedonism, defended American Cold-War foreign policy as justly resisting hostile threats, and viewed American history as generally honorable prior to the moral bankruptcy produced by the intellectual classes during the Progressive era and the New Deal.

These allies differed on taxation, with Objectivists opposing taxation as coercive and arguing that the state could be funded through user-fees or a state lottery. The conservative libertarian might oppose particular types of taxes but saw no practical alternative to taxation *per se*, properly limited. The two groups also parted company on the virtues of atheism and altruism.[78]

Also part of the movement but opposed to any political activity were the Autarchists, or libertarian pacifists, associated with Robert LeFevre's Rampart College.[79] Even more estranged from active engagement with the state were the libertarian survivalists and retreatists, numbering perhaps several hundred to a thousand and living in Canadian backwoods provinces, camping out illegally in National Parks, or crisscrossing the country in mobile homes.[80]

Given such diversity it might be counted a minor miracle that libertarians were capable of coalescing into a political party as they did in 1971. One explanation was their growing awareness of kindred spirits throughout the nation, thanks in part to articles appearing in the national print media between 1969 and 1971. The 1969 YAF split produced comment in the *National Review*, deploring the schism but downplaying its significance.[81] Karl Hess's dramatic journey from right to left through the libertarian movement was the subject of articles in the *New York Times* and *Newsweek*.[82] Both the *New York Times Magazine* and the *National Observer* did major stories on the libertarian movement.[83] Meanwhile the *New York Times* Op-Ed page displayed the intramural rivalry of libertarians and conservatives in articles by Rothbard, Tuccille and Buckley.[84]

Rothbard was enthusiastic about libertarianism's increased visibility. "For the first time in my life, I meet average intellectuals: in colleges, in TV studios, in the press, who are extremely sympathetic toward and interested in the libertarian doctrine."[85] But, ironically, the one person most responsible for coalescing a libertarian political movement was not even a libertarian. He was Richard M. Nixon. His 1971 opening to China and his establishment of wage and price controls alienated anti-communist conservatives and incensed libertarians. Nixon's actions prompted a presidential primary challenge from the anti-communist conservatives and galvanized the libertarians into launching their improbable third-party challenge against the leviathan.

4 The Anti-politics of Market Liberalism: the Libertarian Party, 1972–84

One notable strain of the American character has been a desire, as it were, to "end history" by establishing a utopian order free of strife and hence free of the need for the "conflict resolution" of politics.[1] From the civic republicanism of the Revolutionary generation to the recent communitarian movement, Americans have often sought a social order that denied or minimized conflict.

Libertarianism nicely fitted into this continuing American effort to find a utopian order. The market liberal economist Thomas Sowell quite plausibly identified libertarianism as an example of what he called the "unconstrained vision." Adherents of this vision presume the natural order is harmonious. Thus they "seek the special causes of war, poverty and crime, [while] believers in the constrained vision seek the special causes of peace, wealth, or a law-abiding society." The unconstrained visionaries, argues Sowell, hold to the "conviction that foolish or immoral choices explain the evils of the world."[2] As believers in the natural harmony among men, the founders of the Libertarian Party saw political participation as just an intermediate step to the establishment of a post-political order. Because politics was the realm of unprincipled compromise and rent-seeking, the libertarians from the beginning wrestled with the awful dilemma of how one could be in the world but not of it.

I

The event which precipitated the formation of the Libertarian Party was Richard Nixon's August 15, 1971 decision to "close the gold window" (suspend redemption in gold of foreign-held dollars) and institute a 90-day system of wage and price controls. Nixon's actions confirmed for libertarians what they had been warning would be the results of the "warfare–welfare" policies of both major parties: economic insolvency and curtailment of liberties, both economic and personal. A disgruntled Murray Rothbard wrote at the time that "American fascism arrived on August 15, 1971."[3]

Most libertarians in the early seventies identified with the old isolationist, America First fear that an expansionist foreign policy would ultimately exhaust the nation's treasury and crush economic and political liberty at home.[4] Libertarians spoke with admiration of Senator Robert A. Taft's foreign policy; anarcholibertarians were particularly fond of his exotic 1940 sentiment that American entrance into World War Two would be "more likely to destroy American democracy than to destroy German dictatorship."[5] More mainstream libertarians, at least those who wrote the 1972 Libertarian Party Platform, could envisage, as Taft ultimately did in the 1951 "Great Debate," a judicious resort to collective security arrangements, with Americans providing primarily air and sea forces.[6]

The *sine qua non*, however, for libertarians, as it had been for Taft, was that America's defense policy must not be at the expense of American liberty. A large military establishment might threaten domestic freedoms; it certainly would necessitate high taxes and very possibly a regulated economy.

By the early fifties most isolationists either had died off or had reluctantly made their peace with the perceived necessity of a large defense establishment as the price of liberty during the Cold War. William F. Buckley, Jr., himself a youthful enthusiast of America First in 1940, explained his conversion in a 1952 *Commonweal* article.[7] Buckley resigned himself to the necessity for Americans to "accept Big Government for the duration – for neither an offensive nor a defensive war can be waged, given our present government skills, except through the instruments of a totalitarian bureaucracy within our shores." Buckley believed that there was a greater chance of "ultimate victory against an indigenous bureaucracy" than one imposed by the Soviets. Until the Soviet menace passed Americans would have to support "large armies and air forces, atomic energy, central intelligence, war production boards, and the attendant centralization of power in Washington."[8]

If most market liberal isolationists made their peace with the state's need for a large defense establishment for the duration, they remained alive to its potential for overburdening the private economy and they urged defense policies that minimized costs. As market liberals primarily influenced the Republican Party, it probably was not coincidental that Republican administrations seemed to worry more than the Democrats about the costs of national defense.

As John Lewis Gaddis has noted, the Truman administration, through the adoption of NSC-68 in 1950, ultimately endorsed a comprehensive, symmetrical containment strategy while the Republicans, "given their traditional resistance to Keynesian economics," tended "to see means as less expendable than liberals and hence embrace[d] asymmetrical responses."[9] From the perspective of a libertarian, however, these very real differences between Republican and Democratic foreign and defense policies tended to blur and merge – particularly after the Eisenhower administration's mild reaction to the Hungarian Revolt demonstrated that its "liberation" rhetoric was not to be taken seriously.[10] For libertarians both major parties' policies were too interventionist, too costly, and too restrictive of personal and economic liberty.

Events of the sixties and early seventies only confirmed libertarians in their fear of an interventionist state. Kennedy's rearmament policies, the escalating costs of Johnson's Vietnam war, and the expansion of the social welfare state first unbalanced the federal budget (the FY 1969 budget being the last balanced one) and then prompted the closing of the gold window and imposition of wage and price controls. Rather than cut off the Kennedy–Johnson expansion by allowing interest rates to rise to finance the expanded federal debt, the Federal Reserve "monetized" the debt by expanding the money supply. The result was inflation, followed by European pressures on the dollar that ultimately led to the 1971 crisis.[11]

Although the prompt for the formation of the Libertarian Party was Nixon's closing of the gold window and the imposition of wage–price controls, the founder of the Party, David F. Nolan, had been considering the possibility for some time. A 1965 graduate of MIT with a BS in political science who was working in the advertising business in 1971, Nolan had set up the Liberty Amendment Committee National Youth Council in 1965, been a founding member of the Society for Rational Individualism in 1968, and a participant in the 1969 St Louis YAF convention. In June 1971 he had run for the vice-chairmanship of the Young Republican National Federation but was narrowly defeated.[12]

Ruminating on the state of the nation, Nolan and several fellow Coloradans met several times in the summer of 1971 to consider starting a third party. Meeting together on August 15, they were galvanized into action by Nixon's televised announcement of his "New Economic Policy." Quickly contacting like-minded individuals around the country, Nolan established a Committee to Organize a Libertarian Party which had over 100 members by December 1971 when its leadership decided to transform it into the Libertarian Party.

Nolan had argued that five advantages would be forthcoming from organizing a new party: better news coverage for libertarian ideas, increased outreach to possible new adherents, a testing of actual popular support for libertarian ideas, a focus for movement activities, a rallying point for both left and right-wing libertarians, and a source of pressure on the two major parties to take more libertarian positions.[13]

Not all libertarians, let alone all market liberals, shared Nolan's optimism about starting a new party. Ayn Rand refused to have anything to do with the idea, declaring in 1973 that formation of a third party "on some half-baked or borrowed – and I won't say from whom – ideas is truly irresponsible and in the full modern context close to immoral." After Goldwater's 1964 defeat Rand had announced to her disciples that it was too early to engage in political activism; the battle must first be won in the academy. Her animosity towards the libertarians, however, seemed so intense that probably more than just a difference of strategic visions was involved. Specifically, both Murray Rothbard and Nathaniel

Branden were to be closely associated with the Libertarian Party; their association with it probably would have been enough to earn her opposition.[14] Ironically, Rothbard initially insisted that political organizing was "grossly premature" and also found fault with the temporary platform as being insufficiently radical on taxes, monetary policy and foreign policy.[15]

By later standards both the temporary platform and the one finally adopted at the 1972 Denver convention were relatively moderate documents. Apparently desirous of not alienating Goldwater-type delegates, the temporary platform (prepared by members of the Committee to Organize a Libertarian Party) tacitly accepted the legitimacy of a properly restrained state. The economic reform section called for immediate budget and tax cuts, repudiation of inflationary principles and, ultimately, the termination of the Federal Reserve system. In foreign affairs the temporary platform suggested that the United States might enter into alliances "with countries whose continued free existence is vital to our legitimate national interests," suggesting that those countries would include Japan, Australia, Canada and the "free countries of Western Europe." Reflecting the old continentalism of Herbert Hoover and Robert Taft, the document qualified its support for such alliances by providing that the United States should provide the "protection of its nuclear umbrella" while "our allies provide their own conventional defense capability."[16]

When the 89 delegates from 23 states assembled for a four-day convention, June 15–June 18, 1972, they adopted a platform somewhat more hardline than the Temporary Platform yet not radical enough for the anarcho-capitalists. Because the anarcho-capitalists were to participate in greater numbers in later conventions, future platforms were increasingly radical. As it was, differences among delegates prevented platform planks on the Vietnam war and on trading with "enemy nations."[17]

The 1972 Statement of Principles and Platform certainly distinguished the Libertarian Party's position on most major issues from those taken by the two major parties. Drafted by John Hospers, dean of the School of Philosophy at the University of Southern California, the "Statement of Principles" prefacing the platform began with a brief exegesis of the libertarians' understanding of the sole proper functions for government, namely the protection of the Lockean trilogy of rights to life, to liberty and to property.

> Since government has only one legitimate function, the protection of individual rights, we oppose all interference by government in the areas of voluntary and contractual relations among individuals. Men should not be forced to sacrifice their lives and property for the benefit of others. They should be left free by government to deal with one another as free traders on a free market; and the resultant economic system, the only one compatible with the protection of man's rights is laissez-faire capitalism.[18]

From such assumptions the platform derived specific policy positions proscribing most of the activities of the modern American state. The document called for the repeal of all laws inhibiting voluntary sexual relations, drug use, gambling, or first-trimester abortions. Also opposed were the continuation of broadcast regulation, compulsory arms registration, and the draft, which should be replaced by a voluntary army. State schools and compulsory attendance laws had to go. With the abolition of the welfare system all charity would be provided by the private sector.

The platform called for the reestablishment of "sound money," and immediate reductions in both taxes and government spending. All this was to be accompanied by a balanced budget, an elimination of inflationary policies, and the phasing out "with all deliberate speed" of the Federal Reserve System. The Party's long-range goal was the "eventual repeal of all taxation" and the financing of government services through a "system of voluntary fees for services rendered."

The foreign policy planks condemned all governmental foreign aid or pegging of exchange-rates. Military alliances should be limited to those with countries whose independent existence was vital to American security, but the United States must "disengage from any present alliances which include despotic governments." Allies ultimately would be expected to provide their own conventional defenses with the United States providing a "nuclear umbrella."[19] Foreign and defense policies were to prove perennial subjects of disagreement among libertarians, but subsequent party platforms became even more categorical in repudiating interventionist policies.

Libertarians debated how defense might be financed, whether nuclear weapons were intrinsically immoral, and whether a non-interventionist foreign policy precluded any foreign military involvements.[20] Generally speaking the anarchists took the most uncompromising positions on all of these issues. Rothbard seriously argued for competing private nuclear forces, privately financed. Slightly closer to mainstream thinking was the anarcho-libertarian David Friedman who insisted, *contra* Rothbard, that provision of national defense was a public good and the only function for which a *truly* minimalist state might be necessary. Ayn Rand, an unabashedly minimal-statist, assigned a state monopoly to the provision of national defense (as well as police and judicial services) and suggested that a government lottery or insurance payments for government-provided judicial services could provide the necessary financing without involving coercion.[21]

In all these matters libertarians were shadowed by a seeming paradox: these serious market liberals were simultaneously strongly anti-communist, but opposed the establishment of a military apparatus that others thought necessary to meet the Soviet threat. This mainstream response was not available to the libertarians because they agreed with Randolph Bourne that war was the health of the state. As *any* state, including one's own, was a threat to property and liberty, libertarians generally committed themselves to the proposition that foreign threats, past and present, were grossly exaggerated – necessitating thus only the most modest of defense establishments, preferably one financed by voluntary contributions.

II

Clearly the 1972 Libertarian Party's platform called for a revolutionary transformation of the relationship between the American citizenry and its government. Did the delegates that gathered together at Denver's Radisson Hotel really believe that they could revolutionize America? Judging from the Party's subsequent vigorous debates over strategy and whether candidates properly adhered to a strict libertarianism, many members did think that America could be rallied into a wholesale rejection of the mixed economy and the interventionist state.

Yet for others what was important was the direction of movement. If the Libertarian Party could reverse the modern tendency towards an increasingly powerful state, then even this would be a triumph. In a letter to Samuel Edward Konkin III, a member of the Libertarian Party Radical Caucus, David Nolan argued the strategic superiority of a gradualist approach: "we think more can be gained, in terms of rolling back the State, by convincing 51% of the American people to dismantle the State by 49% than by convincing 1% of the people to dismantle it by 99%."[22] In a 1971 article Nolan had suggested a compromise, noting that "since *anarchy* literally means a condition of no government, I, and any other individual who advocates less government than we have now, would nonetheless have to agree that we want to move *toward* anarchy."[23]

But who as its presidential candidate was to lead the Party "toward anarchy?" Despite Rothbard's skepticism about premature political activity, a poll conducted by the Organizing Committee in late 1971 found Rothbard to be the leading candidate, followed distantly by Alan Greenspan, the future chairman of the Federal Reserve (but then known primarily as an investment banker friend of Ayn Rand who lectured on economics for the NBI and contributed articles to *The Objectivist*).[24] Rothbard declined prior to the convention and it looked for a while that the choice would be between running no national ticket in 1972 or placing a nondescript activist on the ballot.[25]

John Hospers, professor of philosophy at the University of Southern California, emerged as a respectable candidate. The author or editor of seven works on ethics, esthetics and philosophical analysis, Hospers had recently authored a substantial work, *Libertarianism: A Political Philosophy for Tomorrow*.[26] Attending the convention to work on the party platform, Hospers found the gathering "a friendly group, and an idealistic one, bound together by a common purpose: to promote the ideas of freedom and to halt the slide towards big government." He agreed to be the Party's presidential candidate. The Party's vice-presidential candidate was Tonie Nathan, a former "leftist, social-ist liberal" and lifelong Democrat prior to a "long process of re-education." The daughter of the head of Metro-Goldwyn-Mayer's art department, Nathan was a radio-television producer in Eugene, Oregon.[27]

Due to the party's recent organization it proved impossible to get on the ballot in states other than Colorado and Washington. The campaign served primarily to gain some name-recognition and familiarize the press with the party's existence. During the Summer and Fall campaign, Hospers and Nathan made do with a campaign fund of less than $6000, using it, in their mostly sep-arate campaigns, for air travel to urban centers throughout the country including Dallas, Houston, Philadelphia, New York, Boston, Chicago, Los Angeles, San Francisco, Portland, and Seattle. Speeches before Libertarian groups and college audi-ences supplemented media interviews and participation on talk shows along their itineraries.[28]

Inevitably the electoral results were very modest, with the ticket receiving only 3671 votes combined from four states (California, Colorado, Massachusetts, and Washington) plus an unknown number of write-in votes from those states not bother-ing to count them.[29] Projecting an optimism that was to become a hallmark of the Party's official stance, its newsletter analyzed the returns and noted that the Hospers–Nathan ticket received about 20 votes for every party member in Colorado and Washington.

> Thus, if we can increase our membership to 32,000 by 1976 … and can get the election laws revised to eliminate discrimina-tion against minority parties, we can pull 640,000 voters in 1976 – which could easily make us the most significant minor-ity party in America, in terms of numbers (we're already the most significant, in terms of ideas).[30]

As subsequent electoral campaigns were to demonstrate, removing the legal obstacles to ballot-access for a third party was to prove more difficult than this rather confident projection suggested in

1972. The Party was to use a considerable fraction of its campaign funds in simply acquiring the requisite number of signatures for inclusion on the various states' ballots.

The one true 1972 bright spot for the fledgling Libertarian Party came on December 18 when Roger Lea MacBride, a Virginia elector for the Republican Party, bolted and cast his vote for the Libertarian ticket. This action made Tonie Nathan the first woman ever to receive an electoral vote and gave the Libertarian Party some welcome publicity. Seeking publicity for his planned renegade action, MacBride had contacted the columnist Nicholas Von Hoffman through a mutual acquaintance and arranged an interview. Published in the *Washington Post* on the day the Republican electors arrived to cast their votes in Richmond, the interview prompted television stations to dispatch crews to catch MacBride scratching out Spiro Agnew's name on the pre-printed ballot and writing in "Theodora Nathan."[31]

MacBride subsequently indicated that he had hoped to throw the spotlight on Hospers and Nathan, but most of the media attention came his way.[32] His unexpected action made him a hero among most libertarians. When it became known that MacBride had strong libertarian leanings and considerable personal financial resources, he became the odds-on favorite for the party's 1976 presidential nomination.

Born in 1929, MacBride learned at 16 of the writings of the libertarian Rose Wilder Lane from his father, who as a senior editor at Reader's Digest condensed one of her books, *Let the Hurricane Roar*. Lane herself was the daughter of Laura Ingalls Wilder, author of the *Little House on the Prairie* books. Becoming acquainted with Lane because of his father's work on the book condensation, the young MacBride often hiked the 15 miles between Pleasantville, New York, and her home near Danbury, Connecticut, to imbibe the author's philosophy of rugged individualism.[33]

Graduating from Princeton in 1951, MacBride received his law degree from Harvard and took a Fulbright in the Philippines to study comparative constitutional systems. He then returned to join a New York law firm of banking specialists and become Rose Lane's lawyer and business manager. Success in the stock market allowed him in 1960 to purchase 1200 acres near Halifax, Vermont which quickly became quite valuable when the federal government decided to run an interstate highway through it. When Lane died childless in 1968, MacBride was her executor and heir to the rights to the *Little House* books. In the early seventies he briefly became the producer for the NBC series based on the *Little House* series.

Such successful business ventures had allowed MacBride to turn to politics. Winning a seat in Vermont's lower house in 1964, he proposed expenditure cuts that would have diminished the state's budget by 5 to 10 percent. Defeated in a bid for the Republican gubernatorial nomination, he relocated to a farm outside Charlottesville, Virginia and re-entered Republican politics, serving as a presidential elector in 1972.[34]

MacBride represented those libertarians who were least estranged from their own society, who were prepared to play the political game by the established rules, and who were not of the anarchist mentality.[35] These minimal-statists, or "minarchists," found themselves challenged by anarcho-libertarians wanting to do away with the state completely. These political divisions surfaced at the Party's 1974 Dallas convention where the anarchists where strong enough to insist on platform changes removing any implied sanction for *any* state action.[36] No longer would the "Statement of Principles" define the proper limited functions of government, as had the 1972 "Statement." Instead the Statement would speak in negatives, of what governments must not do.[37]

Could the minarchists and anarchists both dwell in the same party? It is a truism that the two major parties in the United States are coalition or umbrella parties, a condition necessitated by a winner-take-all presidential electoral system and single-member congressional districts. Inevitably such coalition parties of disparate elements must be *political*, i.e. they must accommodate divergent interests and live with each other if the prize of victory, office-holding, is to be achieved. What would hold together a coalition such as the Libertarian Party when one group (minarchists) aspired merely to dramatically reduce government while another group (anarchists) supported the total abolition of the state?

The anarchists perceived any "gradualism" in advocacy as a sign that the party was temporizing with the state. Like the abolitionist William Lloyd Garrison, they were prone to call for the immediate and total end of state slavery, lest it merely be "contained" rather than eliminated. Paradoxically, this revolutionary "ultraist" mentality could and did attract even the minarchists. The gap between the size and responsibilities of the American government in the seventies and what even minimal-statists thought appropriate was so large that they too were prone to scrutinizing their own candidates for evidence of "backsliding." The consequence was an ideological anti-politics that ultimately doomed the Libertarians to remain in the margins of American political life.

In the mid-seventies libertarians could by a willful act deny this commonsensical proposition, given the "regime crisis" of Vital Center liberalism and the simultaneous turmoil within the Republican Party in the wake of Watergate. For those who were prepared to be optimistic there were hints of a possible paradigm shift. Thus in 1974 the Swedish Academy of Science awarded Hayek the Nobel Prize in Economics. Equally encouraging, Robert Nozick, who had come to libertarianism through reading Hayek's *The Constitution of Liberty*, received the 1975 National Book Award for his philosophical treatise favoring the minimal state, *Anarchy, State and Utopia*.[38]

At the level of practical politics no libertarians were winning prizes in 1974 but there were ambiguously encouraging signs. In Ohio the founding chairman of the state's Libertarian Party, Kay Harroff, running as an independent against John Glenn for the US Senate, received over 76 000 votes.[39] In New York Jerome Tuccille, gubernatorial candidate of the Free Libertarian Party, sought to get permanent ballot status for the party (requiring 50 000 votes) by running a rather theatrical campaign, challenging his competitors to a game of monopoly, acclaiming Chester Arthur as a great President and sending around Central Park a modern-day Lady Godiva, a blonde in a body-stocking mounted on a horse named "Taxpayer."[40]

The Party was getting better organized. At the 1974 Dallas Convention the 300 delegates had elected Edward H. Crane, III as

Chairman. With a BS in Finance from the University of California at Berkeley and an MBA in Finance from the University of Southern California, Crane was an institutional portfolio manager with Alliance Capital Management Corporation in San Francisco. Crane was an excellent choice. He proved an able manager with a decisive style and a willingness to work long hours.

His involvement with the Party began as a delegate to the 1972 Denver organizing convention. Subsequently he was Toni Nathan's campaign manager in 1972 and, until early 1974, the Vice-Chairman of the California Libertarian Party, probably the Party's largest state organization. Although in the early 1980s he was to be involved in a bitter intra-party dispute, it is difficult to imagine the Party's comparative successes in the 1976 and 1980 Presidential elections without his participation.[41]

A practical individual, Crane did not have a high regard for many of those involved in the formation of the Party:

> They were nice people but they were not really the kind of people who were going to create a new party .... there were very few there who had a sense of what was involved. Most of them were using libertarianism as some sort of rationale for their own failures in life .... But Ed Clark was there. ... And John Hospers was impressive.[42]

Nor did he think much of their political commitment in the early years, comparing party meetings with the old Nathaniel Branden Institute seminars where participants engaged in what, to Crane, were scholastic debates of little practical significance.[43] David Boaz, Research Director for the 1980 presidential campaign, has suggested that Crane was a "political entrepreneur" who, like a successful businessman, acted on "unarticulated knowledge" or hunches in making decisions. Although perhaps the "most important political strategist that the libertarian movement [ever] had," Crane's very decisiveness bred resentment.[44]

Crane persuaded Roger MacBride to provide some "seed money" to set up a National Headquarters office for the Party in San Francisco. Crane called on Robert H. Meier, publisher of *The Libertarian Scholar* and the Party's National Fundraising

Chairman, to serve as national director. The two made a good team. The Party gained a higher profile when it decided to relocate the National Headquarters to Washington, DC. Crane had run for National Chairman at the 1974 Dallas convention on a platform that included a promise never to relocate there. But he and Meier quickly came to the conclusion that it was necessary "if we were going to be a serious party." An important factor in the decision was the recent selection of MacBride, a Virginia resident, as the Party's 1976 presidential nominee.[45]

III

MacBride's nomination had been prefigured as early as the 1973 National Convention when "MacBride for President" banners first appeared. Although MacBride initially rejected the idea, he later in 1974 relented at the urgings of Ed Clark and Ed Crane, then respectively State Chairman and Vice-chairman of the California Libertarian Party. He spelled out the conditions under which he would run for the nomination.

First, whoever was elected as national chair at the 1974 Dallas convention would have to be "professionally minded" and be prepared to run "the campaign of 1976 ... as closely as our resources" would permit to that of a major party campaign. The "whole emphasis" had to "be on outreach." The idea was to "translate the principles in which we believe into the issues of the day that might confront ... the voting public in 1976. Here's a problem – here's a solution. Why does the solution work? Here's the super structure of thinking that lies behind it." MacBride's second condition, which may have worked against his goal of "outreach," was that there be no compromise with the Party Platform. "If I were to be the nominee we would not distill or in any way cloud over what we felt or believed in certain areas because it might be transitorily unpopular to take that point of view." For MacBride, de-emphasizing controversial aspects of libertarianism would ultimately be self-defeating because libertarian ideas were part of a "seamless web." Satisfied that all these requirements were met by the Dallas Convention's rejection of any endorsement of Republican or Democratic candidates with marginally libertarian views, MacBride announced his candidacy at the 1975 California Libertarian Party convention.[46]

MacBride did have opponents for the nomination at the Party's August 1975 convention in New York City. Kay Harroff, who had done comparatively well for a third-party candidate in her 1974 Senate bid against John Glenn, presented herself as the most principled libertarian candidate. Since MacBride – as well as the underdog in the race, Guy W. Riggs, an IBM sales executive – made similar claims, this gave her no clear advantage. MacBride's obvious financial resources, his modicum of public celebrity as the errant Virginia elector, his prior political experience, albeit as a Vermont state senator, and his support by the Party's national chair – all these facilitated his first ballot victory.[47]

Two days of platform debate produced a document that was longer and more detailed than in 1974. The platform now applied its non-interventionist principles to such areas as presidential war powers ("We call for the reform of the Presidential War Powers Act to end the President's power to initiate military action") and the Middle East ("We call upon the United States government to cease all interventions in the Middle East … and to cease its prohibition of private foreign aid, both military and economic.") Perhaps most popular was the addition of a catch-all caveat at the end of the new platform: "Our silence about any other particular government law, regulation, ordinance, directive, edict, control, regulatory agency, activity, or machination should not be construed to imply approval." When the Harvard philosopher Robert Nozick proposed this new plank from the floor, he received a standing ovation, after which the proposal was adopted by acclamation.[48]

The only real excitement at the convention centered around the nominations for the vice presidential position. Jim Trotter, a former SDS member and tax evader, was the leader after the first ballot but lacked a majority. At this point MacBride announced to the delegates that he had strong tactical reservations about the front-runner. MacBride explained that if Trotter became the Vice-presidential candidate, "We will have a one issue campaign …

This is ... not a tax rebel party per se. We have more to say than that ..."[49] Ultimately David Bergland, a Huntington Beach, California, attorney received the nomination.

Despite such intramural contretemps, the Libertarian Party had reason for increased optimism in 1975–76. Delegates from 35 states and the District of Columbia attended the 1975 National Convention which received considerable wire service coverage and network radio reports, as well as several minutes of prime-time coverage on the CBS and NBC nightly news programs. Another bright spot was finance; money was going to be available in 1976 to mount a modest but real campaign. MacBride subsequently poured in sizeable sums of his own, giving the campaign $56 000 for television spots alone by late September 1976.[50] Additionally, Charles Koch, an oil tycoon from Wichita, Kansas provided cash for the operation of the Party Headquarters.[51] Koch, a great admirer of Ludwig von Mises, in a letter to his fellow "Rocky Mountain Oilmen," urged them to support the Libertarian Party and MacBride. Denouncing President Ford's signing of the Energy Policy and Conservation Act as just "one of the many demonstrations of the bankruptcy of the Republican alternative to Democratic interventionism," Koch insisted that MacBride was "far better fitted to be president than any candidate of any party has been in my lifetime."[52]

If Koch had rejected both the Republican and Democratic parties, others were doing likewise in the wake of the scandals associated with Vietnam and Watergate. Voter turnout in the 1974 congressional elections dropped to 38 percent, the lowest since World War Two. Bumper stickers warned the voter: "DON'T VOTE, IT ONLY ENCOURAGES THEM" or "THE LESSER OF TWO EVILS IS STILL EVIL."[53]

MacBride and the Libertarians, hopeful that a grand party realignment was in the works, planned to tap into this dissatisfaction. With the government's moral authority clearly called into question in public surveys, and with the demoralization of the Republican Party evident, some Libertarians saw hopeful parallels between the 1970s and the 1850s. Reviewing the rapid expansion of the Libertarian Party, MacBride concluded its early success "perhaps [was] exceeded only by the period

encompassing the birth of the Republican Party in the 1850s."
Citing an October 1974 *Washington Post* column by Nicholas
Von Hoffman praising the Libertarians as "the only people worth
voting for," MacBride foresaw "a new political tidal wave in
American history."[54]

Murray Rothbard was equally optimistic about the Party's
opportunities thanks to what he perceived as the crisis of the old
order. Reversing his 1972 opinion that it was too early for political organizing, he urged Libertarians to seize the moment.
Everywhere he found evidence of decay. Keynesian economics
had produced "boom and bust *at the same time* in our current
inflationary depression." Government regulation of industry had
been so discredited that "its warmest supporters" were now
calling for the abolition of the Interstate Commerce Commission
and the Civil Aeronautics Board. Government bailouts of businesses in trouble were "increasingly seen to be throttling free
competition" and the "happily imminent bankruptcy of the New
York City government" would be just the start of the urban
financial crisis. Everywhere in the United States a century of
statism had now consumed the "fat" previously generated by free
markets. With no cushion left "[e]very statist act" now produced
"an instant negative feedback." Rothbard exalted at this evidence
of systemic decay and announced that libertarians were "no
longer a remnant." They were now "on the road to the victory of
liberty."[55]

The events of 1976 were to establish that these assessments
were off the mark. Americans generally have been resistant to
revolutionary ideologies in time of crisis. In the aftermath of the
Panic and Depression of 1893 the American electorate turned to
the Republican Party, not the Populists, let alone the Socialist
Labor Party. Similarly, the beneficiaries of the crisis of 1929–33
were the Democrats, not the Communists or Socialists.

MacBride began 1976 with great outward optimism. Writing
to Ralph Raico in mid-February, he was enthusiastic about the
campaign so far.

Oh, its going to be a glorious year all right! I estimate exposure
to be about 20 million people so far, with all thing considered,

the most astounding degree of acceptance of our ideas by reporters and the general public alike. I based my guess as to the general public by the ratio of favorable phone calls to unfavourable ones on the around 50 radio and television programs I've appeared on that have a call-in feature. And it's fun![56]

Travelling around the country in a DC-3 that he rented for the effort, he planned on visiting 30 states and 80 cities by the end of April. A campaign stop in one of the middle-size America cities usually involved a press conference with the local media, participation in a radio talk-show or two, a speech at a banquet under the auspices of the local or state libertarian party and a presentation at the local university.[57] Such activities produced substantial local print and media coverage, but this was transitory in its impact, as MacBride ruefully noted in retrospect. "The difficulty with that sort of coverage, however, is that it's one-shot: when the campaign plane left the runway there was no further news to be reported day-in and day-out, week-in and week-out, in Cincinnati."[58] The only way to overcome this one-shot impact on local awareness would have been regular attention by the national press, something that the Libertarians could not obtain in 1976.

The liabilities of an ideological third party in the United States in 1976 were multiple. In addition to the traditional American suspicion of "extremes," there were institutional barriers to the success of any third party, particularly one that was not led by a prominent national figure. These difficulties included problems of ballot access, federal campaign contribution limits, and dismissal by the national media.

Ballot access had not been a problem in the nineteenth century. Prior to the 1890s political parties rather than states prepared and distributed their own ballots, with party workers distributing ballots at the polling stations on election day. The introduction of the Australian or secret ballot at the end of the century, however, raised the obvious question of what parties were to be included on the official ballots. Ballot access laws quickly made it difficult for minor parties to get on ballots. Additionally, during the Second Red

Scare many states, targeting the Communist Party, made it more difficult for third parties to get and stay on ballots. As there was no uniform, nation-wide law determining what those ballot access requirements would be, this meant that third parties in the seventies were forced to overcome 51 different bureaucratic hurdles.[59]

The process of obtaining ballot access and maintaining it could exhaust and discourage all but the most zealous. National Director Robert H. Meier warned one ballot access director that only relentless pressure would prevent ballot a drive from failing.[60] Although volunteers could drive or fly in from one state to another seeking to help with the drives, the demands for such assistance were always greater than the supply and the party's financial resources. Occasionally a worker went over the edge, as Crane related in a letter to Charles Koch:

Speaking of things going wrong, in North Carolina we turned in 16,600 signatures to meet a 10,000 signature requirement. It turns out that a young man from Atlanta, Georgia who was helping us with the drive had submitted 1100 signatures, of which 400 were forged. ... Our young friend from Atlanta took the discovery of his wrongdoing somewhat hard and tried to kill himself by jumping off a bridge. Being a libertarian, however, he was unsuccessful and is now under the care of a psychiatrist.[61]

Despite such embarrassments and frustrations, the party managed to get on the ballot in 32 states in 1976, more than any other third party or independent candidate. But even this took seven lawsuits and the party did not even try to get on the ballot in California, where new parties had to obtain 600 000 valid signatures in two months.[62] Whatever the success of the party in ballot access efforts in one presidential year, rarely could a state party rest on its efforts. As the party's candidates almost never received a large enough vote to obtain permanent ballot status, the process became a quadrennial sisyphean labor.

The Federal Election Campaign Finance Act of 1974 restrictions on individual contributions were an additional burden.[63] Also, the Act's provision for public funds for the Republican and

Democratic primaries, national conventions, and general presidential campaigns clearly discriminated against minor parties. The law recognized the existence of a political duopoly and sought to perpetuate it by discrimination against new entrants to the competition. If the logic of the anti-trust movement had been applied to the 1974 statute it is difficult to see how it could have survived even cursory examination.

The Libertarian Party in February 1975 joined with Senator James Buckley, former Senator Eugene McCarthy, the New York Civil Liberties Union and others in challenging the law's constitutionality. The suit argued that the Act restricted First Amendment rights of free speech and freedom of association. Numerous other alleged constitutional deficiencies were detected, including the requirement of disclosure of contributions which Ed Crane likened "to the efforts of Southern states to obtain the membership lists of the NAACP during the 1960s."[64]

In January 1976 the United States Supreme Court handed down a ruling in *Buckley* v. *Valeo* that was a partial victory for the Libertarian Party. Although the Court upheld the constitutionality of federal financing of the two major parties' presidential campaigns and the 1974 Act's limits on campaign contributions, the ruling did strike down general spending limits and abolished limits on a candidate's contributions to their own campaign. The later concession was to prove important for the MacBride campaign and absolutely vital for the relative success of the Libertarian Party's 1980 presidential campaign.[65]

Still, the Court's decision to sustain the $1000 limit on an individual's contribution to a campaign precluded wealthy backers such as the Koch family from doing for MacBride what Max Palvesky, a Californian computer millionaire did for McGovern in 1972: give his presidential campaign $350 000 even before the nomination.[66] As minor party candidates were much less likely than McGovern to receive much free national media attention, the 1974 Act's contribution restrictions inhibited their ability to communicate their message; thus the contribution limits, as sustained by the Supreme Court, helped maintain the political duopoly.

Crane explored a variety of ways to increase the national visibility of the MacBride campaign. In January 1976 he began an unsuccessful ten-month campaign to obtain Secret Service Protection for MacBride. Dwight R. MacDonald of the Department of the Treasury rejected the request on the grounds that then current guidelines for Secret Service protection required that the candidate not only be "seriously and actively campaigning on a national basis" – something which MacBride certainly was doing – but he also must "meet the qualifications for matching funds under the Federal Election Campaign Finance Act, as amended." Undaunted by this rejection, Crane pressed on by putting the same protection request to the Secretary of the Treasury William E. Simon. Suggesting that the libertarian philosophy was controversial, he expressed concern for the safety of the candidate in the absence of Secret Service protection. This gambit and all others that Crane subsequently tried failed to budge the Treasury Department.[67]

The Libertarian candidate also had limited success at getting national media attention during the campaign, thanks in part, and rather appropriately, to the highly regulated nature of the communications industry. When the campaign committee sought in April 1976 to purchase five minutes of television air-time from the networks, all three, after consulting legal counsel, refused to do so until after the two major parties had held their national conventions, lest the networks be unfair to the two major parties. Crane protested to Carol Jennings of the Media Access Project, pointing out the disparity between the positions of a third party and the two major parties.

> Simply because we have nominated our candidates does not mean that our candidate will appear on any state ballots. We must raise money and gain publicity in order to conduct successful petition drives around the country. To deny us national television time when we are prepared to pay for it is, in effect to deny us ballot status in many states.[68]

CBS did finally relent to the extent of allowing MacBride one five-minute TV spot and he was quick to point out that he networks in the fall "were ... scrupulously honest in offering us as many five minute political spots as we could reasonably afford."[69]

Perhaps even more handicapping for the MacBride campaign was the impact of the Federal Communication Commission's Equal Time rule stipulating that all candidates for public office be given equal access to free or paid use of radio and television. Because of the Equal Time rule MacBride found it difficult to get television interviews in larger markets. The syndicated "Phil Donahue Show" decided not to have MacBride on for a 60-minute interview after the program's lawyer reviewed the equal time implications. In smaller markets, where there were fewer fears that other candidates would demand access, interview time was often generous.[70]

Seeking national exposure to the "attentive public," MacBride did make it on to ABC's "Good Morning America" and NBC's "Today Show," for three and ten minutes respectively. An appearance on the October 17 edition of "Meet the Press" proved disappointing. MacBride appeared along with Tom Anderson of the American Party, Peter Camejo of the Socialist Workers Party, and Lyndon LaRouche of the United States Labor Party.

LaRouche got the bulk of the questions after early on warning that if Carter were elected, "this nation will be destroyed in thermo-nuclear war before the summer." At another point, Peter Camejo started into an extended discourse in Spanish. Much of the program was spent debating whether the Socialist Worker's party was a revolutionary party and with bantering between LaRouche and Nat Hentoff, one of the panelists.

Despite the zoo-like atmosphere, MacBride did get a couple of questions. His answers illustrated how unprepared the Party was to offer specific incremental policies proposals. Marianne Means of Hearst Newspapers asked MacBride how he proposed to finance national defense, police, and fire protection. "Surely you can't say that charities will support that?" MacBride could only admit that while he believed that "taxation is inherently wrong" it would be cruel to make a straight transition to liberty which "would produce the kind of chaos and suffering that the libertarian philosophy is opposed to."[71]

In another question the syndicated conservative columnist James Jackson Kilpatrick noted that MacBride's campaign book, *A New Dawn for America*, urged total abstention from military intervention. MacBride explained that if Red China put troops in Mexico "we would have to take action," but he seemed to rule out any projection of conventional force beyond immediately contiguous territories. "The point of our policy is to maintain the security of this country and we would do what is necessary to counter the immediate threat if there should be one to this country."[72]

MacBride gave similarly vague answers in other media forums, advocating some idyllic end-state while assuming that the transition would take care of itself. When *Reason* asked MacBride how he would phase out the "moral wrong of taxation," he had to admit that it could not be done immediately. "The markets would be in chaos. People would be without money. ... There would be a situation akin to that in Lebanon at the moment and I am opposed to doing that." When pressed on how long it would take, MacBride indicated that he didn't know.[73]

On Buckley's "Firing Line" program, the host probed the Libertarian candidate's non-interventionist foreign policy, asking how Libertarians would have responded to Soviet support for revolution in Angola and Cuba. MacBride suggested that Soviet influence in Angola and Cuba primarily was "through a set of ideas." It was through advocating an opposite set of ideas, "the reality of human liberty, the necessity of human freedom" that Libertarians would "halt these bit-by-bit bite-offs of the communist empire." Buckley, although certainly supporting the sort of intellectual combat MacBride advocated, found such an approach insufficient.[74]

As with many Libertarians, MacBride seemed to have an ineradicable faith in the incandescent power of ideas to overcome material factors. Most Americans were more skeptical. A Libertarian candidate who did not provide a detailed program for a transition from "welfare–warfare" liberalism found himself at a distinct disadvantage even before the generally sympathetic audience Buckley provided.

Denied participation in the League of Women Voters-sponsored presidential debates, generally ignored by the news weeklies, and able to afford only eight five-minute nationally-

televised spots, MacBride received only 173 019 votes for
President, just 0.2 percent of the national popular vote. A statistical analysis by William Westmiller for the campaign committee
concluded that MacBride "drew no significant support from disaffected Democratic registrants." In those nine states where
Ford's popular vote exceeded Carter by 25 percent or more,
MacBride's percentage increased to 1.072 percent, three times
his national average. Westmiller concluded that MacBride would
have done considerably better if Ford had been assured of election, thus allowing disaffected Republicans to vote Libertarian
with little risk.[75]

MacBride's best showing was in Alaska where he received 5.5
percent state-wide and nearly 10 percent in Fairbanks.
MacBride's relatively impressive Alaskan vote probably was a
by-product of several factors: the attention he gave to the state,
personally piloting his rented DC-3 to Fairbanks; the efforts
made by his Alaska coordinator, Dick Randolph (who subsequently became the first Libertarian elected to a state legislature);
and the general libertarian climate of the state, as evidenced by
its Supreme Court's unanimous 1975 ruling that nothing in the
state's Constitution prohibited the personal use of marijuana.[76]

Generally MacBride, and later Libertarian presidential candidates, did best in the western states. Despite the demonstrable
role that the Federal government had played in the development
of the West, that section of the nation continued to think of itself
as the home of rugged individualism. The older resentment at
being a colony of eastern banks and mining industries had
increasingly given way to resentment at being a colony of the
Federal government, the major landholder in the West, with its
expanding web of social and environmental regulations in the
seventies.[77]

IV

Despite the extremely modest popular vote, Libertarians generally felt a great deal had been accomplished between 1972 and
1976. Although only on the ballot in two states in 1972, at 32

states in 1976 the Party had a broader ballot access than any other third party. The Libertarian Presidential ticket received recorded votes in only four states in 1972 but in 1976 came in third nationally among candidates with a Party identification. (McCarthy running as an independent received far more votes – 756, 631 – than MacBride, but then he was a nationally-known figure.) Starting from only a few state chapters in 1972, the Party now had organizations in all fifty states. Attendance at conventions kept expanding: from less than 100 at Denver, it reached 600 in Washington, DC, in 1976 and was to surpass 1200 in 1977 at the San Francisco convention.[78]

Reviewing the 1976 campaign, Rothbard optimistically declared it a "landmark for our country: for it established the fledgling, new-born Libertarian Party as the biggest 'third party' in America."[79] Ever fearful of moderation, however, Rothbard now detected threats of "right opportunism" from those who insisted that a gradualist reform approach was necessary if the Libertarian Party ever was to have any hopes of electing rather than just fielding candidates.

Robert Poole had advocated precisely this in a August 1976 *Reason* editorial, suggesting that a Libertarian candidate seeking public office must propose "a specific program which can be seen as potentially realizable" during the candidate's term of office. Poole freely admitted this would mean the program "would be evolutionary in nature." Crane took a similar tack in his post-election analysis. Although enthusiastic about what the Party had accomplished in 1976, Crane concluded that a weakness common to all Libertarian candidates in 1976 "was a reluctance to learn the issues of the campaign from the perspective of the media and the major party candidates." Libertarians, warned Crane, had to learn the specific issues of the day and be prepared to offer specific Libertarian alternatives rather than simply speak of the blessings of pure liberty.[80]

Rothbard denounced such a Fabian approach. A gradualist program calling for tax cuts, regulatory reform, and limits on the future growth of government, Rothbard warned, would sound like "simply Reaganite Republicanism, and if that is the case, why in blazes should anyone vote for the new, untried LP when they could vote Reaganite Republican to begin with?" Why indeed?[81]

In truth the Libertarians recognized early on that Ronald Reagan represented a real threat to the growth of their Party. In a 1975 appearance on CBS's "60 Minutes" Reagan had volunteered to Mike Wallace that he was a "libertarian." In an effort at damage control, the *Libertarian Party News* sought to portray Reagan as statist, citing a *New York Times* article indicating that the California state budget more than doubled during his eight years as governor while the sales tax went from 4 to 6 percent and the top bracket for personal incomes went from 7 to 11 percent. The *News* article also suggested that Reagan was no friend of civil liberties as he opposed the legalization of marijuana and prostitution, regretted signing California's abortion law, and "strongly criticized the Warren Court rulings that better secured the civil liberties of the accused." As Reagan did not support unconditional withdrawal of US troops from Western Europe and Korea, had supported escalation in Vietnam in the sixties, and currently opposed normalization of relations with Cuba, the Governor's foreign policy further disqualified him as a libertarian.[82]

Crane subsequently wrote Reagan requesting that he cease calling himself a libertarian.

> As you are no doubt aware, it is most difficult to establish in the public's mind the concept of a specific political philosophy. Given the vastly greater access to media exposure that you have relative to the Libertarian Party, it muddies the waters and confuses the public when you identify yourself as a libertarian.[83]

Reagan was not appreciative of Crane's request that he cease calling himself a libertarian.

> I have used the expression on some occasions that libertarianism is at the very heart of conservatism. That's libertarianism with a small "l" and makes no reference to your party.
>
>   I don't believe that anything I have said can be confusing to Libertarian Party members, but certainly the conservative

approach to individual freedom, in contrast to the liberal's big government philosophy gives validity to my use of the word.[84]

With Reagan in the 1976 race for the Republican nomination, Crane found himself getting headaches from worrying about conservative defections.[85]

Here was the essence of the problem confronting the Libertarian Party in the late seventies: if Reagan were to run and win the Republican nomination in 1980, how many market liberals would adhere to a Libertarian ticket still espousing the anti-politics of an eschatological vision? If the Libertarians were to have any chance at success, they had to design a political strategy that simultaneously appealed to incremental reformers and ideologues while promising some chance of victory, certainly not in 1980 but perhaps by 1992.[86] The vehicle to carry this strategy was the 1980 candidacy of Ed Clark.

V

For a minor party seeking mainstream respectability, Clark was a good choice. As a son of a rock-ribbed Yankee Republican father who had served as Middleboro, Massachusetts' town moderator for 52 years, the younger Clark never doubted that he was a Republican. After an education at Dartmouth College (BA, International Relations in 1952) and at Harvard Law School (JD, 1957), he quickly settled into the comfortable life of a corporate lawyer.[87]

Clark inherited his commitment to free-market ideas from his family, but he had something of an epiphany as a college student when he visited a World War One military cemetery and saw the graves of 40 000 French killed in a 1916 attack that gained about three miles. "I couldn't believe it," Clark recalled in 1980. "I cried. I couldn't understand how those people could have done it – how could the French government have persuaded their tax-payers to have supported it?" Clark remembered having "a very strong emotional feeling that I was looking at one of the great horrors of civilization, a horror that we ought to do away with."[88]

Clark's non-interventionism – a product of these experience and arguments with his father who had been an officer in World War One – prompted him to oppose the Vietnam War. What eventually got Clark actively involved in politics was Nixon's 1971 imposition of wage and price controls. Because the Republicans now were offending against Clark's anti-war views by prolonging the Vietnamese War and his free-market convictions by Keynesian-style economic controls, he was primed for conversion to an alternative political philosophy.

Encountering free-market ideas at a conference sponsored by a libertarian group at Columbia University in the fall of 1971, Clark felt that he had discovered his "new political home." He helped organize the Free Libertarian Party of New York early in 1972 and later that year attended the Denver national organizing convention. Reassigned to Atlantic Richfield's Los Angeles law offices later that year, he was soon involved in libertarian politics there, becoming chairman of the state party in 1973–74; in 1977 he was elected to the Los Angeles Health Systems Agency.[89]

Ed Crane persuaded Clark to run for the California governorship in 1978 as part of the former national chair's plan to convert the Libertarian Party into a viable competitor with the two major parties. Crane recognized in Clark a potential presidential candidate whose academic and professional credentials, conventional upper middle-class family life, attractive personality, and mild demeanor would disarm those skeptical of third parties and take the edge off of his radical proposals. Some 90 percent of the $361 000 raised for this long-shot campaign would be provided by Charles Koch, a Topeka, Kansas-based billionaire libertarian who had been funding market liberal authors and educational institutions since the late sixties.[90]

Clark's 1978 campaign came at an opportune time. Californians were debating Proposition Thirteen to roll back property taxes; libertarians active in the successful anti-tax campaign promoted Clark as the first gubernatorial candidate to endorse the proposition. Clark's straight-arrow appearance took much of the sting out of his more libertarian proposals (such as repeal of "victimless crime" laws). His support for an $800 tax credit for private school expenses, a one-third reduction in the state income tax, and a $500 tax credit for rentpayers naturally appealed to voters caught in the late seventies stagflation and income tax bracket creep.[91]

Clark didn't stand a chance against the better financed Evelle Younger and Jerry Brown – the respective Republican and Democratic nominees – but his campaign frequently received praise for injecting innovative ideas into the political dialogue. Many writers predicted a bright future for the libertarians in an age of anti-politics. As the Clark Campaign's goal was only 5 percent of the popular vote, his 374 000 votes (5.5 percent) seemed a rousing success. Campaigning in a single state, albeit the largest in the country, a libertarian candidate had more than doubled Roger MacBride's 1976 presidential vote total.[92]

Clark's significant expansion on MacBride's vote totals suggested to some libertarians a parallel with the exponential growth of the anti-slavery parties' support between 1840 and 1860. Generally ignored in those comparisons was the fact that while anti-slavery presidential candidates saw exponentially increasing popular votes (even in defeat) after 1840, those mounting totals were just the tip of a broad-based anti-slavery movement of varying fervor and purity within the Congress.

A glance at the 1978 libertarian returns should have raised doubts about this analogizing. Unlike in the 1850s' "liberty" movement, no libertarians had been elected to national office, and exactly one was elected to a state-level office: Dick Randolph, sent by Fairbanks voters to the Alaska House of Representatives. The analogy with the growth of the anti-slavery movement *did* have some merit, however, if the Libertarian party was understood as only the most radical element of a larger political movement committed to revitalizing market liberalism.[93]

Indeed, as utterly implausible as the Libertarian's vision of victory by 1992 seemed in retrospect, commentators in the late seventies could not be fully confident in dismissing the Libertarian Party's claim to be the 'wave of the future.' As the pollster Daniel Yankelovich noted in a 1977 seminar, the general public's distrust of government had reached epidemic proportions: "The change is simply massive. Within a ten to fifteen year period, trust in institutions has plunged down and down, from an almost consensual majority, two-thirds or more, to minority segments of the American public."[94] Who would benefit from such disenchantment? Noting that more than 50 percent of new voters were independents, Leonard Liggio predicted in 1978 that disaffection "among the younger voters is ringing the death-knell of the Republican Party."[95]

At the 1979 Libertarian National Convention, former McGovern advisor and then Washington editor of *Politics Today*, Alan Baron, told an enthusiastic audience that if the trend was not toward pure libertarianism, it was "at least toward classical liberalism."[96] Spurred on by such optimism the Party selected Clark as their Presidential nominee. Adding to the 579 delegates' confidence that 1980 might be the breakthrough year was their choice for Clark's running mate: David Koch, libertarian billionaire Charles Koch's younger brother. The Vice-Presidential candidate promised to make substantial financial contributions to the Party, thus getting around the $1000 dollar limit imposed on contributions to candidates by the 1974 Federal Election Campaign Act. Noting that he had been a libertarian since 1965, the MIT-educated chemical engineer thought "the Libertarian Party [was] at a stage in its development where it could become a very significant force in this country – a truly effective vehicle for rolling back the coercive power of government." Koch ultimately contributed 57 percent of the $3 657 000 raised during the campaign.[97]

Reflecting these augmented resources, the 1980 campaign had a professional look about it. A Steering Committee of eight, including Ed Crane as Communications Director, oversaw a full-time national staff of 20 based in Washington, DC. Policy analysts produced four white papers (on Taxing and Spending, Foreign Policy, Social Security and Education) and 10 position papers (on Inflation, Agriculture, Women's Rights, Housing, First Amendment Freedoms, Federal Election Laws, Government versus the Automobile, a Nuclear Diad, Controlled Substances, and Energy) in an effort to persuade journalists that Libertarians had "done their homework" and had developed plausible "transitional" programs.[98]

On the ballot in all 50 states, Clark visited 36, skipping primarily small rural states, and campaigning on a strategy of "going wherever the most widespread media coverage was likely to occur." He tried to average one college campus appearance per day. Three hundred campus chapters of Students for Clark distributed over one million pieces of literature to students and residents of adjacent neighborhoods. Denied participation in the League of Women Voters-sponsored debates, the campaign purchased 47 five-minute television spots from the three networks.[99]

VI

Despite the expanded effort in 1980, the election results were disappointing. When asked just before the election to anticipate Clark's vote totals, prominent Libertarian Party activists predicted from 500 000 (Murray Rothbard) to 7 percent (David Bergland) with an average projection of about 2 percent. When the Clark–Koch ticket collared only 912 000 votes, a little more than one percent, reactions ranged from disappointment to anger.[100] Most angry were those who felt they had been cut out of the campaign and that the campaign had compromised principles. Rothbard charged that the campaign had been designed to deceive the media and the public into thinking that there were millions of dedicated libertarians. Rather than using the election to "build cadre, or start the march for the long haul," Crane had sought "to reap a quick success by use of mirrors: using lots of money and slick media commercials to con everyone into thinking we are really a mammoth movement. Libscam!" Reviewing the campaign's messages, Rothbard concluded that "libertarian principle was traduced and abandoned in a quest for media respectability and votes." Clark having promised in his acceptance speech to gain "millions" of votes, the ticket and its handlers "sold their souls ... for a mess of pottage, and then they didn't even get the pottage."[101]

David Nolan was outraged by the Clark campaign's "whoring after the media" and its attempt to portray Libertarianism in a non-threatening fashion. A fatal mistake, Nolan argued, was "positioning Clark as a 'liberal reformer' – presenting proposals in the context of making the existing system more humane and benevolent, while avoiding 'controversial' statements (i.e. references to absolute principles) at all costs." What stunned Nolan was Clark's comment during an October 30 ABC "Nightline" interview that "We want to get back immediately to the kind of government that President Kennedy had back in the early 1960s ... much lower inflation, much higher growth rates, much lower taxes." By Clark's citing of John Kennedy, he had identified "himself with one of the most explicitly statist Presidents in modern times ... a grotesque mockery of everything we have fought for and believe in."[102]

How valid were the Rothbard/Nolan criticisms? Granted their premise that the campaign primarily ought to have been an effort to "educate" the public about libertarian principles, their critiques had some merit. But it does not follow that five-minute commercials or 30-second soundbites on the network evening news could do much educating or produce many converts. Stated baldly and without time for exposition, many libertarian principles and proposals would strike many viewers and listeners as absurd. As Hayek had pointed out, the feasibility of a "spontaneous order" is not readily apparent because "such orders as that of the market do not obtrude themselves on our senses but have to be traced by our intellect."[103] And even for Hayek, the application of the market principle to all aspects of social interaction – as Rothbard advocated – seemed inconceivable.[104]

Clark had reminded the Alaska delegation during the 1979 convention that "The world thinks third-party candidates are idiots." During the subsequent campaign he tried to sketch out for libertarians the political context in which he was operating: "I'm running for president of a country with a massive, complex state apparatus in which the forces which have brought that apparatus to its present point are still very much alive and at work." Recognizing this, Clark and Crane sought to present ideas which were "radical but ... not so radical that the audience no longer identifies with them and stops listening."[105]

Even with such caveats, Clark advocated economic positions in 1980 that surely were radical for the times and must have stopped many listeners in their tracks.[106] Clark's first-year budget called for $201 billion of cuts, accomplished by reducing defense spending by $50 billion, abolishing the Education and Energy departments, and taking the knife to all the other executive departments and independent agencies. All business and agricultural subsidies would be terminated. Accompanying the budget cuts would be dramatic tax cuts: income tax rates would be reduced by 50 percent, the zero income-tax bracket would be raised to $7500, inheritance and gift taxes as well as customs duties would be eliminated. Social Security would be privatized. Those under 40 would be taken out of the program. Those between 40 and 65 could opt out and establish their own independent retirement accounts but remain eligible for reduced payments at 65. For those over 65, payments would be continued but financed primarily out of the general fund. These were the economic proposals of a campaign that Rothbard and Nolan found too timid and unprincipled.[107]

The libertarians had made a maximum effort in 1980 yet had fallen far short. The explanations varied. Rothbard and Nolan blamed it on an unprincipled campaign and organized a "Coalition for a Party of Principle" to reclaim the party from the "Craniacs" and the "Kochtopus."[108] Others were inclined to blame the poor showing on Illinois Republican Congressman John Anderson's entrance into the race as an independent. David Boaz, Research Director for the Clark campaign, summed up this argument well in his post-mortem on the election:

> It's not just that Anderson took voters who might otherwise have voted for Clark, though he did in fact get the votes of many independent-minded voters who perceived him as fiscally responsible, socially liberal, and pro-peace. But the problem is also that Anderson took the media attention that might otherwise have been Clark's.[109]

Crane agreed and more recently has stated that "[i]f you do an overlay of Anderson's vote in 1980 and of Clark's in 1978, you find that they were the same people. Anderson got Clark's vote in California."[110]

Crane was accurate in his suggestion that Anderson received most of his 7 percent of the popular vote from the same general audience that the Clark campaign targeted: college-educated young independents. Although Anderson did position himself as economically more conservative than Carter and socially more liberal than Reagan, his deviationism was limited to such ambiguously libertarian positions as support for ERA and an $11 billion budget cut. If this was the "libertarianism" that sizeable numbers of Americans were prepared to endorse in 1980, it was tepid in the extreme. As it was, Anderson's popularity peaked at 20 percent, falling to 7 percent by November.[111]

In fact, most – some 66 percent by one estimate – of libertarian-inclined members of the general electorate supported Ronald Reagan in 1980. As discussed earlier in this chapter, the libertarians had first confronted this potential problem in 1976 when Reagan had unsuccessfully challenged the incumbent Gerald Ford for the Republican nomination. In 1980, as Crane and Chris Hocker noted in their post-election assessment, libertarians found Reagan "regularly portrayed in the news media as a hard-core advocate of the pure free market." Some libertarian activists, including members of the Libertarian–Republican Alliance, actually bolted to Reagan.[112] Although some noted free-market economists endorsed Clark's "White Paper on Taxing and Spending Reduction," most of the prominent market liberal economists – including Milton Friedman – signed on with Reagan.[113] Many, like the Hoover Institution's Director of Domestic Studies, Thomas Moore, probably saw the Libertarian Party primarily as a group to put desirable pressure on the Republican Party.[114] Obviously the gravitational pull of a candidate who might actually win the election – however politically restrained his actual support for market liberal ideas might prove to be – was too strong for the libertarians to overcome.[115]

The post-1980 influence of libertarianism on market liberalism was not to be primarily through presidential politics. The Koch brothers, who had always been skeptical of the political party route, now poured millions into such libertarian educational and lobbying organizations as the Institute for Humane Studies and the Council for a Competitive Economy. The flagship of this Koch-financed libertarian flotilla was the Cato Institute. Founded in 1977, the Cato Institute, with Ed Crane as its president, became a prominent source of libertarian public policy proposals in the 1980s.[116]

Crane and Koch did not permanently forgo the party route until after they were vanquished at the 1983 presidential nominating convention. When the Party selected David Bergland – an avowedly "no-compromise" libertarian – over the more mainstream Georgetown University professor Earl Ravenal, the Koch money disappeared. Bergland received only 228 000 votes in 1984.[117] It appeared clear by 1984 that the Libertarian Party was not destined to be a serious vehicle to elect market liberals.

Some libertarians – Doug Bandow, Dana Rohrabacher, John McClaughry – had reached this conclusion early on and threw in their lot with Reagan, receiving posts in the new administration. Defending his own decision to work as a Special Assistant for Policy Development, Bandow argued that "half a loaf is far better than no loaf." What remained to be determined was whether the Reagan administration could bake up even half a loaf for the market liberals.[118]

5 The Politics of Market Liberalism in the Eighties: Blue Smoke and Mirrors?

In 1980 market liberals had a choice between Libertarian and Republican Presidential candidates, both exploiting the crisis of Vital Center liberalism and committed to freer markets, lower taxes, stable money, and a roll-back of the welfare state. Beyond these programmatic goals the two candidates shared little. Ronald Reagan's orientation was towards the past; his rhetoric evoked images of a vanishing American economic and military pre-eminence that he promised to restore. The Libertarian, Ed Clark, looking to the future, projected a vision of a libertarian utopia and sought to catalyze a political revolution.

Reagan sought to purge the existing system of the excesses of the sixties but intended to leave standing the New Deal order. For Reagan in 1980 there would be no suicidal replay of Barry M. Goldwater's quixotic 1964 assaults on Social Security and the Tennessee Valley Authority. Clark, on the other hand, sought to create a new political order by yoking the free-market political economy of the right to the social liberalism of the left.

The two candidate's proposed foreign policies differed markedly. Where Reagan described the Vietnam adventure as a noble effort and sought to revitalize the military to press the Cold War, Clark repudiated "American interventionism" and echoed George McGovern's 1972 call for America to "come home."

Reagan anticipated coming to power in 1980 by leading a coalition of Republicans, disaffected Democrats, and politicized Protestant fundamentalists; Clark foresaw the ultimate Libertarian victory as the triumph of young, independent voters come to political awareness and committed to the proposition that civil and economic liberties were part of the seamless fabric of freedom.[1]

In a contest to succeed Carter, Clark and the Libertarians had no chance, producing little more than a small blip on the electoral radar screen. Some libertarians took the opportunity to join the Reagan administration, serving in secondary or tertiary policy roles. Most remained outside, serving as skeptical critics and commentators on Reagan's efforts to roll back the state.

Reagan's supporters were quick to claim that he had won an historic mandate comparable to that achieved by Roosevelt, with the implication that a radical downsizing of the state could now be launched. That Reagan received any such mandate seems doubtful. In 1981 the voting specialist Everett Carll Ladd reviewed the relevant polling data and concluded that rather than presaging some great realignment, the 1980 election only confirmed the "dealignment" of American politics. Party loyalties continued to fray. A plurality of voters now identified themselves as independents. Just as the election did not create a new majority party, neither did it give Reagan a mandate to abolish the social welfare state. Although there had been a sharp drop in "confidence in government performance," public "support for government service was at, or near, record levels in 1980." Reviewing much the same material, Gerald M. Pomper suggested that though Reagan had not achieved a mandate in 1980, the election "does provide the opportunity for Republicans to develop an electoral majority that will consistently support a conservative direction in public policy." A majority of the electorate converted to the principles of the New Deal order "when that program improved their lives."[2]

Reagan was not an inflexible dogmatist even if he was perhaps the most ideological of all recent presidents. Reagan's record as Governor of California had been more accommodating than his rhetoric. During the 1980 presidential campaign he consciously sought to disarm those who feared him as Goldwater reincarnate. Subsequently, when his 1981 domestic spending cuts began to hurt, Reagan insisted that, like FDR, he was trying to protect the system rather than transform it:

> I'm doing everything I can to save it; to slow down the destructive rate of growth in taxes and spending; to prune non-

essential programs so that enough resources will be left to meet the requirements of the truly needy.[3]

Reagan never expected to reduce federal spending in the budget's out years; he simply sought to slow the rate of growth. Martin Anderson, Reagan's Assistant for Policy Development, recounts how Reagan would illustrate this point. Raising his arm to about a 45-degree angle, the President would suggest this was the current rate of government spending increase. Dropping his arm to about a 30-degree angle, Reagan would indicate this was his goal. Notes Anderson, the "legendary reputation that Reagan acquired for cutting the budget stemmed almost exclusively from reducing large planned increases to moderate planned increases."[4]

If tax cuts sufficiently energized the private sector and if government spending growth slowed, then the economy might grow its way out of the deficit, producing enough for some expansion of federal spending while reducing the percentage of gross national product consumed by the state. Although the Reagan years saw a reduction in some components of the domestic budget, the growth in spending for entitlements outpaced the economy. Consequently, when Reagan left the presidency in 1989 the Federal Government was consuming about as large a percentage of the GDP as when he entered, 22.1 percent in FY 1989 contrasted with 22.7 percent in FY 1981.[5] In this area as in many others the Reagan years produced no clear victory for market liberalism.

II

The Reagan administration's economic goals were clearly laid out in his February 18, 1981 State of the Union address to Congress:

This plan is aimed at reducing the growth in Government spending and taxing, reforming and eliminating regulations which are unnecessary and unproductive or counterproductive, and encouraging a consistent monetary policy aimed at maintaining the value of the currency.[6]

These four goals – a reduction in the rate of federal spending growth, lower marginal tax rates, regulatory relief and reform, and a moderation of inflation – were widely shared by market liberals.[7] Such incremental reforms, however, couldn't possibly produce a market liberal utopia. At best they would be the first tentative steps to slowing the momentum of government expansion.

While interviewing Murray Weidenbaum, the libertarian Tibor Machan suggested to Reagan's first CEA Chairman that policymakers had to "be guided by ideals." Reagan's chief economic advisor didn't dispute this but insisted that the administration operated in a political context. "As a philosophical matter," Weidenbaum noted, "we share your belief in a free market … [b]ut I just think that when you're in office you have to set some reasonable targets."[8] Even though sympathetic to the goals of the moderate libertarians, most of Reagan's advisors recognized that practical politics limited what could be done.

Although Reagan's advisors all supported his main economic objectives, from the beginning there were competing schools of thought – monetarists, supply-siders and traditional Republican budget-balancers – on how to mesh tax and spending policies to produce a balanced budget in short order, as Reagan had promised during the campaign. Monetarists focused most on getting inflation under control. Supply-siders emphasized the positive effects on productivity produced by lowered marginal tax rates, effects that might make a supply-side tax cut self-financing over the long term. Budget-balancers focused on spending reductions, arguing that deficits produced high interest rates, crowded out private borrowing, and produced inflation.[9]

Complicating the efforts of all three schools to promote "Reaganomics" was the President's insistence on increasing defense spending in order to wage the Cold War more vigorously. Hovering over all these economic considerations was an awareness of the autonomy of the Federal Reserve Board which could derail any administration's economic plans should its Chairman,

Paul Volcker, slow the expansion of the money supply more rapidly than the administration anticipated.

With such a multiplicity of views and factors to be accommodated in any economic plan, economic forecasting in 1981 proved as much a political as scientific exercise. The supply-siders wanted the "biggest possible number for real growth" in the five-year economic forecast because this would show the effects of the anticipated Reagan tax cuts. The monetarists insisted on a more modest estimate of "money GNP" (real GNP growth plus inflation) because this would indicate the achievement of the monetarists' summa: a non-inflationary monetary policy. As the supply-siders wanted to predict a 5 percent real growth rate and the monetarists wanted a prediction of 7 percent money GNP growth, this meant, relates Stockman, that "by the third or fourth year, inflation collapsed to 2 percent because that's what the arithmetic required." When the forecasting team presented Murray Weidenbaum, the Chairman of the CEA, with a projection of a 2 percent inflation rate by the third or fourth year, he rejected it as absurd. Although skeptical of the supply-side projections of a 5–6 percent growth rate, he agreed to accept it in exchange for a projected inflation rate of 7.7 percent for FY 1982.[10]

Out of such compromises was the 1981 Reagan economic forecast cobbled. In the absence of the Administration's assumed only slowly falling inflation rates, the proposed personal tax cuts and provisions for accelerated business depreciations would produce massive deficits in the out years. Even assuming a carefully calibrated slow reduction of interest rates, conventional economics might have predicted a recession. But as Paul Craig Roberts has noted, a distinguishing feature of the supply-side argument was that an economy could enjoy growth while inflation declined. "Monetary policy would first stabilize and then gradually reduce inflation while tax cuts would provide liquidity as well as incentives and prevent the slower money growth from causing a recession."[11] Increased production would facilitate the painless adjustment in inflation as the economy grew its way out of inflation. Relying on "rational expectationist" ideas, administration theorists suggested that if the Federal Reserve could convincingly signal the markets that it was gradually decelerating the money growth, then inflationary expectations could be gradually reduced in lockstep with the Fed's actions. The result would be a soft landing. Whatever its theoretical merits, such an optimistic scenario would have required a precision of execution and coordination of government policies that market liberals – especially the monetarists – had traditionally debunked as impossible.[12]

Many libertarian economists were skeptical of the supply-side position. Richard Ebeling acknowledged that tax reductions could increase investments and ultimately produce more tax revenue but he insisted this couldn't happen in the short term. As the Reagan administration was only slowing the growth of government spending, rather than reversing it, he suggested that the inevitable revenue shortfalls could only be financed by printing more money and increasing inflation or by increased borrowing. Ebeling warned that if the government borrowed the money, "it will inevitably raise interest rates and crowd out the additional private investment demand created by the tax cut." He predicted that the "anticipated capital formation and growth will most likely be thwarted."[13] David Boaz, now a policy analyst at the libertarian Cato Institute, was equally skeptical. Making many of the same points as Ebeling, Boaz insisted that the "Reagan tax program is simply not enough. The economy is in disastrous shape and it will not be saved by these weak reforms."[14]

Murray Rothbard dismissed the Administration's economic medicine as inadequate. He insisted that inflationary expectations were so built into the market that only a dramatic signal from the Federal Reserve would reverse them. Rothbard urged the administration to "forget gradualism and slam on the brakes."

> Only a vivid and dramatic move will work – for example a law prohibiting the Federal Reserve from buying any more assets again. ... Or a return to a genuine, not phoney gold standard. Or abolishing the Federal Reserve. Or, better, a combination of all three. Pussyfooting and fine tuning are like shuffling deck chairs on the Titanic.[15]

Rothbard got his wish for a dramatic slowing of inflation but it may not have been as a result of Volcker's "slamming on the brakes." Indeed Volcker tried to assure the public, as in a mid-April 1981 speech, that the Federal Reserve's goal was a gradual slowing of money growth.[16]

Although the growth rate of the monetary aggregate, M1, declined noticeably in 1981, the broader measure, M2, continued to accelerate through 1981. This continued M2 surge has prompted several economists to suggest that inflation declined so rapidly in the early eighties primarily due to a slowing of the money velocity. The money velocity (the rate at which money is spent) may have declined, as Richard K. Vedder and Lowell Gallaway have suggested, because Volker's public announcements of a changed Federal Reserve policy "had a major effect on the inflationary expectations in the economy." Believing that Volcker was going to vigorously fight inflation, the incentive for the public to quickly spend money diminished, thus lowering the money velocity and reducing inflation – but also prompting a depression.[17] Whatever the exact calibration of the causes of the disinflation – and clearly there were several factors at work[18] – the result was a loss of the "inflation dividend" that the administration had counted on to keep budget deficits within manageable limits.[19] Indeed, of the $310.7 billion shortfall in the Reagan administration's 1981–86 revenue forecast, two-thirds of the shortfall came from overestimating the inflation rate for the out years.[20]

Given Reagan's planned tax cuts and the unanticipated collapse of the inflation dividend, the only way that the Administration could have avoided very large deficits in the short term would have been if it had enacted the massive program retrenchments that Ed Clark and the Libertarians had called for in 1980.

Even if the expected inflation dividend had remained available administrative policies would have produced sizeable deficits, unless a knife were taken to entitlement programs. By early February 1981 – long before anyone knew how dramatically disinflation would reduce anticipated revenue gains – the OMB was predicting sizeable deficits. Stockman's office estimated that the combined impact of just three proposals – the Kemp–Roth 30 percent cut in income-tax rates, the 10–5–3 business-accelerated depreciation reform and the defense build-up – would be a $130 billion deficit by FY 1984. This had prompted the Director to call for additional budget cuts, including those which would impact on the middle class.

"Chapter Two," as Stockman called it, would raise $20 billion by 1984 by imposing user fees on general aviation and yachters, eliminating oil depletion allowances, reducing dairy subsidies, scaling back water projects and capping deductibility of home mortgage payments. As even these proposed savings would not begin to close the deficit gap, and as he had to complete a proposal for Reagan by February 18, he resorted to the "magic asterisk" of "Future Savings to be identified."

The OMB Director anticipated sending two more proposals to Congress after he had time to further review the budget. One would produce perhaps $10 billion of additional savings by a fine-tooth combing of Carter's FY 1982 budget. The second would "entail sweeping reforms of the big middle-class entitlement programs: Social Security, Medicare, and federal retirement pensions."[21]

Although Stockman did get Reagan to approve in May 1981 a proposal to increase the Social Security early retirement penalty from 20 to 45 percent, when this produced a firestorm of Congressional resistance, Reagan disassociated himself from the idea. Stockman later concluded that a "drastic shrinkage of the welfare state was not [the President's] conception of the Reagan Revolution. It was mine."[22]

Libertarians shared Stockman's cynicism. When Reagan acquiesced in tax increases in 1982 to partially compensate for the growing deficit, Sheldon Richman suggested that the reason the deficits were "the largest in history is that Ronald Reagan has proposed federal spending at the highest levels in history. If this administration makes any more history we might not be able to stand it."[23] The Cato Institute prepared a policy analysis showing how the Administration could avoid the 1982 tax increases by making over $200 billion worth of cuts. Out of the window went a myriad of federal agencies devoted to subsidizing business, agriculture, housing, energy, and the transportation sectors. Revenue-sharing was terminated. Even presumptively public goods such as flood control and nature preservation were dispatched as Cato insisted that there was nothing that the Corp of Engineers or the Forest Service did that couldn't be done better and more efficiently by the private sector.

Although the Cato Institute "alternative" budget offered various rationales for the proposed major surgery, perhaps the most penetrating was the libertarian argument that government spending positively damaged the society's overall well-being by subsidizing inefficient businesses, narrowing consumer choice, raising consumer prices, encouraging the over-use of natural resources and promoting government dependency.[24]

Unfortunately for the libertarians and Stockman, Reagan had never given his highest priority to balancing the budget. The President resisted, telling Stockman in November 1981 that "I did not come here to balance the budget – not at the expense of my tax-cutting program and my defense program. If we can't do it in 1984, we'll have to do it later."[25] Meeting privately with money managers several days later, Reagan insisted that a larger deficit was less important than reducing inflation and increasing production and employment. If the economy rebounded, Reagan argued, people would not worry too much about the deficit.[26] To reassure fiscal conservatives he went on television in April 1982 to advocate a constitutional amendment mandating a balanced budget.[27] Thus Reagan could have it both ways, ideological consistency but programmatic flexibility.

Perhaps Reagan could be so casual about a balanced budget because he believed that it was Congress's failure to restrain spending increases on domestic policies that produced the deficits. Surprisingly, Reagan had come to office without any specific plans for budget cuts other than the intention of eliminating waste, fraud, and abuse. During the 1980 campaign Reagan, after meeting with his major economic advisors, made a major speech before the International Business Council spelling out his economic plans. Martin Anderson helped craft the speech and has emphasized that Reagan was not calling for any radical overhaul of federal spending.[28] Control of government spending was to be achieved by slowing the growth of existing programs, rejecting new programs and eliminating wasteful and fraudulent expenditure.

In practice, eliminating unnecessary expenditure proved much more difficult than Reagan anticipated. As William A. Niskanen, a member of Reagan's Council of Economic Advisors and a Public Choice scholar, has noted, there was a good deal of "waste" in the federal budget but most of it was interlarded into programs with considerable political support. It proved almost impossible to excise fat without cutting something that powerful or vocal interests considered sinew.[29]

As Reagan had promised not to touch the major income security programs, was committed to a major military expansion, and had to pay the interest on the national debt (which was running about 10 percent of the budget in FY 1981), this meant that most of Reagan's budget cuts had to be taken out of the remaining 30 percent of the budget.[30] As a student of public choice might have predicted, the Reagan budget cuts in 1981 did the least damage to those constituting the prime Reagan constituency, the broad middle class.

Of the $35.2 billion in cuts made in the 1981 reconciliation package, about $25 billion – some 70 percent of the budget savings – were made in programs targeted on the lower income strata. Reductions took place in Medicaid, housing assistance, food stamps, Aid to Families with Dependent Children, energy assistance, Supplemental Security Income, unemployment insurance, Title XX Social Services, and Legal Services; the CETA public service jobs program was eliminated. As these "poverty programs" constituted less than 10 percent of the budget and as the Reagan budget cuts generally only trimmed their projected growth rates, such "cuts" couldn't possibly suffice to produce a balanced budget by 1984.[31]

It was not that Reagan did not want to reduce the size of government. Rather it was that the President was enough of a politician to recognize resistance and back-pedal in order to gain something that at least marginally advanced his agenda. Martin Feldstein, Reagan's second Chairman of the CEA, recalls Reagan's attitude toward Social Security and the Greenspan Commission's initial recommendations for reform. In those private conversations Reagan wondered why Social Security could not be privatized. He only reluctantly accepted the explanation that continued Social Security taxation was essential to pay future benefits of current retirees.

Reagan recalled that in the thirties the Democrats had promised that Social Security taxes would never exceed 2 percent. He suggested that the best solution to the financial problems facing Social Security in 1983 was a scaling-back of future benefits. Feldstein agreed. He suggested indexing at 3 percent below inflation, but Jim Baker, Reagan's Chief of Staff, warned that this would stigmatize the Republican Party and the matter was dropped.[32]

Needless to say, the Reagan administration was not prepared to advocate an even more radical Social Security reform emanating from the libertarians. Peter Ferrara, who had written Ed Clark's White Paper on Social Security, authored a Cato Institute study in 1980 that proposed the phasing out of Social Security with mandated participation in government-approved private pension plans for those who opted out. In 1982 the Cato Institute published another Ferrara volume on Social Security. When Ferrara shortly afterwards went to work for Martin Anderson in the White House on policy analysis, the Washington press quickly announced that the Administration was considering ending Social Security. Although nothing was further from the truth, the flap produced some welcome publicity for the heretical idea. As Ed Crane and David Boaz noted in 1985, "the conventional wisdom [in 1980] was that privatizing social security was a pipe dream, thoroughly outside the parameters of policy debate." But after the publicity given to Ferrara's ideas, "when the *next* social security [*sic*] crisis occurs, privatization may be seen not as a radical idea but as the only way out."[33]

In 1983 privatization remained politically impossible and Reagan reluctantly forwarded the Greenspan Commission recommendations to Congress for its action. As implemented by Congress, the resultant payroll tax increases for many workers effectively canceled out the Reagan income-tax cuts, leaving them as highly taxed at the end of the decade as at the beginning. The poorest 30 percent of families paid a slightly higher percentage of their incomes in federal taxes in 1988 than they had in 1977.[34]

III

Of Reagan's four major economic reforms, regulatory relief and deregulation perhaps proved the least successful. From the seventies, businesses had incurred major increases in operating costs produced by a wave of new "social" regulations intended to protect consumers and workers and to clean up the environment. Murray A. Weidenbaum co-authored in 1978 a widely-discussed study that estimated the regulatory burden (business compliance costs plus government administrative costs) at $66 billion in 1976. Updating his analysis two years later, Weidenbaum calculated the cost of government regulation at $102.7 billion for 1979. Weidenbaum argued that the concept of a regulated industry had become a quaint idea because *every* industry was now a regulated industry.[35]

Although Weidenbaum's methodology by which he extrapolated his 1976 figures to 1979 was subject to challenge, few economists denied that businesses were being asked to bear unprecedented costs to promote public health and safety.[36] Indeed, many economists who might have served comfortably in a Democratic administration could agree with Weidenbaum's conclusion that "government regulation should be carried to the point where the incremental costs equal the incremental benefits, and no further."[37]

This was an economic philosophy that probably appealed to the Carter administration Chairman of the Council of Economic Advisors, Charles L. Schultze. In his widely-noted 1976 Godkin Lectures at Harvard, Schultze set himself the task of deciding "when and how should government intervene in private markets for the purpose of improving economic efficiencies." He found fault with the sort of command economy approach that the Environmental Protection Agency was forced into by Congressional mandates such as those of the 1972 Federal Water Pollution Control Act. This legislation required the EPA to set pollution levels for more than 62 000 point sources while taking into account equipment and facility age, the manufacturing process involved, the engineering of various types of control techniques, and other factors thought worthy of consideration by the EPA.

Schultze concluded that such mandates presupposed an omniscient EPA. Perhaps even worse, such an approach provided "absolutely no incentives to firms and municipalities to channel technological innovation towards reduction in pollution." Schultze marvelled that "a society that traditionally has boasted about the economic and social advantages of Adam Smith's invisible hand ... has been strangely loath to employ the same techniques for collective intervention."[38]

This attempted mimicking of market pricing mechanisms probably appealed to most market liberals. Even some generally libertarian writers such as William Tucker found it attractive. Tucker proposed that the "bubble concept" – in which the EPA placed an imaginary bubble over a plant site with multiple emission sources, assigned a maximum emission discharge for the site, and then let the owner decide how he would control the individual sources of pollution – be applied to acid rain. The EPA could put an imaginary bubble over the entire Midwest, the source of Acid Rain, and sell the rights to dump sulfur into the atmosphere. The Midwestern utilities, Tucker argued, would buy up some of the rights to pollute and pass on these costs to their customers, who would start to conserve electricity as the price went up – thus resulting in less sulfur discharge and smaller amounts of acid rain. Canada and the New England states would have the option to buy up some of the pollution rights and "retire them" – thus forcing polluters to cut back on their sulfur emissions.

Tucker saw this as an ideal solution to the seemingly interminable arguments over acid rain, its causes, costs, and consequences. Because people on both ends would be paying the "cost of their choices." there would be a strong incentive to get the most scientifically reliable information, "rather than parading out wild exaggerations" for their political effect.[39]

Although "pricing" pollution might seem like a market liberal solution, various libertarian analysts raised objection. Rothbard discussed property rights and air pollution in a 1981 Cato Institute symposium. He argued, in effect, that Tucker's proposed solution to acid rain ignored the ethical dimension. Where a railroad's locomotive belched smoke damaging a farmer's orchard, Rothbard pointed out, "it makes a great deal of difference to both of them who has to pay whom." By extension, it seemed difficult to justify New England's obligation, under Tucker's scheme, to purchase pollution rights so that it could retire them. For Rothbard there was no role for the state in preventing the "trespass" of pollution. Rather, the proper action would be for a private plaintiff (and those who voluntarily joined the plaintiff) to launch a civil suit for damages, provided that (1) the polluter hadn't previously established a homestead easement, (2) the plaintiff could prove actual harm and (3) the plaintiff could prove "strict causality from the actions of the defendant to the victimization of the plaintiff" with clear and convincing evidence.[40]

Even if one wished to dismiss Rothbard's call for a return to the common law and private litigation, libertarians had objections to the proposition that the state regulatory agencies could replicate the price-determining process of a true market. As Fred L. Smith, Jr. pointed out, Schultze's "third way" – the reliance on politically determined pollution taxes – ignored the failure of the socialist command economies. As Hayek had pointed out in the thirties, without the voluntary exchanges which define the market the very information needed to establish a market price would not arise. Smith concluded that "the absence of the market also means that one cannot replicate a market."[41]

Despite these libertarian objections to both command and control and market-mimicking approaches to environmental regulation, most of the market liberals who peopled Reagan's regulatory agencies probably were prepared to acknowledge clean air and water as public goods requiring government intervention. Reagan's election gave them their best opportunity to make some amendments to the seventies legislation that businessmen found most burdensome.

According to Richard N. L. Andrews, the fact that both the Clean Air and Water Acts were scheduled for reauthorization in the early 1980s meant that the "times were favorable ... for both the agencies and regulated industries to digest their responsibilities, reassess those regulations that were unreasonable or ineffective" and enact reformed legislation.[42] Such an approach, however, would have required a protracted struggle with no assured outcome given that the Republicans did not control the House of Representatives.

Stockman, in his famous "Dunkirk" memorandum sent to Reagan in December 1980, had warned that a massive number of new business regulations were scheduled for implementation in the next 18–40 months. They would "sweep through the industrial economy with gale force" unless the new administration launched "an orchestrated series of unilateral administrative actions to deter, revise, or rescind existing and pending regulations where clear legal authority exists."[43] Rather than a long march through the legislative institutions of government to accomplish regulatory reform, Stockman urged relief through the strategy of what Richard Nathan has called the "Administrative Presidency." This entailed selecting cabinet and, particularly, sub-cabinet officers who were ideologically attuned to the Reagan Revolution, and then giving them their marching orders to produce regulatory relief through staff and budget cuts and cost-benefit analyses.[44] Such initiatives could only provide symptomatic relief but they provided the appearance of decisive and effective action that Stockman counted on to boost business morale and prevent an "economic Dunkirk." Real reform could come later.

Zealous proponents of regulatory relief were appointed as heads of the EPA (Anne Burford), the National Highway and Transportation Agency (Raymond Peck) and the Occupational Safety and Health Administration (Thorne Auchter). Budgets, staffs and enforcement efforts were pruned accordingly. To spur on the regulatory relief efforts, Reagan established on January 22, 1981 the Task Force on Regulatory Relief headed by Vice President George Bush. Executive Order 12 291 issued in February 1981 required that all new proposed regulations issued by agencies under the control of the executive branch had to pass a cost-benefit test except where expressly forbidden by law.

What was accomplished by such cost-benefit analyses? Of Carter's 172 "midnight regulations" that were pending when Reagan entered office and "froze" them, eventually 112 were approved without change, 12 underwent major modification, 18 were withdrawn, and 30 were referred back to the originating agencies for revision. During the first two years of OMB's review of regulatory proposals, it rejected only 2 percent of the

5346 it considered. When Bush's Task Force on Regulatory Relief disbanded in August 1983 it issued a report claiming that it had produced $150 billion in regulatory cost savings, but upon closer inspection this claim seemed overstated. The $150 billion included (1) cost savings achieved by previous administrations or by Congress, (2) savings attributed to regulations that had never gone into effect, and (3) savings from the elimination of standards later reinstated by the federal courts.[45]

Clearly the Administration had achieved less regulatory change than the optimists had anticipated. The reasons are not elusive. First of all, no independent regulatory agencies came under the jurisdiction of Reagan's executive order. Secondly, most health and safety legislation explicitly forbade using cost-benefit analysis in evaluating proposed regulations, and the Supreme Court ruled that the enabling act for OSHA in effect prohibited the use of such cost-benefit criteria.[46] The "administrative presidency" could score some tactical victories but any permanent "relief" would require either revising or repealing the regulatory statutes. Any actual elimination of health and safety regulatory agencies, however, was out of the question. Even the Heritage Foundation had to admit in 1981 that there was "widespread support for continued regulation of industry where health and safety conditions are at stake."[47]

Weidenbaum indicated that the Administration made few serious efforts at proposing statute revisions, in part, because the Chairman of the Senate Environment and Public Works Committee "was known to be very protective of the status quo." But an even more important reason for the Administration's "extraordinarily timid" action, notes Weidenbaum, was its "desire to avoid raising controversial legislative questions that could impede the speedy enactment of its tax and budget initiatives."[48] When Bush's Task Force closed up shop in the late summer of 1983 its final report did include a list of proposed legislative reforms but, with one exception, all of the suggested reforms called for the abolition of various economic regulations rather than for revisions of the Clean Air Act, Clean Water Act, or the Occupational Safety and Health Act (OSHA).[49] By the time the Administration did submit proposals for statutory reform, environmental groups had so aroused popular opinion against the Administration that Weidenbaum predicted in 1983 that "we will be lucky if by January 1985 we are back to where we were in January 1981 in terms of public attitudes."[50]

The EPA during Burford's reign found itself in an adversarial relationship with both Congress and the environmental interest groups. Adjusted for inflation, EPA's operating budget dropped by one-third between 1981 and 1983 while its research and development budget was cut in half. The Director first abolished the Office of Enforcement, then re-established it on a smaller scale. One result was that between June 1981 and June 1982 EPA cases referred to the Justice Department dropped by 84 percent and civil penalties imposed by EPA dropped by 48 percent.[51]

These moves assumed that the Reagan administration had received a mandate in 1980 to transform environmental policy. This seems doubtful. Even in 1981, a remarkable 45 percent of the public agreed with the statement: "Protecting the environment is so important that requirements and standards cannot be too high and continuous environmental improvements must be made regardless of cost." The unfavourable publicity associated with the Burford and Watt tenures increased that support to 65 percent in 1986 and to almost 80 percent by 1989.[52]

The inevitable exit of Burford and Watt from the Administration in 1983 put the EPA and Interior in the hands of William Ruckelshaus and William Clark who tacked toward the center in their policies. By the late eighties the EPA was adopting regulations that the OMB estimated would cost $84 billion in 1988 and an additional $95 billion in 1990. Reviewing this record from the vantage of the early nineties, the regulatory economist W. Kip Viscusi concluded that the EPA had not just returned to old habits but "by the late 1980s ... the EPA was undertaking more costly regulatory initiatives than at any time in its history."[53]

Reductions in OSHA costs for business and industry proved equally brief. As OSHA head Reagan appointed his Florida campaign director for special events, Thorne Auchter, who was a 35-year-old vice-president of his father's construction company. Encouraged by Reagan, Congress cut OSHA's 1982 budget by

25 percent, resulting in a 30 percent drop in the number of inspectors. Auchter tried to turn OSHA into a "cooperative regulator," turning over federal inspection to twenty-one states who had their own OSHAs, and exempting from routine safety inspections small firms and larger firms that had fewer workdays lost from injury than the national average. To reduce business and industry compliance costs Auchter weakened or delayed the promulgation of numerous exposure limits.

But after mid-decade, as in the case of many of Reagan's regulatory relief efforts, OSHA reversed field under the direction of a new director, John Pendergrass, who had been Minnesota Mining and Manufacturing's manager of hazards-awareness products. In 1986 OSHA revised its policy to allow spot checks of companies previously excluded from full-scale inspections. The agency significantly tightened its rules governing asbestos exposure. OSHA's staff, although still smaller than in 1980, was once again expanding. Secretary of Labor William Brock established a tougher penalty system for violations and major regulations proposed in 1988 and 1989 would together impose costs of $23 billion, compared to a total burden for 1975–80 of $35–$44 billion. Viscusi concluded that "by the end of the decade OSHA had become more vigorous in its enforcement than ever before. The strategy of deregulation through regulatory neglect had been abandoned."[54]

A disgusted libertarian, Robert Poole, Jr., declared the Reagan "deregulation" effort a sham. Instead of actually carrying through on campaign promises to abolish agencies like the Consumer Product Safety Commission or OSHA, the Administration had settled only for "regulatory reform." The result, noted Poole, had been just an effort to "take the rough edges off the regulations while leaving the agencies and their legislative mandates intact." The libertarian columnist Doug Bandow, who had worked in Anderson's White House Office of Policy Analysis, complained in a 1987 column that "Reagan did virtually nothing to tear out the statutory roots of regulation. What little he did accomplish can be reversed by the stroke of a new president's pen."[55]

One federal agency that undertook regulatory relief that at least lasted for the duration of the Administration was the Federal

Trade Commission (FTC). During the late seventies the FTC, under Chairman Michael Pertschuk's direction, had launched a series of vigorous initiatives that earned it the special animosity of small businessmen. It had proposed to regulate the advertising practices of used-car dealers, morticians, and similar Chamber of Commerce members likely to petition their congressman for relief.

When Pertschuk proposed to regulate children's advertising on television by prohibiting any advertisement directed at children under the age of eight, this drew the fire of even the *Washington Post*, which suggested in a 1977 editorial that the FTC wanted to become the "National Nanny." Congress became so angry that at one point it defunded the FTC and Carter had to intervene to restore funding. The Pertschuk FTC proved equally maladroit in its antitrust prosecutions, winning only fifteen of thirty-five antitrust cases appealed to the federal courts, whereas the agency had won twenty-one of twenty-four appeals in the 1970–76 period.[56]

In one of Reagan's wiser regulatory appointments he selected James C. Miller III to head the FTC. An economist trained in the Public-Choice tradition at the University of Virginia by Buchanan and Tullock, Miller brought a breadth of relevant experience to the FTC chairmanship. The new Chairman had worked for the Ford Council on Wage and Price Stability, served as the co-director of the AEI's Center for the Study of Government Regulation (while serving as the founding editor of *Regulation*) and, until October 1981, directed Reagan's Task Force on Regulatory Relief.[57]

Miller was the first trained economist to chair the FTC and this was reflected in his appointments of economists (including Robert Tollison – another Buchanan student) to key positions. Against some initial resistance from his fellow commissioners, he brought the FTC around to a "rejection of the moralistic approach and the adoption of an economic approach," when evaluating business selling and advertising practices. The Commission established a new policy statement on "unfair" business practices, now requiring that the injury must be greater than the benefit received by the consumer before the practice could be proscribed. Although Miller failed to persuade Congress to enact into law a new "operational unfairness standard," the District of Columbia Court of Appeals approved the FTC's new three-pronged standard in a 1985 test case. Similarly a new "deceptive practices" standard that presupposed that consumers were more intelligent than previous FTC standards was sustained by the courts.[58]

Recognizing that guild and professional regulations enforced by the state often were classic "rent-seeking" activities designed to keep fees above free-market levels by restricting entry and competition, Miller successfully lobbied Congress in 1982 to thwart an effort to exempt professional associations from FTC jurisdiction.[59] A similar logic propelled the FTC's prosecution of taxicab cartels in New Orleans and Minneapolis; these efforts led to taxicab deregulation in such cities as Kansas City, Missouri, and Bloomington, Minnesota.[60] Such opening of local transportation markets may have particularly benefitted minorities because, as the market liberal Walter Williams documented in a 1982 Manhattan Institute publication, medallion requirements for taxi drivers and laws against jitneys effectively denied entry to those without considerable capital.[61]

Chairman Miller also was committed to bringing the FTC's antitrust policies into harmony with the findings of the Chicago School. These included the conclusions that markets need not have many participants to be competitive, that vertical integration seldom was anti-competitive, that past antitrust action on behalf of small businesses was often at the expense of the consumer, and that government-sanctioned cartels should come under the scope of the antitrust laws.

Guided by these precepts the FTC terminated the investigation of the alleged "shared monopoly" of the cereal industry, accepted a merger in a highly concentrated industry when it was shown that there were no barriers to entry, and essentially abandoned the prosecution of vertical price and non-price restraints where there was no evidence of anti-competitive effects. The Commission also drafted a new *Statement on Horizontal Mergers* which gave more recognition to the efficiency defense – that the efficiencies created by the merger would on balance benefit the consumer – while more clearly defining what types of mergers might be deemed anti-competitive and concentrating enforcement efforts in those areas.[62]

Although the former FTC economist William F. Shughart II suggested in 1989 that these FTC changes would be "transitory" because they were shaped by the "personalities of its administrators rather than by fundamental change in the law or institutions of antitrust," there was reason for believing that these innovations would outlast the moment.[63] As Miller himself noted, his policies at the FTC built upon ideas that had been the "dissenting views of the 1960s" but had "become the orthodoxy of the 1980s." By the mid-seventies the Supreme Court, citing articles by Robert Bork and Richard Posner, was beginning to take cognizance of the Chicago school's findings. An increasingly competitive international market made many of the old antitrust arguments seem irrelevant in the eighties.[64]

Generally other administration efforts at deregulation or regulatory relief proved of modest impact or limited duration. Upon entering office Reagan decided to deregulate all oil prices in January but they were scheduled to expire at the end of September anyway.[65] In 1982 the Department of Labor proposed to modify its interpretation of the Davis–Bacon Act so that labor costs on federally-financed projects would more closely approximate market rates. Unfortunately, this initiative was overturned by the US District Court for the District of Columbia. Seeking to build on surface transport deregulation accomplished by the Carter administration, the Reagan Department of Transportation in 1983 proposed legislation that would abolish all remaining economic regulation of trucking, water carriers, and freight forwarders. When advised that the Teamsters, one of the few unions that supported Reagan in 1980, opposed the legislation, the proposed bill was withdrawn from cabinet consideration. A committed market liberal, Thomas Gale Moore, cited this as an example of the "superficiality" of the Reagan White House's support for deregulation.[66]

Although it was anathema to most market liberals and Milton Friedman denounced it in his *Newsweek* column, the Reagan administration negotiated a 1981 "voluntary" agreement to limit

Japanese imports at an estimated cost of $1.1 billion a year to the consumer.[67] Stockman reports that Reagan persuaded himself that this was an issue of regulatory relief because American vehicles had to meet safety, fuel efficiency, and pollution standards mandated by the new social regulation. That Japanese imports had to meet the same standards seemed to have escaped the President.[68] According to the libertarian economist, William Niskanen, the restraint was renewed in 1984 for political reasons. Once Reagan was re-elected, the Administration allowed it to expire in March 1985.[69] Robert Crandall of the Brookings Institution put the cost per job saved at $160 000 per year.[70] The Public Choice economists could hardly have had a better example of rent seeking.

Reviewing Reagan's first-term trade policies, an analyst for the libertarian Cato Institute concluded that the President was "the greatest rhetorical supporter of free trade" in decades. But when short-term political opportunities beckoned, Reagan had "repeatedly forsaken his professed principles and imposed protectionist measures."[71]

Of all the Reagan-era efforts to implement market-liberal ideas, the least successful, perhaps because it had never been one of Reagan's four major economic goals, was the privatization of federal functions and the sell-off of federal assets. These were goals particularly favored by libertarians, who had pioneered in calling for privatization of state and local services and saw no reason why the same remedy ought not to apply at the federal level.[72] Thus, Robert Poole had called for the privatization of the federally-operated air traffic-control system two years before Reagan's 1981 confrontation with the Professional Air Traffic Controllers Organization.[73]

Pursuing a privatization agenda, the Reagan administration established in 1981 a Task Force on Private Sector Initiatives to find business that could take over the work of slashed social-welfare programs. The prospective beneficiaries were not enthusiastic. Urged on by private social service agencies, the Urban Institute quickly brought out two studies showing that the proposed funding cuts would seriously reduce their resources by cutting service contracts. Ironically, due to the increased use of the private or "third sector" to deliver social services in the seventies, these organizations also had become rent-seekers and thus feared privatization initiatives.[74]

The "privatizers" ultimately met with a similar lack of success when they proposed the sale of public lands. Market liberal intellectuals like Steve Hanke and Richard Stroup in Reagan's Department of the Interior proposed selling some public lands. Hanke's libertarian preference was to sell all federally-owned land, explaining that "I'm very much opposed to virtually all the public-sector activities except for some police functions and national defense, and even those could be contracted out." When Reagan proposed to sell "surplus" land Interior Secretary Watt, wanting only to return control of land to the states, construed the mandate narrowly.

Hanke fought back, declaring that government bureaucrats were exhibiting their "asset-hoarding bias" and were "undermining the President's privatization efforts." "The cancer from within," Hanke warned, "must be arrested." Leaving the government in mid-1982 in "a mutual parting of the ways," Hanke proposed that all lands under review that were not yielding the government a real rate of return of 10 percent should be sold.[75] Privatization of federal land initially garnered some support from the anti-Washington "Sagebrush Rebellion" based in the Western states. But when the ranchers learned that they were actually going to have to pay to acquire what they considered an existing property right to use public lands, they joined forces with the environmentalists to defeat the privatization efforts.[76]

Although the Administration accomplished some privatization, such as the sale of Conrail in 1986, the recommendations in 1987 of the President's Commission on Privatization to sell off Amtrak and the Naval Petroleum Reserves, and to privatize the Postal Service went nowhere with Congress.[77] As the United States had never had the degree of state-ownership comparable to England – which pioneered with privatization in the late seventies/early eighties – it was difficult for American market liberals to make the dramatic breakthroughs in asset sales that Prime Minister Margaret Thatcher's government achieved.[78] In this area as in many others, most Americans apparently felt comfortable with the general configuration of their government's responsibilities – if not with its taxes.

IV

How much of a long-term impact did "Reaganomics" have on the political economy of Vital Center Liberalism? Was there a Reagan Revolution? Did market liberalism in the eighties transform the relationship between society and the state? Contemporary and retrospective evaluations of the Reagan era have been markedly diverse. The politically liberal economist James Tobin in 1986 included Reagan with Roosevelt and Johnson amongst those leaders who "manage to shift boldly the whole path of policy. After them, the centrist consensus from which successors will deviate is forever different."[79]

Milton Friedman was more skeptical. While acknowledging in 1984 that Reagan had made "some progress" towards a "smaller and less intrusive government," Friedman argued that Reagan had erred by not being much bolder. Rather than strike at the heart of the interest-group state, Friedman claimed, Reagan had devoted almost all his energy in 1981 to tax cutting while leaving the "iron triangle" of interest-group politics in place.[80]

Retrospective assessments have been similarly divergent. The historian William C. Berman concluded that "not since Franklin Roosevelt had any one president altered the political landscape so radically ... Indeed his impact on the country had been enormous." The political scientist Larry M. Schwab disagreed, devoting a book to debunking the "myth" of a Reagan Revolution and offering the contrarian view that the Carter administration was in many ways the true era of government restraint – producing reductions in post-Vietnam military spending, capping of aid to states and localities, and deregulation of airlines and trucking – while the Reagan years saw an expansion of the percentage of GNP spent by government, attributable to the military build-up and continued growth in entitlement expenditures.[81]

Despite Reagan's success in containing growth in the *scope* of the welfare state, achieving income-tax reduction, maintaining low inflation rates, and providing a measure of regulatory relief, many market liberals were dismayed by how little fundamental reform was achieved and how readily Reagan's limited success could be reversed. Government continued to grow during the eighties as measured both in constant dollars and as a percentage of the total economy. Measuring from the 1979 to the 1989 peaks in the business cycle, the Federal Budget's share of Gross Domestic Product rose from 20.6 to 22.1 percent.[82] The Reagan administration did succeed in reducing significantly civilian spending's share of GNP, which, excluding Social Security payments, dropped from 9.9 percent to 7.6 percent of GNP between 1980 and 1990. Undoubtedly the Reagan deficits put pressure on Congress to reduce these expenditures. Unfortunately, the ballooning Reagan deficits also increased interest payments, which expanded to absorb two-thirds of these savings in civilian programs. The benefits from the downsized or eliminated civilian programs may have been smaller than their costs, but, as Charles Schultze has noted, interest payments on the national debt "provide no benefits whatsoever."[83] Reagan sought to blame Congress for those deficits but the responsibility was a shared one. A comparison of Reagan budget requests for FY 1982–86 with the actual budgets approved by Congress for those years shows the enacted budgets exceeding Reagan's requests by a cumulative total of only $34.5 billion.[84] Despite actions by agency heads to reduce staff size, total Federal civilian employment levels actually increased by 8 percent between 1980 and 1989, contrasted with a growth of only 0.3 percent during the seventies.[85]

Reviewing this decidedly mixed record, many market liberals were discouraged. Milton Friedman concluded in 1988 that the market-liberal intellectual movement had reached middle-age, but "the political movement is in its infancy." The Nobel laureate thought it only a slight exaggeration to say that "we preach individualism and competitive capitalism, and practice socialism."[86] Murray Rothbard, who considered Reagan a "blithering idiot," castigated the Reagan economic policies for leaving the leviathan essentially untouched, tripling the national debt in eight years, and failing to cut federal spending in absolute terms.[87] Christopher DeMuth, who had been Administrator of Information and Regulatory Affairs in Reagan's OMB, thought that the President was the closest thing to a philosophic libertarian likely to ever occupy the White House. Just the same, he concluded that Reagan had "attempted little and succeeded less in cutting domestic spending."[88]

Charles Murray, whom Reagan had admired for authoring a highly critical assessment of the welfare state, found fault with Reagan's continued support for large government programs when they went to the middle class. "The implied message was the Reagan administration was comfortable with government benefits if they went to the right people."[89] David Stockman agreed, having concluded by 1984 that what Americans wanted was "low taxes and substantial public spending." Reviewing the Reagan years from the perspective of 1991 he described a smoking hell: "what we got was $1.5 trillion worth of cumulative deficits, radical deterioration of our internal and external financial health, and a political system that ... now functions like the parliament of a banana republic."[90] Jim Miller, drawing upon public choice ideas, explained Stockman's hypertrophied deficits as the result of a peculiar tragedy of the commons.

> Just as competing sheepherders will overgraze common property, members of Congress will "overgraze" the budget. If a congressman can get a benefit for his district or state and have *all the people* pay for it, he will be compelled to do it.[91]

The neo-Menckenesque editor of the lively monthly, *The American Spectator*, R. Emmett Tyrrell, Jr. attributed Reagan's failure to a character defect in his supporters:

> The conservative's inclination is to acquire worldy possessions and then to purr. By contrast, the ordinary New Age Liberal is given to yelling, to organizing ad hoc committees, to joining in protests! He is political, outgoing, and *outraged!*. ... As his temperature rises he shouts for revolution, thence for Utopia.

By contrast, the conservative was parochial and lacked imagination and literary sensibility. This had denied him the "capacity to dramatize ideas and personalities." Narrowly focused on the political, conservatives had failed to gain control of the culture and the media.[92]

Not all market liberals were equally critical of the Reagan era. When *Policy Review* in 1987 asked various Reaganauts to assess the Reagan record, Martin Anderson acknowledged that the deficit was too high and the government still wasted a lot of money, but he concluded that "the economic glass is 90 percent full and getting fuller." The 1990 publication of a paperback edition of Anderson's memoir of the early Reagan administration, *Revolution*, allowed him to add a glowing retrospective. Pointing out that the US experienced a protracted economic expansion in the eighties while the Soviet system collapsed and capitalism made headway in the Third World, Anderson exalted that "it has been one hell of a decade."[93]

Robert L. Bartley, Editor of the *Wall Street Journal*, certainly agreed, entitling his history of Reagan's economic policy *The Seven Fat Years And How To Do It Again*. Bartley's editorial page had played a prominent role in promoting supply side idea in the late seventies and he was now insistent that any problems with the economy in the eighties were attributable to Federal Reserve policy, not supply-side economics. Indeed, Bartley argued that "if the tax policy had been bolder, if it hadn't been diluted by fear of the deficit, it's likely that the recession could have been avoided."[94]

Even as implemented, supply-side economics had its defenders. Lawrence B. Lindsey, a student of Martin Feldstein's at Harvard, contributed a book, *The Growth Experiment*, in which he sought to show supply-side effects in the post-1982 recovery. While not denying that there were demand-side consequences to Reagan's dramatically unbalanced mid-eighties budgets, he found business investment and savings unexplainable by traditional demand-side models.[95] Lowell Gallaway and Richard Vedder defended supply-side economics against the charge that it was the macroeconomics of greed. Although the 1981 tax legislation did cut the wealthy's marginal tax rates, they pointed out that the share of the tax burden borne by the top 5 percent increased from 34.9 percent to 45.5 percent between 1981 and 1988. Although there was increased inequality of income distribution in the eighties, the two economists noted that this was not a matter of the lowest quintile losing ground but rather "a matter of

gaining *less*, as opposed to *losing more*, than the top quintile."
Drawing on data reported by the Urban Institute, Gallaway and
Vedder found that the most marked upward mobility from 1977
to 1986 came among those starting in the lowest quintile.
Assessing the decade as a whole, they concluded that it was a
time of "substantial, across-the-board economic opportunity, both
in terms of job creation and the potential to improve one's
income position."[96]

Perhaps the most detailed review of the Reagan years from the
perspective of the market liberals was that provided by William
Niskanen, who had served on the Council of Economic Advisors
before becoming Chairman of the libertarian Cato Institute.
Niskanen acknowledged that measured by conventional standards of incremental change a good deal had been accomplished:
reduced inflation, a slowing of the rate of government growth,
some deregulation, a reduction in income-tax rates. On the negative side of the ledger, tax cuts were financed in effect by shifting
taxes to the future via the deficit, modest deregulation was offset
by increased trade restraints, and the federal budget share of
GNP continued to grow. Niskanen concluded in 1989 that there
had been no Reagan revolution, only a Reagan "evolution." At
least among politicians "there has not yet been a fundamental
change in the perceptions about what the federal government
should and should not do."[97]

Arguably the most lasting economic consequence of the
Reagan years has been the structural deficit with its resultant
inhibitions on new spending programs and expansion of existing
government programs. The debate over the causes and consequences of these ballooning deficits has been particularly vigorous, with many mainstream economists blaming them on Ronald
Reagan's commitment to a large-scale military build-up, simultaneous tax cuts and a balanced budget by 1984.

According to this indictment, the Reagan administration in
1981 bought into an extreme version of supply-side economics
("punk supply-sidism" in Herbert Stein's characterization) that
promised self-financing tax cuts.[98] Economists writing for the
popular market have repeatedly insisted that the Reagan budgets
were premised on this assumption.[99] There is little doubt that

popularizers of supply-side principles such as Arthur Laffer, Jude Wanniski and Congressman Jack Kemp occasionally made expansive claims for the benefits of lower taxes.[100]

Defenders of the Reagan supply-side tax cuts, however, indignantly denied that any official economic statement of the Reagan campaign or administration ever suggested that the tax cuts would be self-financing. Martin Anderson has noted that in Reagan's economic plan unveiled during the 1980 campaign supply-side effects were projected to recover only 17 percent of the tax cut over a five-year period. Norman B. Ture, Undersecretary of the Treasury, points out that the "Program for Economic Recovery" submitted to Congress on February 18, 1981 was "expected to reduce tax revenues compared to the amounts that would have obtained under prior law." Defending the 1981 tax cuts against charges of crank economics, Paul Craig Roberts cited the Treasury Department's 1981 public estimate that the tax-cut proposal would cost $718.2 billion in lost revenue over the 1981–86 period.[101]

Despite these projected revenue losses, the Administration anticipated that it could continue the Carter-initiated military build-up and balance the FY 1984 budget simply by slowing the growth of domestic expenditures. These optimistic calculations collapsed when the Administration found it more difficult to contain the growth of domestic spending than initially anticipated and when the unanticipatedly rapid drop in inflation resulted in a $207 billion over-estimation of revenue for FY 1982–86. The 1982 depression expanded government expenditures for relief while simultaneously denying the administration the "inflationary dividend" it had anticipated to help balance the budget.[102]

Senator Daniel Patrick Moynihan was quick to charge in 1983 that the unbalanced budgets were deliberately engineered to force a retrenchment of the social welfare state. Rather than negotiate with the program beneficiaries, Reagan "decided instead [to] create a fiscal crisis in which, will-nilly [sic], they would be driven out of existence."[103] Moynihan probably attributed too much Machiavellian cleverness to Reagan. Perhaps some future historian will review the information in the Reagan Presidential Library and conclude that he, like Eisenhower, was a "hidden-hand" president, but political scientist Fred I. Greenstein's preliminary conclusion is that Reagan was more of a "no-hands" president.[104]

Moynihan suggested that Stockman was the grand schemer to force the reduction in the welfare state by starving it. But the Budget Director apparently saw this more as a beneficial side-effect of the deficits.[105] In his own post-mortem on the Reagan years, Paul Craig Roberts indignantly denied the charge that the Treasury Department had been involved in a plot to cook the books.[106]

As it was, the social welfare state was not starved. Beginning with FY 1983, Reagan's budget proposals were declared "dead on arrival" by Congressional leaders. The result was that Stockman's plans for a "frontal assault on the welfare state" were repelled with minimal damage to the edifice.[107] Reviewing spending on nearly 40 social programs (including AFDC, medic-aid, foodstamps, education and training, and housing subsidies) that particularly benefited women and children, the economist Richard B. Mckenzie found that those programs grew by 18 percent in constant dollars between 1981 and 1989.[108]

What the Reagan deficits *did* produce was an automatic veto on most new liberal initiatives that were not self-financing. Thus when the elderly examined the self-financing 1988 Medicare Catastrophe Coverage Act, they found its coverage defective and not worth the candle if *they*, rather than the general public, had to pay for it. The Act arguably became the first major piece of federal welfare legislation repealed since the termination of the Freedman's Bureau bill in 1869.[109]

Without entirely planning it the Reagan administration thus had established for market liberals, at least temporarily, a new extra-constitutional restraint on policy-makers. Despite the years of Keynesianism there remained a residue of what Buchanan and Wagner in 1977 had called the classical fiscal constitution, the proposition "that public finance and private finance are analogous, and that the norms for prudent conduct are similar."[110] This residue was reflected in the Congress's adoption in 1986 of the Gramm-Rudman Deficit Reduction Act. Unfortunately, the residual sanction against deficit spending proved insufficient to insure compliance with Gramm-Rudman's targets without resorting to gimmickry: shifting government expenditures to the previous or following year, counting Social Security surpluses against the federal deficit, or not counting expenditures used to bail out the savings and loans industry. Gramm-Rudman only modestly restrained deficit growth because virtually all entitlement programs, plus interest on the national debt – some 60 percent of the budget – were declared off limits under the legislation's ground-rules.[111]

If Gramm-Rudman proved a frail reed to force a balanced budget, it did symbolize a modest victory for the market liberals who had long argued for capping government spending. As Aaron Wildavsky had foreseen in 1980, "when expenditure limits take hold, for every major addition to federal expenditures, there will have to be an equivalent subtraction. The doctrine of opportunity costs ... will be alive and well in government."[112]

Although Wildavsky was projecting the consequences of a balanced-budget amendment, something roughly comparable happened in the eighties. With government spending automatically growing because of indexed benefits for entitlement programs, the Reagan-engineered 1981 tax cuts now combined with the indexing of tax rates against bracket creep to produce impressive deficits. This produced an almost automatic containment of spending impulses "without the need for constant new exertions from the advocates of Reaganism."[113]

Although these deficits may have contained the programmatic expansion of the social welfare state, they did relatively little to "roll back" the scope of government involvement in the life of the nation. This failure of the Reagan administration to produce a true market-liberal revolution in public policy is not difficult to explain. At no point did the Administration have either the will or the resources to achieve such a transformation. As we have seen, Ronald Reagan never committed himself to such a transformation. It has been observed that Reagan was the most ideological president in modern times. That this probably was true may say more about the restraints imposed upon the ideological by a center-seeking two-party system than it says about President Reagan. Whatever Reagan's personal preferences, he was too committed to winning to allow ideology to get in the way of a deal.[114]

Reagan's party never had control of the House of Representatives and lost control of the Senate in the 1986 elections. Even if the Republicans had controlled the Congress in the eighties there is little reason to believe that the party was prepared for any radical transformation of the nation's political economy. In the mid-eighties Stockman had reviewed the Republican Party's voting record over the previous 21 years on 13 major additions to the domestic budget, such as Medicare, Medicaid, 1972 Social Security Amendments, and expansion of disability insurance. Collectively the Senate Republicans support had been at the 90 percent level; the House Republicans at the 80 percent level. Stockman was not far off the mark when he concluded that the "Republican party had been the coarchitects over the previous twenty years of this massive and permanent change in the center of the domestic budget."[115]

Republicans were aware that there had been in 1980 no tidal wave change in public sentiment toward the state. As Seymour Martin Lipset has noted, the nation that elected Reagan 1980 was *"ideologically* conservative" but *"programmatically* liberal," reflexively anti-statist in its rhetoric but strongly supportive of most government programs.[116]

The neoconservative James Q. Wilson, in a 1982 article, caught the strategic implications of this contradiction. Noting that "[v]irtually every informed analysis of the 1980 vote" indicated that Reagan won because of dissatisfaction with Carter, and that more than half of those who voted for Reagan described themselves as moderates or liberals, Wilson concluded that "the only mandate Mr. Reagan had was to be different from his predecessor."[117] If he took that victory as a mandate for much smaller government he was mistaken. Although Reagan campaigned in 1980 on the promise to reduce government spending and regulation, cut inflation and pare taxes, the candidate during the campaign did not name any programs that would be cut, let alone eliminated. As the witty Herbert Stein put it, Reagan "had a mandate to provide a free lunch, or as used to be said in more agrarian days, a late fall and an early spring."[118] Although there were those around him who were prepared to launch the crusade against the state, and David Stockman's "Dunkirk Memorandum" provided the justification,

Reagan shied away from any root and branch surgery on the mixed economy and social welfare state.

Rather than a "Reagan revolution" there was a "Reagan evolution."[119] Most of his successes in trimming back the state were further developments of policies begun in the seventies. Jimmy Carter, enthusiastic about economic deregulation as a means to slow inflation, gave a high priority to legislation deregulating first aviation and then trucking. As a result most of the major economic deregulation successes – the Airline Deregulation Act of 1978, the Staggers Rail Act of 1980, and the Motor Carrier Act of 1980 – preceded the Reagan years. This legislation, however, *was* a triumph of market liberal ideas. As Martha Derthick and Paul J. Quirk note in their history of this deregulation, "except for the development of this academic critique of policy, the reforms ... would never have occurred."[120]

Similarly, the effort to "raise consciousness" about regulatory cost began before the Reagan era, starting with Nixon's 1971 requirements that OMB conduct "quality-of-life" reviews of the cost and benefits of new social regulations. The Ford administration established an Inflation Impact Statement program in 1974 requiring that all new legislation and all proposed agency regulations be accompanied by an inflationary impact evaluation. If Ford had been re-elected in 1976 he had planned on making deregulation one of his highest priorities.[121] President Carter in 1978 created the Regulatory Analysis Review Group to review and make recommendations regarding the economic impact of high-cost executive agency proposals. Thus Reagan's Task Force on Regulatory Relief and the OMB's OIRA cost-benefit requirements were not without precedent.[122]

Arguments for lower marginal tax rates had been developed in the seventies by both mainstream economists such as Martin Feldstein, Lawrence Summers and Barry Bosworth as well as by supply-side enthusiasts.[123] Political groundwork for reduced taxes already had been done in Congress in the late seventies. Thus the Joint Economic Committee, chaired by Senator Lloyd Bentsen, argued in its 1979 Report for a "supply side" emphasis and urged (1) monetary restraint, (2) reduced taxes and regulatory burdens, and (3) spending restraint. The JEC's 1980 report carried the title "Plugging in the Supply Side." Paul Craig Roberts plausibly called this "Reaganomics before Reagan."[124]

Clearly the Reagan administration could build upon established support for economic deregulation, tax reform, currency stabilization, and budget trimming. When it sought to go beyond these areas it ran into trouble. Arguably, not too much should be made of Reagan's failure to fully implement the market liberals' agenda. As the political scientist Walter Dean Burnham has pointed out, "presidential 'creators' of new regimes typically have failed to solve the problems that brought them into office." Instead they succeed in "capturing the intellectual high ground, in authoritatively defining the agenda of politics, and in organizationally building the revolution by institutionalizing it."[125]

Measured by such standards, the eighties were success years for market-liberal ideas. The Chicago school already was riding high, but such Law and Economics scholars as Bernard H. Siegan and Richard Epstein gained a new visibility as advocates of an activist jurisprudence that would seek to restore economic liberty to parity with personal liberties and restrain the use of the Constitution's takings clause.[126] Epstein was widely discussed as a possible judicial nominee and Siegan did receive the nod for the Ninth Circuit Court of Appeals, but was rejected by the Senate.[127] Reagan succeeded in appointing Richard Posner and Frank Easterbrook, another Law and Economics scholar, to the Seventh Circuit Court of Appeals. Reviewing Posner's judicial and scholarly record in 1994 *The New Republic*'s legal affairs editor, Jeffrey Rosen, concluded that in a "perfectly meritocratic world, a delegation of senators from both parties would fly to Chicago with a signed Supreme Court commission and lay it respectfully at Posner's feet."[128]

Public Choice ideas increased in visibility and influence in the eighties at Washington University, the University of Maryland, the Political Economy Research Center in Bozeman, Montana, the Workshop in Political Theory and Policy at Indiana University, and most importantly, the Center for the Study of Public Choice at George Mason University where both Buchanan and, initially, Tullock resided.[129] Public Choice scholars were winning awards. In 1983 the American Political Science Association designated

Mancur Olson's *The Rise and Decline of Nations: Economic Growth, Stagflation and Social Rigidities* the co-winner of the Kammer Award for the best book on US national policy. Olson had found that mature nations were particularly prone to inefficiencies produced by the luxuriate growth of special-interest groups. Three years after Olson's recognition, the Swedish Academy of Sciences awarded James M. Buchanan the 1986 Nobel Prize for Economics for his challenge to welfare economics.

The Austrians also were energized in the eighties. The revival had gained an institutional home in 1974 when New York University established an Austrian Economic Program under Israel Kirzner's direction. Four years later, Richard Fink, a Ph.D in Economics from the NYU Austrian program, established at Rutgers University the Center for the Study of Market Process. The Center transferred in 1980 to George Mason University, fast becoming a locus of market liberalism. Added to the Austrian list in 1982 was the Ludwig von Mises Institute at Auburn University.

Despite their internal disagreements over Ludwig M. Lachmann's radical subjectivism, and quarrels over whether to emphasize Mises's apriorism or Hayek's undogmatic empiricism, these neo-Austrians could unite in casting anathemas upon Keynesians macro-economics and all other forms of government economic intervention. Seeking common ground with adherents of other schools, Austrians at the NYU and George Mason programs entered into dialogue with the public choice, post-Keynesian and Institutionalist schools. Reflecting their new institutional strengths and the rekindled interest in Hayek and Mises's criticism of command economies in the light of the implosion of Eastern-bloc economies, the number of Austrian symposia and books increased almost exponentially in the eighties.[130]

The transmission belts for these market-liberal ideas, the think-tanks and advocacy organizations, grew in number and size during the Reagan years. Heritage, AEI, and Hoover all expanded their staffs and budgets while providing personnel to man the policy positions in the Republican administration. These organizations were joined on the firing line by new market-liberal think-tanks like the Independent Institute, the Pacific Research

Institute and the Cato Institute. In a town where few actors had the time to actually read the reports they debated, credibility could be enhanced by sheer tonnage and market-liberal ideas now descended on Washington in a density that just overwhelmed the opposition. Writing in *The Atlantic Monthly* in 1986, Gregg Easterbrook concluded that market liberal thinking "had not only claimed the presidency; it has spread throughout our political and intellectual life and stands poised to become the dominant strain in American public policy." Liberals had little in place to counteract it. Democratic Senator Daniel Patrick Moynihan gloomily concluded that the Republican party had become the "party of ideas and we were left, in Lord Macaulay's phrase, 'the stupid party.'"[131]

The battle was played out at the state and local level as well. State government expenditures grew rapidly in the eighties and market liberals had to warn conservatives against "favouring states' rights as an end in itself, rather than as a means to the greater end of protecting individual liberty."[132] Much of this state-spending growth was explained by the increasing power of public employee unions, now the most powerful special-interest groups in many capitals. Starting in the mid-eighties a group of state-based think-tanks developed to do combat with these rent-seekers. Lead by young enthusiasts possessing the "earnestness and verve that sent missionaries to China in the 19th century," these grass-root groups rapidly proliferated. By 1989 there were some 55 market liberal organizations in 22 states, organized into the Madison Group and publishing, after 1990, their own bimonthly newsletter, *Intellectual Ammunition*. Their growing influence could be seen in the term-limits crusade, school choice initiatives, the privatization movement, and the resistance to costly federal mandates.[133]

Perhaps the single most important new transmission belt in the eighties for the dissemination of free-market economic analysis and education was the libertarian empire constructed by Charles and David Koch. Both billionaires, they had financially supported the Libertarian Party in 1976 and 1980. After Clark's modest showing in 1980 it was obvious that the Libertarian Party was not an effective mechanism to promote a vision of a radical market utopia. Always skeptical of the party route, the Koch brothers now poured millions into such advocacy, lobbying and education groups as Citizens for a Sound Economy, the Council for a Competitive Economy, and the Institute for Humane Studies.[134]

The flagship of this Koch-financed flotilla ("Kochtopus" to its critics) was the Cato Institute. Initially set up in San Francisco in 1977, Cato came east to Washington in 1981 and quickly established itself as a remarkably effective advocate for very specific proposals for incrementally rolling back the state. Its president, Ed Crane, had recognized during the 1976 Libertarian campaign that radical market liberals spoke about idyllic end-states but were not prepared to grapple with the specifics of the day-to-day policy debates that would make libertarian proposals credible alternatives to mainstream solutions.

Cato, under Crane's leadership, proved to be "among the most energetic think tank entrepreneurs and the most skillful in employing intellectual marketing techniques." Its arsenal of weapons extended from the light artillery of op-ed pieces in national newspapers and a radio commentary program, "Bylines," to the medium ordinance of a series of "Policy Analysis" on current policy issues, on to the heavy guns of policy conferences on law and economics, privatization of money, pollution, and Social Security reform. Papers delivered at such symposia frequently were published in the *Cato Journal* or reworked into monographs published either by Cato or other presses.

Cato tried to keep just ahead of the more mainstream free-market think-tanks, staking out positions that perhaps were not acceptable at the time but could be within a decade if the mainstream shifted in its direction. Thus Cato studies called for replacing Social Security with Super IRAs, privatization of bank and savings and loan insurance programs, tax credits for schools, grazing fees on public lands set at market levels, a constitutional jurisprudence that applied a "strict scrutiny" standard to laws restricting economic liberty, and a host of other market liberal desiderata.[135] While Cato focused on policy questions, the IHS continued with its primary emphasis on education. With its relocation to George Mason University in the Virginia suburbs of

Washington in 1985, Liggio had an opportunity to realize F. A. Harper's dream of a libertarian Institute for Advanced Studies. The new university affiliation had other advantages. Liggio argued that "[a]ll access to hegemonic positions is through networks."[136] The George Mason location provided IHS with something of a "web-site." The Institute could now network with other GMU-based institutes representing the Chicago, Public Choice and Austrian branches of the market liberal revival: Henry Manne's Law and Economics Center, James Buchanan's Center for the Study of Public Choice, and Richard Fink's Center for the Study of Market Process. In 1988, after Sir Antony Fisher's death, the Atlas Foundation relocated near GMU. With such an array of market liberal institutes in close proximity, Fairfax Virginia was beginning to resemble Calvin's Geneva, or perhaps more aptly, given its growing influence in Eastern Europe, an Anti-Comintern headquarters.

Reviewing in 1988 the progress that the market liberals had made, Cato President Ed Crane and Chairman William S. Niskanen expressed a certain satisfaction. Ironically, they noted, the influence of market-liberal ideas was most visible overseas. "The massive privatization programs in Great Britain, the economic miracle in the Pacific Rim, and the remarkable erosion of the commitment to Marxism in the Soviet Union," they observed, "makes the eighties a watershed decade." Paradoxically, those success were less visible at home where in 1988 government spending at all levels had reached a "peacetime record" of 41.3 percent of national income. "Clearly," the Cato executives observed, "there is a need to develop a better understanding of the systemic biases that fuel the growth of the state."[137] By the end of the eighties market liberals had assembled powerful arguments against the leviathan and had organized new research, educational and advocacy centers that had made the statists' dominance of the academy increasingly irrelevant (although even here there were serious inroads). Supporters of an ever-expanding government were demoralized both by events and their own seeming inability to mount an effective counter-argument against the market liberals. Yet for all the market liberals' successes they had yet to assemble a winning political coalition. Vital Center liberals had succeeded by organizing groups committed to rent-seeking. What the market liberals had to build was perhaps much harder: a political coalition committed to self-denial. During World War One the writer Anatole France had reacted skeptically to Woodrow Wilson's unavailing call for a "Peace without Victors," suggesting that such a pallid victory would be about as appealing as a "village without [a] brothel."[138] If successful politics similarly involved the construction of coalitions committed to the "spoils of victory," then how could the market liberals, with their calls for abstinence, ever collar an electoral majority?

6 The Future Politics of Market Liberalism: "Are We a Permanent Minority?"

In the eighties Ronald Reagan often compared himself with Roosevelt and Republican partisans certainly hoped that his 1980 electoral victory heralded an equivalent mighty political realignment. One close student of the liberal tradition did characterize Reagan as "The Roosevelt of the Right," but Alonzo Hamby was quick to add that if Reagan and Roosevelt shared certain qualities – buoyant personalities, heavy reliance on communication skills to energize their presidencies, an ideological rhetoric tougher than actual policy, and a relative indifference to details and policy contradictions – Reagan ultimately accomplished less than did Roosevelt. "The one goal," noted Hamby, "that consistently eluded him, and the one that Roosevelt achieved, was that of an enduring political realignment in the form of a broad coalition of interest groups loosely held together by an ideology."[1] The Reagan Presidency was a coalition of disparate and competing elements: New Rightists, libertarians, neoconservatives and paleoconservatives. Of these groups only the libertarians supported an across-the-board market liberalism.[2]

New Rightists were preponderantly Christian social conservatives who believed that government expansion had usurped traditional authority, undermined the family, and provided unorthodox lifestyles with preferential status before the law. For the social conservatives the New Class's emphasis on personal fulfillment and liberation was a fundamental threat to the old patriarchal order. Government support for these changes through the proposed Equal Rights Amendment and the Supreme Court abortion rulings made the state seem a co-conspirator against the normal moral order.[3]

185

Libertarians could support the social conservative's call for squeezing welfare programs, lowering of anti-family taxes, and promotion of educational choice, but for fundamentally different reasons. The social conservatives emphasized the revitalization of moral authority; libertarians saw liberty as the highest value. Thus the two groups' ultimate visions conflicted. Indeed the social conservatives were not inherently anti-statists. Although they insisted that government must promote and protect the traditional moral order, evangelicals differed very little from the rest of Americans regarding support for the basic social welfare functions provided by the modern American state.[4]

The market liberals also received only partial support from the neoconservatives. Although Irving Kristol's journal *The Public Interest* had published some of the most effective critiques of the Great Society's social program, Kristol was not an unqualified supporter of a capitalist order, offering only *Two Cheers for Capitalism*.[5] Kristol argued the inevitability of some sort of welfare state, accepted the need for government regulation of business, endorsed a decentralized censorship, and worried about the corrosive effects of capitalism on bourgeois morality.[6] Writing to Roy Childs, he suggested that libertarians were too optimistic about the nature of man:

> Basically the issue between us is whether or not our bourgeois-capitalist society needs the Judeo-Christian tradition to function or whether human beings can, out of their existing liberties, create a new morality and a new set of beliefs that can replace this tradition. Obviously, I believe that the latter effort is doomed to failure. Rationalism can subvert traditional beliefs, but it cannot of itself create beliefs that human communities can or will accept as codes of moral and social conduct.[7]

Kristol was not the only neoconservative who expected a conservative government to promote public morality and provide for the general welfare. James Q. Wilson cautioned libertarian conservatives that the major conflicts of American history had been not about the size of government but rather about "right principles." The arguments had been about "union, slavery, liquor, war, welfare, the franchise, and currency." Wilson warned that if conservatives evaluated all policy in terms of whether it reduced government size, then they would be "engaging in a debate that most people believe is irrelevant."[8] George F. Will agreed, insisting in his 1981 Godkin Lectures that two conservatives, Otto von Bismarck and Benjamin Disraeli, pioneered the welfare state "and did so for impeccably conservative reasons: to reconcile the masses to the vicissitudes and hazards of a dynamic and hierarchial industrial state."[9]

Tensions also existed between traditional conservatives, paleoconservatives in the argot of the 1980s, and the libertarians. Although both opposed the growth of the modern state, they differed on the greatest threat to freedom. Libertarians argued that societal efforts to promote the "public good" often resulted in tyranny. Traditionalists like Russell Kirk or Robert Nisbet warned that totalitarianism could arise from too much individualism; in an atomistic, rootless society the alienated individual would ultimately opt for some sort of false community promulgated by the state. Nisbet cautioned against the siren songs of either national community or unrestrained individualism.[10] Kirk insisted that "genuine libertarians are mad – metaphysically mad."[11]

Most libertarians hesitated to support Nisbet's call for revitalized local communities. Murray Rothbard noted that for "traditionalists the central object of concern and of imputed rights or obligations is the 'community'; for libertarians it is the individual." For Rothbard communities were "simply voluntary groupings" with no independent authority of their own. Between these two positions Rothbard found "no middle ground".[12]

The tensions between these varying approaches were momentarily muted at the beginning of the Reagan administration. With a banquet of liberal programs before them the various factions could devote themselves to the feast. The harmony did not last. Although Reagan's decision to emphasize economic reform could garner the support of all factions, his failure to achieve dramatic downsizing of government expenditures only confirmed the libertarians in their original skepticism.

The social conservatives withheld their criticism longer than the libertarians but ultimately they realized they were getting little more than rhetorical support from the Administration. Thus the President told the National Association of Evangelicals in 1983 that the Soviet Union was the "focus of evil in the modern world," and he reminded a prayer breakfast for 17 000 at the 1984 Republican National convention that "politics and morality are inseparable."[13]

Beyond such symbolic politics, Reagan seem unable to go. In 1982 the President did support a proposed constitutional amendment to permit voluntary prayer in public schools. Reagan pushed this rather unthreatening proposal more than any other item on his "social agenda." But the Republican-controlled Senate never even brought the proposal to the floor, partly because the Administration failed to force the merger of two competing versions of the school prayer amendment.[14] Observing that Reagan never attended church, was the first divorced man to be president, and maintained close friendships with Hollywood friends, William A. Niskanen concluded that Reagan was a "closet tolerant."[15]

Frustrated by Reagan's failure to deliver on the New Right's social agenda, Richard Viguerie and Howard Phillips denounced Reagan in 1983 as an apostate and threatened to form a new populist party.[16] Cal Thomas, Vice-President of the Moral Majority, complained that if Reagan managed to balance the budget but "we keep murdering a million and a half babies every year, there's no way we can say that we're better off than we were four years ago." Reagan, Thomas declared, always said the right thing when he talked to conservative leaders, but then failed to "follow through relentlessly."[17] Yet Reagan could not as a matter of politics ally himself so strongly with the New Right's social agenda that he alienated Republican cosmopolites and the baby-boomers.

As for the neoconservatives, who might have been thought of as natural allies for the social conservatives, they had their suspicion that the evangelicals were rednecks and anti-Semites.[18] If some social conservatives were suspicious of the neoconservatives' traditionalist rhetoric, it may have been, as Paul Weaver suggested, because the neoconservatives were not really traditionalists but actually modernists. "They may believe in the traditional family, but they practice women's liberation and all the other modes of modern liberation. Intellectual defenders of religion, they are themselves nonbelievers and nonpractitioners."[19]

Neoconservatives had their difficulties with the paleos. Where paleos could trace their intellectual lineage back to Richard Weaver, Russell Kirk and the Southern Agrarians, the modernist neoconservatives felt more comfortable with Reinhold Niebhur and Joseph Schumpeter.[20] The paleos' first battle with the neoconservatives may have been the 1981 contest for the Chairmanship of the National Endowment for the Humanities. Neoconservative philosopher and former anti-war Democrat William Bennett bested the University of Dallas English Professor M.E. Bradford. Irving Kristol led the campaign against Bradford on the basis of the professor's opposition to the 1964 Civil Rights Act, his endorsements of George Wallace in 1968 and 1972, and his portrayal of Lincoln as a tyrant.[21]

Resentful of the number of positions that the neoconservatives collared in the Reagan administration, Bradford complained that the neoconservatives were "interlopers" and "opportunists" whose agenda remained "essentially statist, pacifist and coercively egalitarian."[22] When Bradford became president of the conservative Philadelphia Society he organized the 1986 meeting around the theme of neoconservatism and gave the traditionalists a platform to indict the interlopers. Stephan Tonsor, a monarchist and professor of history at the University of Michigan, decreed that the true conservative world-view was "Roman or Anglo Catholic" whereas neoconservativism was the province of "secularized Jewish intellectuals." When Arnold Beichman of the Hoover Institution asked Tonsor if he would reject James Burnham, Whittaker Chambers, Frank Meyer and other converts because they were not born to the faith, Tonsor replied: "Would you accept an ex-Nazi?"[23] Tonsor's disparagement of neoconservatives as secularized Jews may have been evidence of a residual anti-Semitism within the conservative movement, made manifest by the paleo and neo tensions.[24]

Where the neoconservatives and paleoconservatives debated the true conservative lineage and argued over who should receive

Reagan's patrimony, the libertarians entirely repudiated his estate. The only differences in the various libertarian critiques of Reagan were their degrees of vehemence. The *Libertarian Review* assessed the President's first ten months in office as proof that Reagan was a neoconservative for whom "'free enterprize' is not a system of political economy [but] *packaging*; a tissue of rhetoric wrapped around whatever happens to be the status quo." Ed Crane, now president of the Cato Institute, insisted that Reagan was a non-ideological politician who used ideology "as a vehicle for returning to center stage." Reaganomics was not a failure, argued Crane, because there never had been any Reaganomics. About the only prominent libertarian who came close to supporting Reagan was *Reason* publisher Robert Poole, who suggested critical support for Reagan's anti-government efforts. Then when the voting public finally realized that Reaganomics was not a "fundamental break with the New Deal philosophy" the Libertarian Party plausibly could stand forth "as the middle class's true ally."[25]

Any chance that the Libertarian Party could effectively present itself in 1984 as an alternative to Reagan for disaffected middle-class voters was seriously damaged by the party's fratricide at its 1983 national presidential convention. The selection of the long-time activist David Bergland over the "outreach" candidate Earl Ravenal prompted the Koch family to withhold financial support, dooming any chance of building on the Party's 1980 vote total. Bergland never had the resources to mount an effective campaign. The paid staffers from the 1980 Clark campaign, many now employed within the Koch libertarian empire, refused to work for him. Initially his campaign had to rely entirely on volunteers, although a small paid staff was in place by early 1984. Only able to raise about $600 000, and pledged not to go into debt, the Bergland organization had no paid advance men, produced no white papers, and attained ballot status in only 38 states.

Receiving less than 230 000 votes, Bergland attributed this great vote implosion to a lack of resources and Ronald Reagan's ability to bamboozle the public. The Libertarian candidate also attributed the Party's weakness to the "rising tide of nationalism" that Reagan promoted and exploited. "Young people," Bergland concluded, "remember Grenada, not Viet Nam."[26]

Don Ernsberger, Co-Director of the Society for Individual Liberty, blamed the inevitable post-election depression among libertarians on the withdrawal of the Koch money. "Like the Federal Reserve Board," Ernsberger suggested, "the Koch family pumped millions of dollars into the libertarian economy, distorted all the signals, and changed all the expectations. 1980 was the binge ... 1984 was the contraction."[27]

The contraction lasted three years. National Directors came and went with alarming speed, three in as many years. The inevitable staff upheavals damaged efficiency, fund-raising efforts, and membership services. In 1986 acting LP Director Terry Von Mitchell reported that because of the high costs of prospecting and fulfilling information requests, the Party was actually losing money on each membership it solicited! By 1987 paid national party membership was down 20 percent from the 1985 figure of 7600.[28]

Prospects brightened for the Libertarians when Ronald E. Paul, a former Republican four-term (1976–84) Congressman from Texas, repudiated his party and announced his candidacy for the Libertarian Party's presidential nomination. Paul denounced Reagan for having betrayed his own free-enterprise philosophy through massive deficits and a skyrocketing debt. "Thanks to the President and the Republican Party," Paul declared, "we have lost the chance to reduce the deficit and the spending in a non-crisis fashion." What was even worse, Reagan had legitimized big government. "It was tragic," the former Congressman noted, "to listen to Ronald Reagan on the 1986 campaign trail bragging about his high spending on farm subsidies, welfare, warfare, etc. in his futile effort to hold on to control of the Senate."[29]

A staunch economic conservative when on the House Banking Committee, Paul had championed the gold standard and called for the abolition of the Federal Reserve System. After he was defeated in the 1984 Texas Republican Senatorial primary won by Phil Gramm, Paul had launched Ron Paul Coins and the Ron Paul Investment Letter; his subscribers and coin customers subsequently proved to be a major source of money for his presidential quest.

Although his support for social libertarianism was not as vigorous – he opposed abortions – as his economic libertarianism, a Paul candidacy promised the Libertarians an infusion of money, enhanced credibility, and the chance to regain the electoral ground loss in 1984.[30] Ultimately, these practical considerations overrode many libertarians' doubts about Paul's commitment to civil liberties. Beating back a strong challenge for the nomination by Russell Means, the eloquent American Indian Movement activist, albeit convicted felon, Paul won on the first ballot. Yet even his strongest supporters, like Murray Rothbard, admitted that the victor never won the convention's affection. If Paul "won the heads of the LP," Rothbard concluded, "he did not win their hearts." Another commentator suggested the candidate had "the charisma of a baked potato."[31]

Paul promised to raise $6 million, and conduct "a highly professional media-type campaign," but the results were disappointing.[32] Despite his tireless campaigning for 18 months, Paul only raised about $3 million, failed to gain ballot status in four states, lacked funds to buy television time, and received only about 430 000 votes.

Many libertarians had expected much better, predicting from 650 000 to 1 500 000 votes for Paul.[33] Rothbard certainly had anticipated a better showing; in the summer of 1987 he had gleefully insisted that as a result of "Iran/contragate, or Gippergate, the carefully crafted return to trust in government lies in shambles." As a consequence, he saw "an unprecedented chance [for the Libertarian Party] to leap into the mainstream of American history, to have a strong and even decisive influence on American politics."[34]

In his assessment of the campaign, *Liberty*'s political analyst, "Chester Alan Arthur" (a pseudonym), more realistically assessed the resistance to libertarianism. "Americans do not vote for ... sweeping change except in times of social or economic crisis .... In addition, most Americans believe that the only way change will be effected is through the two major parties." Reagan had provided the country with just about as much change as it was prepared to accept. That Libertarian Party candidates were not winning many offices was not evidence that the Party was a failure. "Rather," Arthur concluded, "it is evidence of how early we are in the struggle for liberty."[35]

In a perhaps bizarre example of how complex the politics of liberty could become, the disappointed anarcho-libertarian Rothbard now joined with the paleoconservative M. E. Bradford in 1990 to form the John Randolph Club, devoted to fighting "big government conservatives" like Jack Kemp, Newt Gingrich, and William J. Bennett. Its goal was to reconstitute "the Old Right as it stood in 1945." In an improbable invocation Bradford told the Society's organizing meeting that "[o]ur troubles with each other as conservatives and libertarians stand a better chance of being resolved if we observe an order of priorities and focus with renewed joy at freedom from contamination by pragmatists."[36] Although Llewellyn H. Rockwell, Director of the Ludwig von Mises Institute, also made the case for a paleo-libertarian alliance, it appeared that few libertarians found the match plausible. Rockwell's emphasis on cultural conservatism found few takers among libertarians.[37] While some paleos flirted with the possibility of an alliance with libertarians, some paleos were identifying with the "American First" nationalism of Pat Buchanan.[38]

II

Clearly the diversity of the Reagan core constituency had prevented any exclusive concentration on a market liberal agenda. Other than a dislike of liberalism, only anti-communism had held it together. With the 1989 collapse of the Berlin Wall that cohering glue began to weaken. Some neoconservatives suggested that support for global democracy should replace the anti-communist impulse as an organizing principle for American foreign policy. The New Rightist, Patrick Buchanan, responded that this was just an updated version of Henry Wallace's liberal vision of the century of the common man: "Our going away gift to the globalist ideologues should be to tell the Third World we are not sending the gunboats to collect our debts, but nor are we sending more money. The children are on their own."[39]

Iraq's 1990 invasion of Kuwait and President Bush's response, demonstrated how divisive foreign policy could be for the old market liberal coalition. The Heritage Foundation's *Policy Review* exalted that Bush would "go down in history as one of America's great commanders-in-chief." Although raising doubts about the wisdom of such a massive commitment to the Gulf, wondering if it could realistically be replicated for every possible Middle-Eastern crisis, the editor of the neoconservative *The National Interest* also applauded Bush's decision to intervene.[40]

Buchanan and the new nationalists, however, saw it a replay of 1941, with Israel playing the role of England in persuading America to 'fight their fight.' At the January 1992 meeting of the pro-Buchanan John Randolph Club, the shortly to be dismissed *National Review* columnist, Joseph Sobran, conjectured that perhaps "the United States had killed more people outside its borders than any other [country]."[41]

When the libertarian Cato Institute denounced the Gulf Intervention, William E. Simon, President of the John M. Olin Foundation, fired off a letter to Edward Crane filled with indignation:

> You cannot imagine how astonished I was – indeed "outraged" would be a better word – to read in your memorandum your description of the recent war in the Gulf as a conflict in which "the world's most advanced military power laid waste to a Third World nation …" and your lament that "It really is a tragedy that so many good free-market conservatives have signed off on the Gulf war."[42]

Simon promised to use his influence with the Olin Foundation to terminate financial support for the Cato Institute.[43]

In a seven-page response Crane sought to persuade Simon that he had over-reacted to a single memo. While assuring Simon that he supported a resort to war when the nation's independence or geographical integrity were at risk, the invasion of Kuwait, "while indisputably an odious event," did not "come close to meeting" that test. Citing studies done by Cato economists that the oil rationale was specious, oil being a "fungible commodity,"

Crane argued that no fundamental national interest was at stake. What was at stake, warned Crane, was the collapse of the movement for limited government in America:

> After eight years of Reagan and after signing on with George Bush, conservatives now face a federal government more intrusive, more inclined to disregard basic civil liberties, consuming more taxes as a percentage of GNP, and intentionally re-regulating business in a manner more oppressive than at any time in American history.[44]

Reviewing this disarray in the coalition, John B. Judis cheerfully concluded that "[c]onservatism appears to be returning to what it was before 1956 ... a welter of contradictory and inconsistent beliefs."[45] Certainly George Bush was not the man to hold this fractious group together. Never a true believer in the Reagan Revolution, considering himself only a "moderate conservative," President Bush enthusiastically signed into law the 1990 Clean Air Act and the Americans with Disabilities Act. In 1991 he presided over a 25 percent single year expansion of the *Federal Register*.[46]

When the *New Republic* senior editor Fred Barnes looked at the prominent conservatives in the Bush Administration – Drug Czar William J. Bennett, Vice President Dan Quayle, and Jack Kemp, Secretary of Housing and Urban Development – he concluded that big-government conservatism had won the day. "People, it turns out, like big government," Barnes concluded, "not bigger, but roughly as big and as expensive as it is now."[47] Perhaps so, but they apparently did not wish to pay for it. Bush's agreement to the 1990 tax increases, a reversal of a campaign pledge, so alienated his conservative supporters that a November 1990 canvas of seven prominent conservative activists representing most factions produced an average grade of "D" for his presidency. By the Winter of 1990–91 *Policy Review* was suggesting that conservatives "decide if they will stand against their party's leader."[48]

Paradoxically, Bush's defeat by Governor William Clinton of Arkansas in 1992 provided the necessary ingredients for the revitalization of the fraying conservative coalition. Given their animus towards government and their own internal disagreements on priorities, conservatives generally have cohered more effectively in opposition than in power. President Clinton's tolerance for gays in the military, a foreign policy widely perceived as weak, the role of the First Lady in drafting a national health insurance plan financed by higher taxes and featuring increased regulation – all produced an astonishing growth in the indices of support for conservative organizations.

The evidence of a reinvigorated conservative opposition was overwhelming. Emblematic of the revival was the phenomenon of Rush Limbaugh. By mid-1994 this anti-government talk-show host was on 659 radio stations and 250 television stations, denouncing the Clinton agenda and declaring that "I am equal time." Broadcasting for three hours each day on radio, Limbaugh presided over a "shotgun wedding between the *National Lampoon* and the *National Review*." His influence was remarkable. When he mentioned a Heritage or Cato study, their switchboards would be jammed with incoming calls, driving secretaries to distraction. Aided by Limbaugh's vocal endorsement, the neoconservative monthly, *The American Spectator*, was reborn as an anti-Clinton vehicle, with a circulation of 340 000 by the end of 1994.

Other elements of the old Reagan coalition benefited from the groundswell. Thus the social conservative Family Research Council received $4.5 million in contributions in the first six months of 1993, exceeding its entire 1992 income. The Heritage Foundation found itself getting a remarkable 10 percent rate of response on a fund-raising letter to purchasers of William Bennett's "Index of Leading Cultural Indicators." Even the Libertarians could report good news with a 1993 increase of 15 percent in revenues for Laissez-Faire Books while the editor of *Liberty* reported that the new journal's circulation, now at 12 500, had exceeded all expectations. Pointing to the source of this new-found health, David Keene, Chairman of the American Conservative Union, observed that conservatives "have identified a new enemy. We used to have communism. Now we have Bill Clinton."[49]

The remarkable Republican victory in the 1994 Congressional elections provided the market liberals with another opportunity to advance their agenda. In 1994, for the first time in 40 years, the Republicans gained control of both the House of Representatives and the Senate. The victory was reminiscent of the 1894 Congressional election. In that late nineteenth-century electoral rout not a single Democrat was elected to national office in 24 states, anticipating the 1896 "critical election" and political realignment which made the Republicans the majority party until the thirties.[50]

Although some pundits and editorial writers were quick in 1994 to claim the arrival of the long-awaited post-Roosevelt realignment, others were more skeptical, suggesting that the new majority party-designate would not be able to accommodate the diversity of interests reflected in the country. The result, warned John B. Judis, might be for both parties "to remain in the minority while more and more Americans cast about among third parties or abandon politics altogether."[51]

If so, this would be a reflection of a difficulty that the market liberals had not been able to overcome in the eighties. As David M. Ricci has noted, by the end of the seventies the traditional conservative-liberal single dimension continuum did not seem to explain the choices being made by many voters:

> the particular nature of one problem or another encouraged people to favor more government action today and less tomorrow, or vice versa depending on the specific matter ... more and more Americans came to espouse options that were, strictly speaking, contradictory.[52]

What Ricci saw as contradictory could be made more comprehensible by assuming that the old single-dimensional (liberal-conservative) ideological continuum was too simple to catch the diversity of viewpoints in the electorate.

In the early eighties William S. Maddox and Stuart Lilie had suggested that more sense could be made out of polling data and electoral behavior if political scientists used a two-dimensional measure of preferences, where one axis would reflect attitudes (negative or positive) towards government economic intervention, while the other axis would measure attitudes towards expansion of personal freedoms. Each of the resultant four quadrants could represent a different ideological position: those who favored government economic intervention and expansion of personal freedom were liberals; voters who favored expansion of personal freedom but opposed government economic intervention were libertarians; members of the electorate who opposed government economic intervention and expansion of personal freedoms were conservative; finally, those who favored government economic intervention but opposed expansion of personal freedom were populists.

Using responses on questions pertaining to economic and personal freedom found in the longitudinal survey data from the Center for Political Studies at the University of Michigan, Maddox and Lilie produced a breakdown of ideological preferences in the United States (see Table 1).

Table 1　Distribution of ideological types in the seventies (%)

Ideological Category	1972	1976	1980
Liberal	17.3	16.4	24.4
Populist	30.0	23.7	26.3
Conservative	18.3	18.0	16.5
Libertarian	9.4	13.0	17.7
Inattentive	5.7	9.6	4.6
Divided	19.2	19.2	10.6

Such data suggest something of the difficulty that market liberals encountered in the 1980s. Even when using the most optimistic assumption (namely that all conservatives and libertarians were staunch market liberals), only 34.2 percent of the electorate in 1980 favored any thoroughgoing privatization of most government functions.[53]

III

What would it take to produce a dramatic victory for the market liberals in America? William A. Niskanen suggested in 1994 that libertarians, conservatives and populists ought to be able to form a coalition in support of "limited, constitutional, *smaller* government." While admitting that these groups would not agree on some issues, he argued that only such a coalition would be broad enough to "constrain our democratic leviathan."[54]

The feasibility of revitalizing and broadening the market liberal coalition may have been greater by the mid-nineties than several years earlier. Out of power the anti-statists showed evidence of a willingness to acknowledge their own statist codependency. The Heritage Foundation's Burton Pines, reconsidering the impact of the Cold War on American domestic life, noted that it had forced a Faustian bargain upon conservatives: to insure security in the post-war years they had acquiesced in the construction of an American leviathan, consisting of a social-welfare state and a military-industrial complex. With the Cold War over a new bargain could be struck and in the negotiations conservatives could "redeploy their most formidable artillery – strong philosophical principles rooted deeply in the lessons of history – to besiege the state grown fat during the Cold War."[55]

Similar arguments were heard from George F. Will and William J. Bennett, both formerly identified as big-government conservatives. Will now advocated term-limits and Bennett called for a revitalization of traditional values as therapies for what seemed in the early nineties to many conservatives an increasingly dysfunctional society.[56] Where Charles Murray in 1984 had written only of the destructiveness of the welfare state for the lower classes, the conservative journalist David Frum in 1994 now sounded the tocsin against the debilitating effects of entitlement programs on members of the middle-class: "Big government ... enables them to engage in destructive behavior without immediately suffering the consequences."[57]

This new emphasis on the supposed cultural and social consequences of departing from a market liberal economy might permit the economic conservatives to make common cause with the religious conservatives. Ralph Reed, Jr., Executive Director of the Christian Coalition, acknowledged that the religious conservatives had been unnecessarily narrow in their focus, noting that surveys showed that regular churchgoers' chief public concern was not abortion, prayer in school or pornography but rather the state of the economy and the need for reducing the deficit and controlling government waste. He concluded that "in an essentially conservative society, traditionalist ends can be advanced through libertarian means."[58]

Republican Congressman Richard Armey, a former professor of economics at the University of North Texas (and House Majority Leader after the 1994 elections), tendered an offer of cooperation from the "economic conservatives." Armey insisted that there was no need for the economic conservatives and libertarians to fear an aggressive religious agenda because the Religious Right had only been energized in the late seventies when the federal government threatened to remove the tax exempt status of religious schools. Left alone the Religious Right would at most seek to implement their values through local governments "where they are more likely to reflect the general wishes of the governed" and can be comparatively easily escaped by relocating to a more "liberal" jurisdiction. In effect, Armey was suggesting that where there were true disagreements among Americans, the "Party of Freedom" should support a market in cultural values by invoking a form of antitrust action against the single national moral monopoly decreed by Washington.[59]

William Kristol, son of Irving Kristol and Chief of staff for Vice-President Dan Quayle, and, beginning in 1993, Chairman of the Project for the Republican Future, sounded a similar note, calling for a "politics of liberty and a sociology of virtue." The politics of liberty would seek to limit government through a balanced budget amendment, term limits, and devolution and privatization of government functions. The sociology of virtue would involve reinventing or restructuring social institutions to "promote virtue and to foster moral character." Much of this character-building could be done by non-political institutions like schools and churches which would mimic the functions of state institutions but invest them with new values. If the exercise were successful public institutions would be required to emulate the private alternatives or wither and die.

At one point the separate tracks of the politics of liberty and the sociology of virtue would intersect: at the family. It would be impossible, Kristol admitted, for the state to be neutral about this fundamental institution and the sociology of virtue would need some government support, as only so much "can be done in the civil sphere absent legal or public policy support."[60]

Of all the elements of the small-government coalition, the libertarians would find such talk of moral regeneration and state support for a "patriarchal" institution most problematic. Although there was nothing intrinsically hedonistic about libertarianism as a credo, it applied the doctrines of market liberalism more comprehensively and vigorously than any other elements of the conservative coalition. Perhaps for precisely that reason it seemed to attract a disproportionate number of the socially and religiously heterodox. When in the early eighties political scientists John C. Green and James L. Guth surveyed contributors to the Libertarian Party, they found them overwhelmingly secular, and "more concerned with the value of personal freedom and less concerned with material well-being, doing God's will, friendship and social recognition, and working to better America." Other surveys confirmed the essential accuracy of the Green/Guth study.[61] Although social conservatives and libertarians remained skeptical of each other, there were opportunities to work together on specific issues – such as school choice – where they shared common goals despite the difference in their rationales.[62]

Whether such a coalition of the various conservative factions, libertarians, and those populists more driven by the social question than by economic redistribution would be broad enough and coherent enough to achieve Niskanen's restraining of the democratic leviathan seemed problematic. At a minimum it would require the participants to join in a self-abnegating pledge to eschew the state's proffered entitlements. This seemed doubtful. Most Americans by the eighties had developed a proprietary attitude toward government entitlements; the result was a "libertarian welfare state" committed to self-aggrandizement.[63] For a coalition to succeed against such strong tidal forces it would have to persuade its members to react as taxpayers and not as tax-consumers. As Jonathan Rauch noted recently, "We have met the special interests and they are us."[64] Indeed one might wonder if an unrestrained democracy and a market liberal order were fully compatible.[65]

As the political scientist James L. Payne has recently suggested, much of the modern American social welfare state was a system of "self-subsidies" under the guise of public goods. Although a public good traditionally meant a "socially beneficial thing that individuals could not purchase for themselves," such as national defense, over time it shifted "to include *any* socially beneficially expenditure." This revised definition "opened the floodgate to self-subsidy" through government programs.

Although such self-subsidization might seem harmless, there were problems with such an expanded definition of a public good. Inevitably there were efforts to transfer the costs to someone else, as through intergenerational transfers. Additionally, notes Payne, self-subsidization resulted in inefficient use of resources as groups spent money trying to capture the "rents," taxpayers consumed or misallocated resources trying to avoid the costs, and governments invested money in enforcement measures. The end result wasn't even a zero-sum game; it was a negative-sum contest which left the economy the poorer for the exercise.[66]

The nineteenth-century classical liberal Frederic Bastiat defined the state as that "great fictitious entity by which everyone seeks to live at the expense of everyone else." Such rent-seeking was tolerable when the rent-seekers were comparatively few and when the United States government could function as the equivalent of a geographically isolated monopolistic provider of rents along with public goods.[67] Under such circumstances the system could "afford" such inefficiencies because non-beneficiaries were not heavily burdened and could not readily relocate.

Unfortunately, at the same time as the government markedly expanded the number and size of entitlement programs in the sixties and seventies, most substantially through the creation of Medicare and Medicaid and the indexing of improved Social Security payments, the American economy found itself meeting new competition from abroad. This increasingly competitive trade environment and the ability of high-tech firms to relocate or subcontract overseas with comparative ease forced governments to consider shedding "unworthy" rent-seekers while searching out more efficient means of delivery of basic services.[68]

As the greatest increase in government expenditures since the mid-sixties however, had been to pay for middle-class entitlements, radical downsizing of government expenditures could not be achieved without an assault on those programs. Although market liberals by the seventies had made a compelling case for the inefficiencies and irrationalities of much economic regulation and subsidization, they were much less successful in persuading their peers or the American public that the state's other functions might properly "wither away."

As Richard C. Cornuelle, a Mises student in the late forties and then administrator of the William Volker Fund, has recently noted, market liberals had a "roadmap" for extricating the state from operation or regulation of the strictly economic institutions of American society. What they lacked was a consensus on how, and even if, the market might provide for the social functions of the state. Noted Cornuelle,

> [i]f there are alternatives to the state's failing efforts to get rid of Skid Row, eliminate involuntary employment, eradicate illiteracy, provide reasonable pensions, treat the indigent sick, detoxify the environment ... there is only the dimmest awareness of them, and certainly no confidence that they would work.[69]

There *were* vague memories of thriving private charitable organizations of the nineteenth and early twentieth centuries but little confidence that they, where still extant, could ever fully reclaim their prior autonomy.[70]

Despite all their identifications of "government failures," market liberals might be forced, at best, to settle for a continued government financing of local public services and national health, education and social welfare programs while it resorted to increased use of the market and mediating institutions for delivery through contracting-out, vouchers and other choice mechanisms.

The system would remain a mixed one but with somewhat greater reliance on market and third sector (non-profit) delivery systems.[71]

V

In the years before market liberalism's revival, some adherents despaired that capitalism ever could compete with the siren song of socialism. Thus at the 1974 meeting of the Mont Pelerin Society, Ernest van den Haag gloomily anticipated the demise of the market order. Where the market still existed, noted van den Haag, "it is under bitter and perpetual attack by the great majority of intellectuals, and its mechanism is distorted by inflation, controls and welfare measures." What was the market's future? While he admitted that "extrapolation never has been predictive," there seemed little hope. Although the market might be saved, van den Haag sadly concluded that "I'm dammed if I know how."[72]

In his 1978 Presidential Address to the Mont Pelerin Society George Stigler was equally gloomy. After reviewing some theories of the expansion of the modern welfare state, he pondered an unpleasant possibility: "Suppose the rational theory of government is correct ... [that] democratic majority rule likes what we have been doing." Stigler suggested this would leave the market liberals only three choices: become collectivists, advocate constitutional reforms producing different outcomes, or hope for the turning of the tide of public opinion. Although he hoped that the tax rebellion signified by California's Proposition Thirteen indicated the turning of the tide, he thought this unlikely: "surely changes of political tastes are more convenient than probable, and I doubt that they will allow us to escape the hard question: are we a permanent minority?"[73]

Some eighteen years later, although no unqualified answer could be given to Stigler's query, prospects appeared brighter. The true alternative paradigm to market liberalism, socialism, *had* been discredited – for the moment. By the end of the eighties, events in the Soviet Union had effectively ended the debate between socialists and the market liberals. Hayek and Mises had bested the advocates of centralism. Keynes's biographer, Robert Skidelsky, recently summed up the lesson:

> Collectivism – the belief that the state knows better than the market, and can improve on the spontaneous tendencies of civil society, if necessary by suppressing them – has been the most egregious error of the twentieth century.[74]

It had not always been thought so. As the economist Robert Heilbroner recollected in 1990, when he had gone to college in the thirties socialism seemed quite feasible. It would merely necessitate the nationalizing of the 500 largest industrial corporations which then could be run by a central planning agency for the general welfare. Although experience subsequently demonstrated to Heilbroner that the various socialist systems constructed under communism never worked all that well, the collapse of the planned economies in the eighties produced the final shock for the remaining true-believers:

> As a semireligious vision of a transformed humanity, [socialism] has been dealt devastating blows in the twentieth century. As a blueprint for a rationally planned society, it is in tatters. What then is left?[75]

Assessing the causes of this collapse of scientific socialism and the end of the Cold War, John Lewis Gaddis now offered an almost deterministic interpretation of capitalism's seeming triumph: Marx was wrong about history being linear; rather, it was cyclical. Drawing an analogy from geology, Gaddis suggested that "one set of tectonic forces – industrialization, the emergence of class-consciousness and the alienation that flowed from it" – had "undermined liberal, democratic, bourgeois, market capitalism" which gave way in the early twentieth century to communism and fascism. Then in the second half of the twentieth century new tectonic forces – "postindustrialization, the emergence of communications-consciousness and the alienation that flowed from it" – undermined authoritarian regimes. These new forces, Gaddis concluded, "brought us around to our next historically determined phase, which turned out to be the liberal, democratic, bourgeois, market capitalism all over again."[76]

Milton Friedman, deploying an oceanographic image, was equally enthusiastic about the world-wide prospects for what he called the "Hayek Wave." Reviewing the economic history of the past 200 years, Friedman saw three "waves:" the Adam Smith Tide, the Fabian Tide, and now the Hayek Tide. Each tide had produced major shifts in social and economic policy and each tide had been preceded "by a shift in the climate of intellectual *opinion*, itself generated, at least in part, by contemporaneous social, political, and economic circumstances."[77]

Even in the United States the intellectual support for the Hayek Tide was only a counter-current during the dominance of the older paradigm. Indeed, after Hayek published *The Road to Serfdom* he concluded it was one of the intellectual disasters of his life. He believed that in the eyes of many of his academic colleagues he now was merely a propagandist for capitalism. At a late forties meeting of the American Economic Association when Hayek publicly praised a young economist's work, the latter's friends told him he had just received the kiss of death.[78]

That Hayek may not have exaggerated the negative response to his writings is suggested by the difficulty he had getting a position at the University of Chicago. Rejected by the faculty of economics in 1950, Hayek obtained a position with the University's Committee on Social Thought where his salary was paid by the Volker Fund. Karen I. Vaughn speculates that Hayek's views "made him too controversial to employ on regular appointment."[79]

Austrians found difficulty getting their ideas accepted within the economics profession after World War Two not just because of their passionate commitment to a free market but also because of their extreme apriorism, disdain for quantitative mathematics, opposition to central banking and other deviations. Thus when Murray Rothbard insisted on incorporating Mises's business-cycle theory into his doctoral thesis on *The Panic of 1819*, he couldn't get it approved by Arthur F. Burns. Ultimately Burns left Columbia to become Eisenhower's CEA Chairman and Rothbard received his degree in 1956. As it was, Rothbard found little demand for his Austrian ideas, eventually landing a position teaching at the Brooklyn Polytechnical Institute in 1963, but only because a left-wing faculty member liked his vocal opposition to the Cold War.[80]

Public Choice and Chicago economists also encountered resistance to their ideas. The *American Economic Review* rejected Gordon Tullock's articles "The Welfare Costs of Tariffs, Monopolies and Theft" (1967) and "The Costs of Transfers" (1971), explaining in the later case that "[t]his paper does not have anything to offer."[81] Friedman was similarly under-appreciated in the early years of the developing Hayek Tide. Although his 1963 book, *A Monetary History of the United States, 1867–1960*, was a major accomplishment, with its message that "money counted" and Federal Reserve mismanagement probably caused the Great Depression to be so severe, Friedman only began to be listened to after the "New Economics" edifice began to crumble in the late sixties.[82]

By the mid-seventies the time in the wilderness for the free-market liberals was ending. Hayek received the Nobel Prize for Economics in 1974; Friedman in 1976. The same year (1978) that Stigler lamented market liberalism's minority status brought additional hopeful signs that the academy was beginning to listen. In a preface for the second edition of *The End of Liberalism*, Lowi now acknowledged his "belated thanks" to Hayek. Although not ending up an Hayekian, Lowi found himself "confirming, by process of elimination and discovery, many of his fears of the modern liberal state." Giving the Richard T. Ely Lecture at the 1978 convention of the American Economic Association, the Chairman of the Civil Aeronautics Board acknowledged the contributions of members of the Chicago school – Henry Simons, George Stigler, and Richard Posner – in identifying the deficiencies of regulated monopoly.[83]

When that same year Congress adopted the toothless Full Employment and Balanced Growth Act (the Humphrey–Hawkins Act), possibly the "last legislative gasp of the Keynesian persuasion," the legislation, ironically, heralded the new order. Included in the act was a monetarist provision requiring the Federal Reserve to announce publicly its target ranges for the monetary aggregates.[84]

With the eighties came new prominence for members of the public-choice school as Niskanen, Tollison and Miller took economic policy-making positions in the Reagan administration. When Buchanan received the Nobel Prize for Economics in 1986, some liberals tried to trivialize his contribution by suggesting that it had always been obvious to them that, just as markets could fail, so could governments! That the public-choice perspective now seemed "self-evident" suggested just how effectively it had been incorporated into the "conventional wisdom."

In the late eighties Friedman illustrated the changing market-liberal fortunes by describing the different responses two of his books had received:

> The first, *Capitalism and Freedom*, published in 1962 and destined to sell more than 400 000 copies in the next eighteen years, was not reviewed at the time in a single popular American periodical – not in the *New York Times*, the Chicago Tribune, *Newsweek, Time*, you name it. The second, *Free to Choose*, published in 1980 was reviewed by every major publication ..., became the year's best-selling nonfiction book in the United States, and received world-wide attention.[85]

What had produced the differing reactions to the two books? Although Friedman acknowledged the power of market-liberal ideas, he insisted that experience had been an even better teacher. The excesses of the Great Society and the Vietnam débâcle gave anti-statists in America a larger audience but the truly catalytic event, according to Friedman, was the "worldwide wave of inflation during the 1970s, originating in excessively expansive monetary growth in the United States in the 1960s." This failure at fine-tuning the economy and the subsequent stagflation and tax-bracket creep damaged the credibility of Keynesian monetary and fiscal policy and imposed taxes on the middle class that previously had only applied to the rich.[86]

Friedman's analysis of the causes of the crisis of the old paradigm surely was substantially correct, but he may have been too optimistic in forecasting the market liberals' ultimate success in the public arena. Although Americans had a long history of opposing taxes, there was little evidence that the American public was disposed to deny itself social welfare programs. If median family incomes had continued to grow in the seventies, perhaps Vital-Center liberalism could have weathered the crisis of confidence relatively unscathed. What the Democrats lacked most in 1980, noted Bennett Harrison and Barry Bluestone, were credible plans "for restoring productivity and economic growth."[87]

Market liberals, offering explanations for these "government failures" and proffering alternative policies during liberalism's crisis, gained some influence in the Reagan administration. But as Carter's defeat was primarily, in Walter Dean Burnham's characterization, a *"landslide vote of no confidence in an incumbent administration,"* rather than an affirmative vote for drastic surgery on main-line liberal programs, all the market liberals were able to accomplish was the paring of some expenditures, modest (often temporary) deregulation, and income-tax reduction.[88]

The ideas of market liberalism had been only partially incorporated into the United States political economy by the end of the eighties; the Hayek Tide had not yet swept away much of the New Deal order. But the market liberals *had* "reshaped political discourse. Governmental options were conceived and talked about differently. The differences shifted expectations and the burden of proof against those who would argue for an authoritative government role."[89] As Peter Drucker, coiner of the neologism "privatization," succinctly put it: "No one except a mere handful of Stalinists believes anymore in salvation by society."[90] Where Paul Samuelson in the 1955 edition of *Economics* had warned that the capitalist system suffered from a bad income distribution, monopolistic tendencies, and irregular employment levels – all of these defects capable of amelioration by government policy – by the twelfth edition he was warning students that "we must be alert to *government failure* – situations in which governments cause diseases or makes them worse."[91]

All mixed economies in the post-war era had suffered from these economic inefficiencies to some degree. As the social democratic states of Western Europe generated even greater inefficiencies than the United States did, their forced response to international market pressures was a much more dramatic sell-off of nationalized properties and some scale-back of the social insurance programs. Because the European socialist parties had articulated an elaborate argument for nationalization and the comprehensive welfare state, their repudiation of those doctrines was equally explicit. "What had been adopted seriously," noted Seymour Martin Lipset, "could only be removed seriously, and serious consequences followed from doing so – organizational as well as ideological ones."[92]

No such "debate" occurred in America; US political parties are traditionally decentralized and non-ideological. Thus a withdrawal from exposed positions would likely be much less dramatic, systematic and coherent. Given the continued roughly equal division of American voters into the populist, liberal, conservative, and libertarian camps, it seemed unlikely that any resolution of these issues would be arrived at shortly.[93]

Surveys in the wake of the 1994 Republican victory suggested that most Americans still believed that the fundamental problem with government was not that it provided entitlements and subsidies but that it provided them to the "unworthy."[94] In his postmortem on the mid-term election, House Republican Whip Newt Gingrich offered a challenge to those grown skeptical of government: "The New Hampshire slogan is 'Live Free or Die.' It is not 'Live free or whine.'"[95]

Despite Gingrich's admonitions to eschew the state, it is unlikely that anything like a market-liberal utopia will ever be established in the United States.[96] Market liberal thinking just assumed that individuals placed the highest value on liberty and prosperity. But as Norman P. Barry has suggested, "people normally hold a plurality of mutually incompatible ends and ... political judgement is pre-eminently concerned with a satisfactory ranking of these ends."[97] Clearly, any successor political economy to the battered Vital Center liberalism will of necessity require an appeal to more than market-liberal values.

Market liberals have not been able to persuade the general public or economists that the unrestrained market provides "social justice" and sustains community. Some 63 percent of economists and 72 percent of political scientists still identified themselves as liberals in the late eighties.[98] Public opinion polls continue to show strong support for social welfare spending.

The communitarian social philosopher Amitai Etzioni insisted that market-liberal thinking was ethically deficient because it excluded the moral dimension in its calculus.[99] This assertion ignored the arguments of libertarian from Rand to Rothbard that the *only* moral order was that constituted by a market-liberal society.

Yet some market liberals were sufficiently sensitive to this criticism to advocate a modest welfare state, witness Friedman's support for the negative income tax. Similarly, despite his insistence that the concept of social justice was nonsensical, Hayek did acknowledge the need for some income support for the unfortunate.[100] A market economy dissolved the "ties of the local community," Hayek noted, producing a "highly mobile society," and breaking the association with those "groups whose help and support they [could] count upon in the case of misfortune." Thus the "assurance of a certain minimum income," Hayek concluded, would be a guard against "great discontent and violent reaction" focused on the market order.[101]

Although a minimum welfare state would be an insurance policy for a market order, Hayek argued that more was needed. In one of his most frequently cited passages, he had urged the market intellectuals to build a "new liberal programme which appeals to the imagination. We must make the building of a free society once more an intellectual adventure, a deed of courage."[102]

Despite Rand's portrayal in *Atlas Shrugged* (1957) of the businessman as a heroic titan, and George Gilder's more recent efforts to picture him as an altruist, there was little evidence that the intellectual class was any more disposed to glorify the bourgeois in 1996 than it was in 1949.[103] As the sociologist Peter L. Berger has written, capitalism stands at a disadvantage to socialism at the "mythic level." This "mythic deprivation" of capitalism is explained by the "fact that capitalism is an economic system and nothing else," whereas "socialism is a comprehensive view of human society."[104]

The libertarians, recognizing this allure of socialism, sought to offer an alternative comprehensive vision.[105] In its most extreme form libertarianism amounted to a capitalist anarchy. This version seems as improbable in 1996 as when Rothbard and his merry band of followers pumped for it in the late sixties. Buchanan dismissed anarcho-capitalists in 1979 as "romantic fools, who have read neither Hobbes or history." Viewed from the perspective of the mid-nineties there seems to be very little evidence that the state is about to "wither away."[106] Similarly, those libertarians who would seek America's return to Herbert Spencer's beau ideal of the "nightwatchman state" of courts, constabulary and common defense are likely to be disappointed. There is little evidence that any sizeable minority of the public presently supports such a proposition. The anarcho-libertarian Roy Childs, having found a new moderation by the early eighties, admitted to Irving Kristol that no revolution was in the offering: "Never mind that we aren't going to get any kind of libertarian utopia ... Every generation of intellectuals needs its paradigmatic vision, even if it is moderated and adapted to the real world over time."[107]

Taking a pole position in efforts to radicalize America into a *true* market-liberal revolution had been the Libertarian Party. Despite repeated rebuffs from the electorate, the Party soldiered on in its improbable quest. Rejecting arguments for compromise it remembered Rothbard's warning: "who in blazes would go [to] the barricades" just for a tax reduction?[108] Who indeed! What Rothbard counted upon was a systemic crisis of the state that would so alienate Americans from their government that they would consider a thoroughgoing market liberal paradigm. Although Americans in the seventies and eighties did feel themselves over-taxed and over-regulated, libertarians did not grasp how difficult it would be to persuade most Americans that they were oppressed by all forms of "statism."

After a recent book-length review of the case for libertarianism, the generally sympathetic writer Jan Narveson remained skeptical that it would ever triumph. He doubted that libertarianism ever would be able to convince the average voter that most of the things that governments did were violations of fundamental rights. Certainly the taxes are compulsory and always unpopular, noted Narveson, but most of the "services in question are, [the modern citizen] would claim, necessary or important ... And then, you know, there's the fact that when the State does them, they are *done* and one doesn't have to think about them." Narveson warned that the "libertarian's battle" – and by extension that of all market liberals – "is an uphill one: his enemies are apathy, affection for the State and lack of rallying cries."[109]

Narveson may have been too pessimistic. In drawing the attention of the intellectual classes and the attentive public to the deficiencies of the old Vital-Center liberalism while proposing alternatives, market liberals have had a significant influence on the public discourse in the last twenty years – and libertarians have made their contribution. Those libertarians who have been most influential have been those who, forgoing revolutionary rhetoric, have taken a leaf from the Fabian socialists in advocating *specific* reforms rather than grand chiliastic visions – witness the Reason Foundation and the Cato Institute's promotion of privatization, school choice, and Social Security reform.[110]

The Reagan administration acted as a carrier of this message even while never consistently adhering to it. Only a fellow-traveller of the libertarians, Reagan routinely infuriated them. Yet the President's anti-statist rhetoric added credibility to the libertarian message. By the end of the decade, noted E. J. Dionne, "libertarian attitudes enjoyed a prominence in the American political discussion they had not had since at least the 1940s."[111] The electoral analyst Everett Carll Ladd found that supporters for Ross Perot's 1992 independent presidential candidacy "were disproportionately libertarian-inclined independents and Republicans, who were angered by government excesses and wanted a more restricted government role."[112]

The election of Republican majorities to the House of Representatives and the Senate in 1994 gave the critics of the modern liberal state an opportunity to take up where the Reagan administration left off. Despite House Speaker Gingrich's self-identification as a revolutionary, the 104th Congress impact on the modern liberal state proved less than revolutionary. Efforts to pass a balanced-budget amendment, rein in the growth of entitlement spending, lower capital-gains tax rates, adopt a market-driven health-care policy, and abolish various cabinet offices all failed. A combination of Gingrich's over-confidence and prickly personality, resistance in the more moderate Senate, and key vetoes by the President prevented any dramatic scale-back of government responsibilities. Congress did reject Clinton's proposal for national health insurance, calling it a grab for control of one-seventh of the economy. The President had his retaliation. When the Republicans proposed cuts in Medicare expenditure growth rates, Clinton successfully portrayed his opponents as grinches trying to steal Christmas.

Despite these misadventures the 104th Congress was not without its considerable victories for the market liberals. Privatization made headway with the sell-off of the US Enrichment Corporation, the Naval Petroleum Reserve, and the Alaska Power Marketing Administration. Deregulation made some progress as agricultural programs were revised to give farmers more freedom over planting while reducing government subsidies. Additionally, the telecommunications industry benefitted from legislation permitting competition, albeit regulated, between cable, local telephone companies and long-distance carriers.

Operating on the assumption that liberty and efficiency would be enhanced by restraining the federal government's power over the states, the 104th Congress enacted legislation checking federal unfunded mandates, restoring state authority over highway speeds and, most importantly, giving states primary responsibility for operating welfare programs. Whether the states would be able to substantially reduce the size of the underclass remained to be determined, but the elimination of welfare benefits as a federal entitlement reversed a policy whose roots extended back to the very beginnings of the federal social welfare state in the thirties.

At the federal level Congress terminated 270 programs, agencies, offices and projects, including the grand-daddy of all regulatory agencies – the Interstate Commerce Commission. Most of the programs eliminated, however, had tiny budgets of a few million dollars each. Targeted programs that survived (e.g. the Appalachian Regional Commission, Corporation for Public Broadcasting, and the Legal Services Corporation) often saw their budgets cut dramatically, but as they had only modest budgets to begin with, no dramatic individual savings were achieved. Yet these cuts when added to savings achieved by several brief government shut-downs and the use of continuing resolutions during the wrangling over budget bills, combined to produce in FY1996 the first decline in discretionary spending in 27 years. Additionally, it now appears that as a percentage of GDP, federal spending in both FY1996 and FY1997 will be lower than any of the Reagan years.[113]

In his 1996 State of the Union address President Clinton announced, "the era of big government is over." Almost certainly the President's adoption of the market liberals' mantra reflected studied political calculation in an election year, for he was quick to add that "we cannot go back to the time when our citizens were left to fend for themselves."[114] Yet his or any other future president's room for maneuver may be seriously circumscribed. As "free trade and electronic commerce allow capital to flow around the world," notes Richard B. McKenzie, "the discretion of government to regulate, manage, and exploit economic resources is shrinking."[115]

As a result of these considerations the burden of proof for an increase of government responsibility now clearly rests with the advocates of expansion. Indeed the combined effect of international economic competition, national demographic pressures, and the catalyst of market-liberal ideas ultimately may force the federal government to more dramatically shed load, casting off many rent-seekers, while focusing more clearly on the provision of plausible public goods. The powerful American resistance to paying European-level taxes combined with the fast increasing entitlement spending caused by the "graying of America" suggests continuing turmoil in American politics.

For the moment the United States has experienced only a paradigm lost – thus the efforts of the communitarians, neo-liberals, "new paradigmers" and some libertarians to synthesize a new order.[116] As the New-Deal system was ideologically inconsistent, so will any likely successor political economy offend against the sensibilities of the monists. Despite this defeat for the radical enemies of the leviathan, a newly delimited state may prove to be the considerable legacy of a revitalized market liberalism.

Notes

1 THE TRIUMPH AND CRISIS OF VITAL-CENTER LIBERALISM

1. Michael D. Reagan, *Regulation: The Politics of Policy* (Boston, MA: Little, Brown, 1987), 9.
2. Nigel Ashford, "Liberalism," in *Dictionary of Conservative and Libertarian Thought*, Nigel Ashford and Stephen Davies, eds (London: Routledge, 1991), 160.
3. Ronald D. Rotunda, "The 'Liberal' Label: Roosevelt's Capture of a Symbol," *Public Policy* 17 (1968): 39. Modern devotees of nineteenth-century liberalism, frustrated by this appropriation of "liberalism" by advocates of the mixed economy, were forced to use such circumlocutions as "classical liberal," "libertarian," or, in Friedrich A. Hayek's case, "old Whig." See Milton Friedman, *Capitalism and Freedom* (Chicago: University of Chicago Press, 1962), 5–6; Louis M. Spadaro, foreword to *Liberalism in the Classical Tradition*, 3rd ed. by Ludwig von Mises, trans. Ralph Raico (Irvington-on-Hudson, NY: Foundation for Economic Education, 1985), xiv–xv; and Friedrich A. Hayek, *The Constitution of Liberty* (South Bend, IN: Gateway Editions, 1972), 407–11.
4. Alonzo L. Hamby, *Liberalism and Its Challengers: F. D. R. to Bush*, 2nd ed. (New York: Oxford University Press, 1992), 4.
5. Carl M. Degler, "The Ordeal of Herbert Hoover," *The Yale Review* 52 (Summer 1993): 563–83. Richard K. Vedder and Lowell E. Gallaway recently have argued that unemployment during the Great Depression was so severe precisely because Hoover's support for high tariffs and maintenance of nominal wages during a deflation resulted in an actual *increase* in real wages at a time of decreasing labor demand. See Richard K. Vedder and Lowell E. Gallaway, *Out of Work: Unemployment and Government in Twentieth-Century America* (New York: Holmes & Meier, 1993), 89–92.
6. Otis L. Graham, Jr., *Toward a Planned Society: From Roosevelt to Nixon* (New York: Oxford University Press, 1976), 22–3.
7. William E. Leuchtenburg, "The New Deal and the Analogue of War," in *Change and Continuity in Twentieth Century America*, John Braeman, Robert H. Bremmer and Everett Walters, eds (New York: Harper & Row, 1966), 129.
8. Graham, *Toward a Planned Society*, 30.
9. Graham, *Toward a Planned Society*, 30.
10. Ellis W. Hawley, *The New Deal and the Problem of Monopoly* (Princeton, NJ: Princeton University Press, 1966), 470.

11. Paul K. Conkin, *The New Deal*, 2nd ed. (Arlington Heights, IL: Harland Davidson, 1975), 72.

12. Hawley, *The New Deal and the Problem of Monopoly*, 484.

13. Robert Higgs, *Crisis and Leviathan: Critical Episodes in the Growth of American Government* (New York: Oxford University Press, 1987), 192; Andrew Kull, "The Stealth Revolution," review of *The Supreme Court Reborn: The Constitutional Revolution in the Age of Roosevelt*, by William E. Leuchtenburg, *The New Republic*, 22 January 1996, 41.

14. Arthur M. Schlesinger, Jr., *The Coming of the New Deal* (Boston, MA: Houghton Mifflin, 1958), 193–4.

15. Thomas K. McGraw, "The New Deal and the Mixed Economy," in *Fifty Years Later: The New Deal Evaluated*, Harvard Sitkoff, ed. (New York: Alfred A. Knopf, 1985), 58.

16. Quoted in ibid., 63.

17. *The Public Papers and Addresses of Franklin D. Roosevelt*, Vol. V (New York: Random House, 1938), 148.

18. Louis Galambos and Joseph Pratt, *The Rise of the Corporate Commonwealth: United States Business and Public Policy in the 20th Century* (New York: Basic Books, 1988), 153–4.

19. Arthur M. Schlesinger, Jr., *The Politics of Upheaval* (Boston, MA: Houghton Mifflin, 1960), 172, 176, 544, 611.

20. Alonzo M. Hamby, "The Democratic Movement: FDR to LBJ," in *Democrats and the American Idea: A Bicentennial Appraisal*, Peter B. Kovler, ed. (Washington, DC: Center for National Policy Press, 1992), 256.

21. Conkin, *The New Deal*, 69.

22. Michael Barone, *Our America: The Shaping of America from Roosevelt to Reagan* (New York: Free Press, 1990), 97–8.

23. George H. Nash, *The Conservative Intellectual Movement in America Since 1945* (New York: Basic Books, 1976), 5–9.

24. Manfred Jonas, *Isolationism in America, 1935–1941* (Ithaca, NY: Cornell University Press, 1966), Ch. 3, passim.

25. Richard Polenberg, *War and Society: The United States, 1941–1945* (Philadelphia, PA: J. B. Lippincott Company, 1972), 180–1.

26. See Vedder and Gallaway, *Out of Work*, 150–9 for a skeptical view of this Keynesian explanation of World War Two "prosperity" and the post-war recovery.

27. Robert M. Collins, *The Business Response to Keynes, 1929–1964* (New York: Columbia University Press, 1981), 69–71.

28. Ibid., 6.

29. Alan Brinkley, "The Idea of the State," in *The Rise and Fall of the New Deal Order, 1930–1980*, Steve Fraser and Gary Gerstle, eds (Princeton, NJ: Princeton University Press, 1989), 87–100.

30. Alan Brinkley, *The End of Reform: New Deal Liberalism in Recession and War* (New York: Alfred A. Knopf, 1995), 266, 268–9.

31. Arthur M. Schlesinger, Jr., *The Vital Center: The Politics of Freedom* (Boston, MA: Houghton Mifflin, 1949).

32. Nelson Lichtenstein, "From Corporatism to Collective Bargaining: Organized Labor and the Eclipse of Social Democracy in the Postwar Era," in *The Rise and Fall of the New Deal Order*, Fraser and Gerstle, eds, 122–45.

33. Alonzo L. Hamby, *Beyond the New Deal: Harry S. Truman and American Liberalism* (New York: Columbia University Press, 1973), 270–4, 505–16.

34. Ibid., 299–303.

35. Schlesinger, Jr., *The Vital Center*, 38, 45.

36. John Kenneth Galbraith, *American Capitalism: The Concept of Countervailing Power* (Boston, MA: Houghton Mifflin, 1952), Ch. IX, passim.

37. Richard Hofstadter, *The Paranoid Style in American Politics* (New York: Vintage Books, 1967), 226–7.

38. Charles Alexander, *The Eisenhower Era, 1952–1961* (Bloomington: Indiana University Press, 1975), Ch. IV and Richard H. Pells, *The Liberal Mind in a Conservative Age: American Intellectuals in the 1940s and 1950s* (New York: Perennial Library, 1985), Chs. 3–4 provide excellent overviews of this phenomenon and its contemporary critics.

39. Alexander, *The Eisenhower Era*, 105.

40. Lynn Hanrahan, "In Praise of Prosperity: Liberals Reevaluate American Capitalism in the 1950s" (Master's thesis, Ohio University, 1991), 39.

41. Bruce Miroff, *Pragmatic Illusions: The Presidential Politics of John F. Kennedy* (New York: David McKay Company, 1976), 9, 291.

42. Godfrey Hodgson, *America in Our Time* (New York: Doubleday & Company, 1976), 76.

43. Herbert Stein, *Presidential Economics: The Making of Economic Policy from Roosevelt to Reagan and Beyond* (Washington, DC: American Enterprise Institute, 1988), 71–4.

44. Collins, *The Business Response to Keynes, 1929–1964*, 133–7, 152–8, 250.

45. Ibid., 153.

46. Irving Bernstein, *Promises Kept: John F. Kennedy's New Frontier* (New York: Oxford University Press, 1991), 126–7.

47. John F. Kennedy, *Public Papers: 1962* (Washington, DC: United States Government Printing Office, 1963), 470–1, 473.

48. Collins, *The Business Response to Keynes, 1929–1964*, 186.

49. John Brooks, *The Great Leap: The Past Twenty-five Years in America* (New York: Harper Colophon, 1968), 68.

50. Walter S. Salant, "The Spread of Keynesian Doctrines and Practices in the United States," in *Economics and Policy*, Omar F. Hamouda and John N. Smithin, eds, vol. 1 of *Keynes and Public Policy After Fifty Years* (New York: New York University Press, 1988), 71.

51. Paul A. Samuelson, "Economics in My Times," in *Lives of the Laureates: Ten Nobel Economists*, William Breit and Roger W. Spencer, eds (Cambridge, MA: MIT Press, 1990), 68.

52. *Time*, 31 December 1964, 64.
53. Walter Heller, *New Dimensions of Political Economy* (Cambridge, MA: Harvard University Press, 1966), 12.
54. Doris Kearns, *Lyndon Johnson and the American Dream* (New York: Harper & Row, 1976), 285.
55. John Mueller, *Retreat from Doomsday: The Obsolescence of Major War* (New York: Basic Books, 1989), 170–3, 177–9.
56. Allen J. Matusow, *The Unraveling of America: A History of Liberalism in the 1960s* (New York: Harper & Row, 1984), 159–61, 169–73.
57. Arthur M. Okun, *The Political Economy of Prosperity* (Washington, DC: The Brookings Institution, 1970), 119.
58. Friedman, *Capitalism and Freedom*, 77.
59. Ibid., Chs. III and V, passim.
60. Matusow, *The Unraveling of America*, 177.
61. Milton Friedman, "The Role of Monetary Policy," *The American Economic Review* 58, no. 1 (March 1968): 11.
62. Paul Krugman, *Peddling Prosperity: Economic Sense and Nonsense in the Age of Diminished Expectations* (New York: W. W. Norton, 1994), 45.
63. *Journal of Post Keynesian Economics* 1, no. 1 (Fall 1978): 2.
64. James Dean, "The Dissolution of the Keynesian Consensus," *The Public Interest* (Special Edition, 1980): 29.
65. Daniel Patrick Moynihan, *Maximum Feasible Misunderstanding: Community Action in the War on Poverty* (New York: Basic Books, 1969), 24–5.
66. Nicholas Lemann, "The Unfinished War," *The Atlantic Monthly*, December 1988, 39, 43–4. For a recollection that suggests a greater Kennedy sense of urgency, see Arthur M. Schlesinger, Jr, *A Thousand Days: John F. Kennedy in the White House* (Boston: Houghton Mifflin Company, 1965), 1012.
67. Lemann, "The Unfinished War," 39.
68. "Opinion Roundup," *Public Opinion* (February/March 1984): 20.
69. Hamby, *Liberalism and Its Challengers*, 261, 264, 265.
70. Quoted in Alfred L. Malabre, Jr, *Lost Prophets: An Insider's History of the Modern Economists* (Cambridge, MA: Harvard Business School Press, 1994), 77.
71. John Kenneth Galbraith, *The Affluent Society* (New York: Mentor Books, 1958), 257.
72. Robert Wood, *Whatever Possessed the President? Academic Experts and Presidential Policy, 1960–1988* (Amherst, MA: University of Massachusetts Press, 1993), 33–4.
73. Quoted in Randall Rothenberg, *The Neoliberals: Creating the New American Politics* (New York: Simon & Schuster, 1984), 111.
74. James S. Coleman, "Equal Schools or Equal Students?," *The Public Interest* 4 (Summer 1966): 73.
75. David J. Armor, "The Evidence on Busing," *The Public Interest* 28 (Summer 1972): 95.

76. Ibid., 99.
77. Matusow, *The Unraveling of America*, 104–5, 238–9.
78. William E. Leuchtenburg, *In the Shadow of FDR: From Harry Truman to Ronald Reagan* (Ithaca, NY: Cornell University Press, 1983), 142–3.
79. Richard Goodwin, *Remembering America: A Voice from the Sixties* (Boston, MA: Little, Brown, 1988), 258.
80. Thomas S. Langston, *Ideologues and Presidents: From the New Deal to the Reagan Revolution* (Baltimore, MD: Johns Hopkins University Press, 1992), 134.
81. Robert A. Dahl, *A Preface to Democratic Theory* (Chicago: University of Chicago Press, 1956), 138.
82. James T. Patterson, *America's Struggle against Poverty, 1900–1985* (Cambridge, MA: Harvard University Press, 1986), 135.
83. Thomas Bryne Edsall and Mary D. Edsall, *Chain Reaction: The Impact of Race, Rights, and Taxes on American Politics* (New York: W. W. Norton, 1991), 68.
84. Michael B. Katz, *The Undeserving Poor: From the War on Poverty to the War on Welfare* (New York: Pantheon Books, 1989), 92.
85. Patterson, *America's Struggle against Poverty, 1900–1985*, 153.
86. Vaughn Davis Bornet, *The Presidency of Lyndon B. Johnson* (Lawrence: University Press of Kansas), 61.
87. Dr George A. Wiley, introduction to *Welfare Mothers Speak Out* by Milwaukee County Welfare Rights Organization (New York: W. W. Norton, 1972), 12.
88. Henry J. Aaron, "Six Welfare Questions Still Searching for Answers," *Brookings Review* 3, no. 4 (Fall 1984): 13.
89. Charles A. Reich, "The New Property," *The Public Interest* 3 (Spring 1966): 58–9; 83, 88.
90. Charles R. Morris, *A Time of Passion: America 1960–1980* (New York: Penguin Books, 1986) 141–2.
91. Samuel H. Beer, "In Search of a New Public Philosophy," in *The New American Political System*, Anthony King, ed. (Washington, DC: American Enterprise Institute, 1978), 12.
92. Lemann, "The Unfinished War," *The Atlantic Monthly*, January 1989, 62; Edsall and Edsall, *Chain Reaction*, 18. In the late eighties some convergence was evident, but black members of the middle class were still employed disproportionately by government. Whereas 28.5 percent of whites holding professional or managerial positions were in the public sector, the figure for blacks was 53.5 percent. Edsall and Edsall, *Chain Reaction*, 290, fn. 13.
93. Hugh Davis Graham, "The Origins of Affirmative Action: Civil Rights and the Regulatory State," *Annals* 523 (September 1992): 51.
94. Steven M. Gillion, *Politics and Vision: The ADA and American Liberalism, 1947–1985* (New York: Oxford University Press, 1987), 224.
95. Steve M. Gillion, "The Travails of the Democrats: Search for a New Majority," in *Democrats and the American Idea*, Kovler, ed., 288.

96. Austin Ranney, "The Political Parties: Reform and Decline," in *The New American Political System*, Anthony King, ed. (Washington, DC: American Enterprise Institute, 1978), 231–2, 235.

97. *National Party Conventions 1831–1976* (Washington, DC: Congressional Quarterly, 1979), 115–16; Theodore H. White, *The Making of the President 1972* (New York: Athenaeum, 1973), 160.

98. Laird Hart, "'Stagflation' Reminds Economics Professors How Little They Know," *The Wall Street Journal*, 6 September 1974, A1 (E).

99. Quoted in "Social Science: The Public Disenchantment," [a symposium] *The American Scholar* 45 (Summer 1976): 349.

100. Quoted in Richard P. Nathan, *Social Science in Government: Uses and Misuses* (New York: Basic Books, 1988), 43.

101. Benjamin Ginsberg and Elizabeth Sanders, "Theodore J. Lowi and Juridical Democracy," *PS: Political Science and Politics* 23, no. 4 (December 1990): 563.

102. Theodore J. Lowi, *The End of Liberalism: The Second Republic of the United States*, 2nd ed. (New York: W. W. Norton, 1979), xvi, 57.

103. David A. Stockman, *The Triumph of Politics: Why the Reagan Revolution Failed* (New York: Harper & Row, 1986), 33.

104. Burton I. Kaufman, *The Presidency of James Earl Carter, Jr.* (Lawrence: University Press of Kansas), 28–9.

105. "Transcript of the President's Address Saying that the State of the Union is 'Sound'," *New York Times*, 20 January 1978, A12(L).

2 THE REVITALIZATION OF MARKET LIBERALISM

1. Quoted in Richard H. Pells, *The Liberal Mind in a Conservative Age: American Intellectuals in the 1940s and 1950s* (New York: Perennial Library, 1985), 135.

2. William C. Berman, *America's Right Turn: From Nixon to Bush* (Baltimore, MD: Johns Hopkins University Press, 1994), 20.

3. E. J. Dionne, Jr., *Why Americans Hate Politics* (New York: Simon & Schuster, 1991), 56; Alonzo L. Hamby, *Liberalism and Its Challengers: F.D.R. to Bush*, 2nd ed. (New York: Oxford University Press), 204, fn. 1.

4. Charles K. Wilber and Kenneth P. Jameson, *Beyond Reaganomics: A Further Inquiry into the Poverty of Economics* (Notre Dame, IN: University of Notre Dame Press, 1990), 33–5.

5. Friedrich A. Hayek, *The Road to Serfdom* (Chicago: University of Chicago Press, 1944), 69–70.

6. Peter J. Boettke, "Hayek's *The Road to Serfdom* Revisited: Government Failure in the Argument Against Socialism," *Eastern Economic Journal* 21, no. 1 (Winter 1995): 11, 12.

7. George H. Nash, *The Conservative Intellectual Movement in America Since 1945* (New York: Basic Books, 1976), 8–9.

8. Herman Finer, *Road to Reaction* (Chicago: Quadrangle Books, 1963), v, 33, 67.

9. For an argument that Vital-Center liberals and Hayek were not all that far apart regarding fears of totalitarianism and concerns about central planning, see Theodore Rosenof, "Freedom, Planning and Totalitarianism: The Reception of F. A. Hayek's *Road to Serfdom*," *Canadian Review of American Studies* 5, no. 2 (Fall 1974): 156–8, 161.

10. By the early seventies a mainstream historian, John A. Garraty, could acknowledge certain similarities between the New Deal and the Third Reich's economic programs, noting that the "worse horrors of nazism were unrelated to Nazi efforts to overcome the depression." "A Comparative Approach: The New Deal, National Socialism, and the Great Depression," in *The New Deal: Analysis & Interpretations*, Alonzo L. Hamby, ed. (New York: Longman, 1981), 221.

11. Julian Joseph Delgaudio, "Refugee Economist in America: Ludwig Von Mises and American Social and Economic Thought, 1940–1986" (Ph.D. dissertation, University of California, Irvine, 1987), 96–101.

12. John Patrick Diggins, *The Rise and Fall of the American Left* (New York: W. W. Norton, 1992), 192–3.

13. Karl Polanyi, *The Great Transformation* (Boston MA: Beacon Press, 1957), 249, 251.

14. Joseph A. Schumpeter, *Capitalism, Socialism, and Democracy*, 3rd ed. (New York: Harper & Row, 1950), 143–55.

15. R. M. Hartwell, *A History of the Mont Pelerin Society* (Indianapolis: Liberty Fund, 1995), 45–6.

16. F. A. Hayek, *Studies in Philosophy, Politics and Economics* (Chicago: University of Chicago Press, 1967), 149.

17. Ibid., 151.

18. Hartwell, *A History of the Mont Pelerin Society*, 35–6.

19. 'Taxation, Poverty and Income Distribution' in "Minutes of Discussion, Economic Issues," Friedrich A. von Hayek Collection, Box 81, Hoover Institution Archives, Stanford, CA. Hereafter cited as Hayek Collection.

20. Martin Anderson, *Welfare: The Political Economy of Welfare Reform in the United States* (Stanford, CA: Hoover Institution Press, 1978), 77–9.

21. Hartwell, *A History of the Mont Pelerin Society*, 37.

22. Quoted in Fritz Machlup, ed., *Essays on Hayek* (New York: New York University Press, 1976), xii.

23. Ibid., xiii.

24. William Breit and Roger L. Ransom, *The Academic Scribblers*, rev. ed. (Chicago: Dryden Press, 1982), Ch. 14, passim.

25. George J. Stigler, *The Citizen and the State: Essays on Regulation* (Chicago University of Chicago Press, 1975), 114.

26. Ibid., 72–3.

27. Yale Brozen, "The Antitrust Task Force Deconcentration Recommendation," *The Journal of Law and Economics* 13 (October 1970), 292.

28. Yale Brozen, "Is Government the Source of Monopoly?," *The Intercollegiate Review* 5, no. 2 (Winter 1968–69): 78.

29. Dominick T. Armetano, *Antitrust and Monopoly: Anatomy of a Failure*, 2nd ed. (New York: Holmes & Meier, 1990), 63.

30. Harold Demsetz, "Industrial Structure, Market Rivalry and Public Policy," *Journal of Political Economy* 16 (April 1973): 2, 5.

31. Lester Telser, "Advertising and Competition," *Journal of Political Economy* 72 (December 1964): 537–62; Lester Telser, "Some Aspects of the Economics of Advertising," *Journal of Business* 41 (April 1968): 166–73.

32. John Kenneth Galbraith, *The Affluent Society* (Boston, MA: Houghton Mifflin, 1958), 149.

33. "John K. Galbraith's *The Affluent Society*," *The Mont Pelerin Quarterly* 3, nos. 1–2 (April–July 1961): 15, R. M. Hartwell Collection, Box 3, Hoover Institution Archives, Stanford, California. Hereafter cited as Hartwell Collection.

34. Ibid., 18.

35. George J. Stigler, *Memoirs of an Unregulated Economist* (New York: Basic Books, 1988), 79–80, 162–4.

36. R. H. Coase, "The Problem of Social Cost," *The Journal of Law and Economics* 3 (October 1960): 8.

37. David R. Henderson, "Ronald H. Coase," in *The Fortune Encyclopedia of Economics*, David R. Henderson, ed. (New York: Warner Books, 1993), 782; Henry G. Manne, *An Intellectual History of the School of Law, George Mason University* (Arlington, VA: Law and Economics Center, George Mason University School of Law, 1993), 8.

38. Harold Demsetz, "Toward a Theory of Property Rights," *American Economic Review* 57, no. 2 (May 1967): 355.

39. David Friedman, "Law and Economics," in *The New Palgrave: The Invisible Hand*, John Eastwell, Murray Milgate and Peter Newman, eds (New York: W. W. Norton, 1989), 173.

40. "Are Government Programs Worth the Price?," *Business Week*, 30 June 1975, 114–15.

41. Herbert Hovenkamp, "Law and Economics in the United States: A Brief Historical Survey," *Cambridge Journal of Economics* 19 (1995) 333–4.

42. Lionel Robbins, *An Essay on the Nature & Significance of Economic Science*, 2nd ed. (London: Macmillan, 1952), 139.

43. James M. Buchanan, *What Should Economists Do?* (Indianapolis: Liberty Press, 1979), 151.

44. Richard A. Posner, *Economic Analysis of the Law*, 4th ed. (Boston: Little, Brown, 1992), 13–15, 251, 523–4.

45. Richard A. Posner, *The Problems of Jurisprudence* (Cambridge, MA: Harvard University Press, 1990), 360.
46. Ibid., 358.
47. Posner, *Economic Analysis of the Law*, 252. For a skeptical view of Posner's claim that courts can mimic markets, see Jeffrie G. Murphy and Jules L. Coleman, *Philosophy of Law: An Introduction to Jurisprudence* (Boulder, CO: Westview Press, 1990), 219–29.
48. Ibid., 375.
49. Coase, "The Problem of Social Cost," 18.
50. James M. Buchanan, *Better Than Plowing, and Other Personal Essays* (Chicago: University of Chicago Press, 1992), 72.
51. James M. Buchanan, "Political Economy: 1957–82," in *Ideas, Their Origins, and Their Consequences* (Washington, DC: American Enterprise Institute, 1988), 120, 122.
52. Henri Lepage, *Tomorrow, Capitalism*, trans. Sheilagh C. Ogilvie (Lasalle, IL: Open Court, 1982), 95.
53. Anthony Downs, *An Economic Analysis of Democracy* (New York: Harper & Row, 1957), 208–9, 298–9.
54. Mancur Olson, "Collective Action," in *The New Palgrave*, Eastwell, Milgate, and Newman, eds, 61–9.
55. Buchanan, *Better than Plowing, and Other Personal Essays*, 106–7.
56. James M. Buchanan, "Economic Policy, Free Institutions, and Democratic Process," Hayek Collection, Box 83: 2, 7.
57. James M. Buchanan and Gordon Tullock, *The Calculus of Consent* (Ann Arbor: University of Michigan, 1965), 72.
58. Ibid., 304, 306.
59. Ibid., 82, 143.
60. Ibid., 303.
61. James M. Buchanan, *The Limits of Liberty: Between Anarchy and Leviathan* (Chicago: University of Chicago Press, 1975), 162.
62. William A. Niskanen, Jr., "Competition Among Government Bureaus," in *The Economics of Politics* (London: Institute of Economic Affairs, 1978), 164.
63. Quoted in Lepage, *Tomorrow, Capitalism*, 104.
64. Gordon Tullock, "The Welfare Costs of Tariffs, Monopolies, and Theft," *Western Economic Journal* 5 (June 1967): 231.
65. Gordon Tullock, "The Charity of the Uncharitable" (Paper presented at the 1971 Annual Meeting of the American Political Science Association, 7–11 September 1971), 10.
66. James M. Buchanan, "From Private Preference to Public Philosophy: The Development of Public Choice," in *The Economics of Politics*, 14.
67. James M. Buchanan and Richard E. Wagner, *Democracy in Deficit: The Political Legacy of Lord Keynes* (New York: Academic Press, 1977), 3.
68. Ibid., 21.

69. Ibid., 49–50.
70. James M. Buchanan, "Markets, States, and the Extent of Morals," *American Economic Review* 68, no. 2 (May 1978): 367–8.
71. Thomas C. Taylor, *The Fundamentals of Austrian Economics* (San Francisco: Cato Institute, 1980), 1–4.
72. Israel M. Kirzner, "Austrian School of Economics," in *The New Palgrave*, Eastwell, Milgate, and Newman, eds, I, 148.
73. Ludwig von Mises, *Socialism; An Economic and Sociological Analysis*, 2nd ed., trans. J. Kahane (Indianapolis: Liberty Classics, 1981), 101, 102.
74. Friedrich A. Hayek, *Individualism and Economic Order* (South Bend, IN: Gateway Editions, 1977), 187, 188, 206.
75. David Ramsay Steele, *From Marx to Mises: Post-Capitalist Society and the Challenge of Economic Calculation* (Lasalle, IL: Open Court, 1992), 166–7.
76. Ludwig von Mises, *Human Action: A Treatise on Economics*, 3rd rev. ed. (Chicago: Contemporary Books, 1966), 32.
77. Quoted in Delgaudio, "Refugee Economist in America," 202, 205.
78. Dionne, Jr., *Why Americans Hate Politics*, 154.
79. Quoted in Steele, *From Marx to Mises*, 95.
80. Karen I. Vaughn, *Austrian Economics in America* (Cambridge: Cambridge University Press, 1994), 99–100.
81. Edwin G. Dolan, "Austrian Economics as Extraordinary Science," in *The Foundations of Modern Austrian Economics*, Edwin G. Dolan, ed. (Kansas City: Sheed & Ward, 1976), 3.
82. Ibid., 6, 7.
83. Israel M. Kirzner, *Competition and Entrepreneurship* (Chicago: University of Chicago Press, 1973), 42.
84. Israel M. Kirzner, "Competition, Regulation, and the Market Process: An 'Austrian' Perspective," *Policy Analysis* (Washington, DC: Cato Institute, 10 August 1982): 3.
85. Israel M. Kirzner, "Divergent Approaches in Libertarian Economic Thought," *The Intercollegiate Review* 3 (January–February 1967), 108.
86. F. A. Hayek, *The Constitution of Liberty* (Chicago: University of Chicago Press, 1960), 113.
87. Of 74 economists that President Ronald W. Reagan employed in six task forces, 20 were members of the Society. Lindley H. Clark, Jr., "Reaganomics Reassessed: What Went Right – and Wrong," *Wall Street Journal*, 24 September 1987, A26(E).
88. Friedman, writing to the neoconservative Edward C. Banfield, observed that the Prize demonstrated the truth of his adage "that there is no free lunch. The consequences of the award have been an incredible pressure of papers, requests, and the like …. But in this case I have to admit the price is low relative to the reward." Milton Friedman to Edward Banfield, 16 November 1976, Milton Friedman Collection, Box 20, Hoover Institution Archives, Stanford, CA. Hereafter cited as Friedman Collection.

89. James M. Buchanan, "The Examined Politics and an Emergent Public Philosophy," in Hayek Collection, Box 89: 3, 5.
90. Milton Friedman, "Presidential Circular to all members," October 1970, Hartwell Collection, Box 5: 1–2; Hartwell, *A History of the Mont Pelerin Society*, 161–2.
91. Milton Friedman, "Presidential Circular to all members," October 1971, Hartwell Collection, Box 5: 1; Hartwell, *A History of the Mont Pelerin Society*, 164.
92. R. M. Hartwell, "The Re-emergence of Liberalism?" The Role of the Mont Pelerin Society," Hartwell Collection, Box 4: 21.
93. Ibid., 22, 33, fn. 20; "Questionnaire of Members," Hartwell Collection, Box 1. (See especially the responses of Ralph Harris, Guy Plunier, Antonio Martino and George Stigler.)
94. Antony Fisher, *Fisher's Concise History of Economic Bungling* (Ottawa, IL: Caroline House Books, 1978), 79–80.
95. Ibid., 80–8, 113; Arthur Seldon, *Capitalism* (Oxford: Basil Blackwell, 1990), 41–4; David Graham and Peter Clarke, *The New Enlightenment: The Rebirth of Liberalism* (London: Macmillan, 1986), 18–21; Richard Cockett, *Thinking the Unthinkable: Think-Tanks and the Economic Counter-Revolution, 1931–1983* (London: Fontana Press, 1995), 171–7; 195–9.
96. Antony Fisher to Friedrich A. Hayek, 14 July 1975, Hayek Collection, Box 20: 1–2.
97. Antony Fisher to Friedrich A. Hayek, 12 August 1975, 1; Antony Fisher to Friedrich A. Hayek, 13 April 1976, pp. 2–3; Antony Fisher to Friedrich A. Hayek, 15 July 1977, ibid.
98. Quoted in Guy Wright, "The Power of Ideas," *San Francisco Examiner*, 24 June 1980 [press clipping with no page number], Hayek Collection, Box 20; Cockett, *Thinking the Unthinkable*, 306–7.
99. Richard Cockett, *Thinking the Unthinkable*, 307; "Sir Antony Fisher," *Atlas Economic Research Foundation Highlights* (Summer 1998): 1.
100. Dian Berlanger, [draft] "History of the Institute for Humane Studies," part one, 4–5, Harper Library, Institute for Humane Studies, George Mason University, Fairfax, VA; Arthur Kemp, foreword to Bruno Leoni, *Freedom and the Law*, expanded 3rd ed. (Indianapolis: Liberty Fund, 1991), x–xii.
101. "Directory of Earhart Fellows 1957" and Milton Friedman to James A. Kennedy, 27 January 1953, Friedman Collection, Box 26.
102. Hayek, *Studies in Philosophy, Politics and Economics*, 179.
103. Margit von Mises, *My Years with Ludwig von Mises*, 2nd ed. (Spring Mills, PA: Libertarian Press, 1984), 90–2; Mary Sennholz, *Leonard E. Read: Philosopher of Freedom* (Irvington-on-Hudson, NY: Foundation for Economic Education, 1993), 60–70.
104. Sennholz, *Leonard E. Read*, 70–3; Hayek, *Individualism and Economic Order*, 108.
105. von Mises, *My Years with Ludwig von Mises*, 99–106, 149, 171.

106. Nash, *The Conservative Intellectual Movement in America Since 1945*, 24.
107. Sennholz, *Leonard E. Read*, 87–95; William H. Peterson, "A Free-Market University," *The Freeman*, April 1994, 164–5.
108. Belanger, "History of the Institute for Humane Studies," 1, 3–6, 15–16, 21–6; Ralph Raico, *Classical Liberalism in the Twentieth Century* (Fairfax, VA: Institute for Humane Studies, n.d.), 18.
109. Charles H. Hamilton, introduction to *Fugitive Essays: Selected Writings of Frank Chodorov*, Charles H. Hamilton, ed. (Indianapolis: Liberty Press, 1980), 13–19; 27–9; Nash, *The Conservative Intellectual Movement in America Since 1945*, 16–18.
110. Hamilton, ed. *Fugitive Essays*, 157.
111. Ibid., 415.
112. Nash, *The Conservative Intellectual Movement in America Since 1945*, 30–1. Among the works that the ISI distributed in the early years were Henry Hazlitt's *Economics in One Lesson*, Frederick Bastiat's *The Law*, F. A. Hayek's *The Road to Serfdom* and William Graham Sumner's *What Social Classes Owe to Each Other*.
113. E. Victor Milione, "Ideas in Action," *The Intercollegiate Review* 29, no. 1 (Fall 1993): 55.
114. Ibid., 55.
115. Sidney Blumenthal, *The Rise of the Counter-Establishment: From Conservative Ideology to Political Power* (New York: Perennial Library, 1988), 46–7.
116. Milton Friedman, introduction to *New Individualist Review* (Indianapolis: 1981), ix.
117. Manne, *An Intellectual History of the School of Law, George Mason University*, 10–13; Walter Guzzardi, Jr., "Judges Discover the World of Economics," *Fortune*, 21 May 1979, 59–61; William Landes and Richard A. Posner, "The Influence of Economics on Law: A Quantitative Study," *Journal of Law and Economics* 36 (April 1993): 404–7. By 1993 more than 400 federal judges and 600 law professors had taken at least one of the courses sponsored by the Law and Economics Center, located at George Mason University since 1986.
118. David R. Henderson, "Armen Alchian," in *The Fortune Encyclopedia of Economics*, David R. Henderson, ed. (New York: Warner Books, 1993), 773–4; "Spotlight," *Reason*, July 1976, 49; Robert Poole, Jr., "Regulation Reformer," *Reason*, March 1979, 41; Patrick Cox, "Environmentalist cum Economist," *Reason*, November 1980, 54–5; Patrick Cox, "Property Rights in Print," *Reason*, November 1983, 50.
119. Peter Duignan, *The Hoover Institution on War, Revolution and Peace: Seventy-five Years of Its History* (Standford, CA: Hoover Institution Press, 1989), 35, 38, 41–2, 67, 74–7; Jon Weiner, "Old-time Hustlers," *New Statesman & Society*, 17 January 1992, 20; "The Joys of Detached Involvement," *The Economist*, 21 December 1991–3 January 1992, 53.
120. Robert W. Poole, Jr., "Reason Interview: Robert W. Poole, Jr.," interview by David Brudnoy, *Reason*, May 1983, 60–1.

121. Robert Poole, Jr., "Getting Legislators to Listen," *Reason*, January 1978, 43–4; Alan Crawford, *Thunder on the Right: The "New Right" and the Politics of Resentment* (New York: Pantheon, 1980), 11; Patrick Cox, "Canadian Walker Makes Market Talk," *Reason*, January 1982, 49; John R. Lott, "Economics Educator," *Reason*, December 1978, 52; David Remnick, "The Lions of Libertarianism," *Washington Post*, 30 July 1985, E4.

122. The story of the Center for Libertarian Studies can be followed in the Williamson Evers Collection, particularly Boxes 5, 6 and 13, Hoover Institution Archives, Stanford, CA. Hereafter cited as the Evers Collection.

123. Berlanger, "History of the Institute for Humane Studies," part two, 1–2, 4–14.

124. Randy E. Barnett, "One Cheer for the Reagan Years: Economic Liberties and the Constitution," in David Boaz, ed., *Assessing the Reagan Years* (Washington, DC: Cato Institute, 1988), 380.

125. Leonard P. Liggio, "Toward a More Effective *IHS*," Evers Collection, Box 6: 1–9.

126. Kuhn's concept of a paradigm is subject to a variety of understandings. One friendly critic, Margaret Masterman, found that Kuhn used the term in 21 different ways. Subsequently the term has taken on a life of its own. Martin Landau, *Political Theory and Political Science: Studies in the Methodology of Political Inquiry* (New York: Macmillan Company, 1972), 63–9. Whether Libertarianism and liberalism are separate paradigms or whether the former is just, as Stephen L. Neuman has suggested (*Liberalism at Wit's End: The Libertarian Revolt Against the Modern State* (Ithaca: Cornell University Press, 1984)), an extreme form of liberalism probably depends on one's understanding of "paradigm," "liberalism," and "libertarianism."

127. Leonard Liggio, "Kuhn's Paradigm," *The Libertarian Forum* 9, no. 11 (November 1976): 4, Libertarian Party Archives (#10187), Box 7, Special Collections Department, University of Virginia Library, Charlottesville, VA. Hereafter cited as LPA.

128. David Vogel, *Fluctuating Fortunes: The Political Power of Business in America* (New York: Basic Books, 1989), 8–9, 13, 25, 54–5, 98–9.

129. Gary Dorrien, *The Neoconservative Mind: Power, Culture and the War of Ideology* (Philadelphia: Temple University Press, 1993), 69–70, 72, 79, 88, 96, 102.

130. Irving Kristol, "On Corporate Capitalism in America," *The Public Interest* 41 (Fall 1975): 134.

131. Quoted in Vogel, *Fluctuating Fortunes*, 221.

132. William E. Simon, *A Time for Truth* (New York: Reader's Digest/McGraw-Hill, 1978), 223, 233, 244.

133. J. Allen Smith, *The Idea Brokers: Think Tanks and the Rise of a New Policy Elite* (New York: The Free Press, 1991), 174–84, 263–4.

134. Niels Bjerre-Poulsen, "The Heritage Foundation: A Second-Generation Think Tank," *Journal of Policy History* 3, no. 2 (1991): 159–64.

135. John S. Saloma, III, *Ominous Politics: The New Conservative Labyrinth* (New York: Hill & Wang, 1984), 24.

136. Ibid. Robert Poole, Jr., "Regulation Reformer," *Reason*, March 1979, 41; W. John Moore, "Wichita Pipeline," *National Journal*, 16 May 1992, 1172–3.

137. Paul Kuntz, "Heir Turned Publisher Uses Financial Largess to Fuel Conservatism," *Wall Street Journal*, 12 October 1995, A1, 12(E); Saloma, *Ominous Politics*, 25–30.

138. World Research Institute, *Campus Studies Institute Program Summary 1973*, Evers Collection, Box 25: 3–4.

139. Saloma, *Ominous Politics*, 28; "Persona Grata: Theodore B. Loeffler on WRI," *World Research, INK* (March 1977): 3; [Hayek quote] *World Research, INK* (August 1977): 1; Don Markely, "Beginning Decade II: Happy Anniversary WRI," *World Research, INK* (April 1979): 10; Patricia Morris, "INK Grows Older and Better," *World Research, INK* (June 1979): 3 in David Walter Collection, Box 19, Hoover Institution Archives, Stanford, CA. Hereafter cited as Walter Collection.

140. Don Lipsett to F. A. Hayek, 1 July 1975, Don Lipsett to F. A. Hayek, 29 December 1976, Hayek Collection, Box 25. The book derived from the conference was Fritz Machlup, ed., *Essays on Hayek* (New York: New York University Press, 1976).

141. Saloma, *Ominous Politics*, 34–5.

142. Peter W. Bernstein, "The Man Who Brought You Milton Friedman," *Fortune*, 25 February 1980, 109, 111; Robert Chitester to George Shultz, [n.d.], Robert Chitester to Charles Koch, 6 October 1977, Friedman Papers, Box 61.

143. Friedman later insisted that in such actions "I wasn't doing it as a scientist; I was doing it as a citizen deeply concerned about a public issue." Milton Friedman, "My Evolution as an Economist," in *Lives of the Laureates: Ten Nobel Economist*, William Breit and Roger W. Spencer, eds (Cambridge, MA: MIT Press, 1990), 91.

144. Milton Friedman, *Capitalism and Freedom* (Chicago: University of Chicago Press, 1962), 35–55, 85–107, 190–5.

145. Robert H. Nelson, *Reaching for Heaven on Earth: The Theological Meaning of Economics* (Lanham, MD: Littlefield Adams, 1991), 240.

146. Breit and Ransom, *The Academic Scribblers*, 259.

147. "Free to Choose to be Revised and Telecast," *The Palmer R. Chitester Fund Newsletter* (November 1989): 1 in Roy A. Childs, Jr., Collection, Box 7, Hoover Institution Archives, Stanford, CA. Hereafter cited as Childs Collection.

148. Milton Friedman and Rose Friedman, *Free to Choose: A Personal Statement* (New York: Harcourt Brace Jovanovich, 1980), 284.

149. Ibid., 285.

150. For an illustration of this disillusionment see Mickey Kaus's reflections in his *The End of Equality* (New York: Basic Books, 1992), 1–2.

151. Herbert Stein, *Presidential Economics: The Making of Economic Policy from Roosevelt to Reagan*, 2nd rev. ed. (Washington, DC: American Enterprise Institute, 1988), 15.
152. Arthur M. Schlesinger, Jr., *The Crisis of Confidence: Ideas, Power and Violence in America Today* (New York: Bantam Books, 1969), ix.
153. Peter F. Drucker, "The Sickness of Government," *The Public Interest* 14 (Winter 1969): 4–5.
154. "Opinion Roundup," *Public Opinion* (February/March, 1984): 20.
155. James L. Sundquist, "The Crisis of Competence in Our National Government," *Political Science Quarterly* 95, no. 2 (Summer 1980): 185–6.

3 MARKET LIBERAL VISIONS: THE LIBERTARIAN MOVEMENT

1. Daniel Patrick Moynihan, "The Most Important Decision-Making Process," *Policy Review* 1 (Summer 1977): 90.
2. Kenneth J. Heineman, *Campus Wars: The Peace Movement at American State Universities in the Vietnam Era* (New York: New York University Press, 1993), 76.
3. For a recent statement of this libertarian view of modern conservatism see Justin Raimondo, *Reclaiming the American Right: The Lost Legacy of the Conservative Movement* (Burlingame, CA: The Center for Libertarian Studies, 1993).
4. Julian Joseph Delgaudio, "Refugee Economist in America: Ludwig von Mises and American Social and Economic Thought, 1940–1986" (Ph.D. dissertation, University of California, Irvine, 1987), 187–90, 390.
5. Murray N. Rothbard, *For a New Liberty: The Libertarian Manifesto*, rev. ed. (New York: Collier Books, 1978), 301.
6. Patrick Cox, "Tender of the Tradition," *Reason*, March 1982, 48; Leonard P. Liggio, "Towards a More Effective *IHS*," Evers Collection, Box 6: 2, 3; Leonard P. Liggio memo to Chris Hocker, 3 March 1982, Evers Collection, Box 35: 6, 7; Leonard P. Liggio, "President's Report," in *Institute for Humane Studies 1984 Annual Report*, 1; IHS Institution History, part two, 15; Charles G. Koch, *An Investment in Change* (Fairfax, VA: Institute for Humane Studies, 1993), 7–8.
7. Delgaudio, "Refugee Economist in America," 458.
8. Margit von Mises, *My Years with Ludwig von Mises*, 2nd ed. (Spring Mills, PA: Libertarian Press, 1984); quoted on back cover of George Reisman, *The Government Against the Economy* (Ottawa, IL: Jameson Books, 1979).

9. Ralph Raico, "Speech Introducing Murray N. Rothbard", LPA (#10187), Box 2; M. Stanton Evans, *Revolt on the Campus* (Chicago: Henry Regnery Company, 1961), 173–4; *New Individualist Review* (Indianapolis, 1981), 711; quoted in von Mises, *My Years with Ludwig von Mises*, 136.

10. The two groups briefly overlapped. In the mid-fifties Rothbard, Raico, Reisman and Liggio were members of a group of New York City libertarians who met for discussion, calling themselves the "Circle Bastiat." After Rand published *Atlas Shrugged* in 1957 Rothbard wrote Rand a fan letter which led to perhaps six months of meetings between members of the Bastiat group and Rand and her followers. Rand's intimate, Nathaniel Branden, expelled Rothbard in 1958, accusing him of plagiarizing Randian ideas for a conference paper. Murray N. Rothbard, "My Break with Branden and the Rand Cult," *Liberty 3, no. 1 (September 1989): 27–32.*

11. "Opinion Results Surprising," *Individual Liberty*, May 1979, 2, Walter Collection, Box 3, Hoover Institution Archives, Stanford, CA. Hereafter cited as Walter Collection.

12. "The Liberty Poll: Who We Are and What We Think," *Liberty*, July 1988, 41.

13. Ayn Rand, *For the New Intellectual: The Philosophy of Ayn Rand* (New York: Random House, 1961), 161.

14. Ludwig von Mises, *Liberalism in the Classical Tradition*, 3rd ed., trans. Ralph Raico (Irvington-on-Hudson, NY: Foundation for Economic Education, 1985), 19–20, 30.

15. Ayn Rand, *Capitalism: The Unknown Ideal* (New York: Signet Books, 1967), 20–1.

16. James T. Baker, *Ayn Rand* (Boston, MA: Twayne Publishers, 1987), 18–22.

17. For a discussion of the many persons of accomplishment influenced by Rand's ideas see Barbara Branden, *The Passion of Ayn Rand* (Garden City, NY: Doubleday, 1986), 407–22.

18. Jerome Tuccille, *It Usually Begins with Ayn Rand* (New York: Stein & Day, 1971), 15.

19. Tibor Machan, "Ayn Rand and I," *Liberty*, November 1989, 50.

20. Roy Childs to Nathaniel Branden, 25 July 1969, Childs Collection, Box 4.

21. John B. Judis, *William F. Buckley, Jr: Patron Saint of the Conservatives* (New York: Simon & Schuster, 1988), 160.

22. Sharon Presley, "Individualist Libertarians: A Psychological Study," Evers Papers, Box 4.

23. Roy A. Childs, "Ayn Rand and the Libertarian Movement," *Update*, April 1982, 4.

24. F. A. Hayek, *Studies in Philosophy, Politics and Economics* (Chicago: University of Chicago Press, 1967), 194.

25. Nathaniel Branden, *Judgement Day: My Years with Ayn Rand* (Boston, MA: Houghton Mifflin, 1989), 256.

26. "The Neutralizers," *Freedom's Way*, 26 April 1965, reprinted in *The Rational Individualist*, April 1969, 3–4, in *Peace Plans No. 975*, a microfiche available from John Zube, 7 Oxley Street, Berriman, NSW Australia 2577. Hereafter newsletters and journals used from Mr Zube's microfiche collection will be cited as "PP (no.)".

27. Jarret B. Wollstein, "Objectivism: A New Orthodoxy?" *The Rational Individualist*, April 1969, 8–14, PP. 975.

28. LeFevre, during a colorful and varied life, was a radio announcer, religious cultist, Army officer in World War Two, and, finally, an editor for the Hoiles Freedom Newspaper chain. He founded Freedom School (1957) and Ramparts College (1965) to spread the "freedom philosophy." Located just outside Colorado Springs, Colorado, the short-lived College (1965–68) awarded no degrees, although it tried to develop graduate programs in history and economics. Among the market liberals speaking at Freedom School/Rampart College were Rose Wilder Lane, Milton Friedman, Ludwig von Mises, F. A. Harper, Frank Chodorov, Leonard Read, Gordon Tullock, G. Warren Nutter, Bruno Leoni and James J. Martin. LeFevre "graduates" who later had an influence on the libertarian movement include Dana Rohrabacher, Roy Childs, Fred and Charles Koch, and Roger MacBride. Ethan O. Waters, "The Wonderful Wizard of Liberty," *Liberty*, March 1989, 57–60; Carl Watner, *Robert Lefevre: "Truth is Not a Half-way Place"* (Gramling, SC: The Voluntaryists, 1988), 187–8, 199–200, 208.

29. Rand, *Capitalism*, 334.

30. *The Rational Individualist*, August 1969, 7, Walters Collection, Box 15.

31. Ibid., 3–4.

32. Jarret B. Wollstein, "Introduction," *The Rational Individualist, November 1968-March 1969* (Silver Springs, MD: n.p., 1970), PP 975; Dave Walter, "Interview: Dave Walter the SIL Story," interview by William A. McDonald, *Toward Liberty*, April 1981, 4, Walter Collection, Box 12.

33. Branden, *Judgement Day*, 259.

34. Rand, *Capitalism*, 331.

35. Ludwig von Mises, *Human Action: A Treatise on Economics*, 3rd rev. ed. (Chicago: Contemporary Books, 1966), 719–24, 804–5, 835–40.

36. Ibid., 148.

37. F. A. Hayek, "Freedom and Coercion: Some Comments and Mr. Hamowy's Criticism," *New Individualist Review* (Indianapolis: Liberty Press, 1981), 70; Friedrich A Hayek, *The Constitution of Liberty* (South Bend, IN: Gateway Editions, 1972), 258.

38. David Friedman's argument for anarcho-capitalism's feasibility is developed in *The Machinery of Freedom; Guide to a Radical Capitalism*, 2nd ed. (La Salle, IL: Open Court, 1989), Part III.

39. Milton Friedman, "An Interview with Milton Friedman," interview by Tibor Machan, Joe Cobb and Ralph Raico, *Reason*, December

1974, 9, 13; Milton Friedman, *Capitalism and Freedom* (Chicago: University of Chicago Press, 1962), 27, 30.

40. Murray N. Rothbard, "What's Wrong with the Liberty Poll; or, How I Became a Libertarian," *Liberty*, July 1988, 53.

41. Murray N. Rothbard, *Man, Economy and State* (Los Angeles: Nash, 1970), 883–8. For most economists a "collective good" requires at least two elements: nonexcludability and nonrivalrous consumption. That which is nonexcludable, such as national defense, cannot be denied to non-payers. A nonrivalrous good, such as clean air, is one which simultaneously may be consumed by many (if not an infinitude) without any one individual's consumption being reduced. Tyler Cowen, "Public Goods and Externalities: Old and New Perspectives," in *Public Goods & Market Failures: A Critical Examination*, Tyler Cowen, ed. (New Brunswick, NJ: Transaction Books, 1992), 3–4.

42. Ibid., 883.

43. Ibid., 619; Rothbard, *For a New Liberty*, 219. See Chapters 11 and 12 of *For a New Liberty* for Rothbard's sketch of how he envisaged the privatization of defense, police and judicial services.

44. Murray N. Rothbard, *Power and Market: Government and the Economy*, 2nd. ed. (Kansas City: Sheed Andrews and McMeel, 1977), 8.

45. "The General Line," *Left and Right*, no. 1 (Spring 1965): 3, PP 984.

46. Murray N. Rothbard, "Left and Right: The Prospects for Liberty," *Left and Right*, no. 1 (Spring 1965): 7, PP 984.

47. Ibid., 12.

48. Ibid., 41.

49. Murray N. Rothbard, "Harry Elmer Barnes RIP," *Left and Right* 4, no. 1 (1968): 7–8, PP 984.

50. Murray N. Rothbard, "Liberty and the New Left," *Left and Right* 1, no. 2 (Autumn 1965): 38, 41–3, 61, 67, PP 984.

51. Ronald Hamowy, "Left and Right meet," *The New Republic*, 12 March 1966, 15.

52. Quoted in James Miller, *"Democracy is in the Street": From Port Huron to the Siege of Chicago* (New York: Touchstone, 1987), 363–4. The Port Huron Statement is included as an appendix on pp. 329–74.

53. Quoted in *Western World Review Newsletter*, October 1969, 2, Walter Collection, Box 18, "NLN".

54. Murray N. Rothbard, "SDS: The New Turn," *Left and Right* 3, no. 1 (Winter 1967): 13–14, PP 984.

55. Murray N. Rothbard, "Confessions of a Right-Wing Liberal," *Ramparts*, June 1968, 48, 52.

56. Karl Hess, *Dear America* (New York: William Morrow, 1975), 151.

57. "For Revolutionary Anarchocapitalism," Evers Collection, Box 4, "Libt Movement, National." Walter Block earned a Ph.D. in Economics at Columbia University and authored one of the more novel introductions to libertarianism, *Defending the Undefendable: The*

Pimp, Prostitute, Scab, Slumlord, Libeler, Moneylender, and Other Scapegoats in the Rogue's Gallery of American Society (New York: Fleet Press, 1976).

58. "The Radical Libertarian Alliance" [n.d.], Evers Papers, Box 4:1.

59. Samuel Edward Konkin III, "A Cram History of the Libertarian Movement, Part II Post 1969," *The Southern Libertarian Messenger*, October 1972, 3, LPA (10187), Box 9.

60. Quoted in Evans, *Revolt on the Campus*, 111.

61. George Thayer, *The Farther Shores of Politics: The American Political Fringe Today* (New York: Simon & Schuster, 1967), 169.

62. "Moise Tshombe YAF," Evers Collection, Box 36: 1.

63. Bill Evers, "From Goldwater to the Filthy Speech Movement: A Neglected Chapter in Libertarian History," Evers Collection, Box 36: 1, 6–8; W. J. Rorabaugh, *Berkeley at War: The 1960s* (New York: Oxford University Press, 1989), 115.

64. Tom McGivern, "Up from Statism," *Daily Californian*, 10 October 1966 [newspaper clipping], and *The Libertarian Iconoclast*, May 1967, 1–2, both in Evers Papers, Box 36.

65. Dave Walter, "The Activist Origins of the New Libertarian Movement," *New Libertarian Notes*, November 1974, 21, Evers Collection, Box 24; David F. Nolan, "The Road to Liberty," *Reason*, May 1978, 39–40.

66. "Listen YAF," *The Libertarian Forum*, 15 August 1969, 2, reprinted in *The Libertarian Forum (1969–1971)* (New York: Arno Press & New York Times, 1972); Don Ernsberger to Murray Rothbard, 25 August 1969, Evers Collection, Box 24.

67. Malcom G. Scully, "Conservative Students Lay Plans to 'Sock It to the Left,'" *The Chronicle of Higher Education*, 15 September 1969, 4; Norm Pressman, "Left Moves In On YAF," *College Press Service*, 12 September 1969, 6; Jerome Tuccille, *Radical Libertarianism: A Right Wing Alternative* (Indianapolis: Bobbs-Merrill, 1970), 101–6.

68. Walter, "The Activist Origins of the New Libertarian Movement," 22.

69. Tuccille, *Radical Libertarianism*, 108; "We Made a Deal," *Society for Individual Liberty News*, November 1972, 1, Walter Collection, Box 3.

70. Ronald Reagan to David A. Keene, 8 October 1969; David A. Keene to Ronald Reagan, 30 October 1969, Evers Collection, Box 24. That Keene considered M. Stanton Evans a representative of the "libertarian" wing of YAF suggests the limits of the "trads'" tolerance for libertarians. In 1975 Evans suggested that "far more young lives have been ruined by smoking pot than by laws attempting to prevent them from smoking it." M. Stanton Evans, *Clear and Present Dangers: A Conservative View of America's Government* (New York: Harcourt Brace Jovanovich, 1975), 342.

71. Ronald Reagan to William E. Saracino, 19 December 1969, Evers Collection, Box 24.

72. "Libertarian Festival Planned," *Los Angeles Free Press*, 13 February 1970, 9.

73. Murray N. Rothbard, "The Conference," *The Libertarian Forum*, 1 November 1969, 1–3, reprinted in *The Libertarian Forum (1969–1971)*. For a humorous description of the conference by one of the participants see Tuccille, *It Usually Begins with Ayn Rand*, 113–25.

74. Murray N. Rothbard, "Ultra-Leftism," *The Libertarian Forum*, 15 November 1969, 2; Karl Hess, "Cults and Criticisms," *The Libertarian Forum*, 15 December 1969, 2–3; Murray N. Rothbard, "The New Left RIP," *The Libertarian Forum*, 15 March 1970, 3, reprinted in *The Libertarian Forum 1969–1971)*.

75. David DeLeon, *The American as Anarchist: Reflections on Indigenous Radicalism* (Baltimore, MD: Johns Hopkins University Press, 1978), 130.

76. Vincent McCaffrey and Mark C. Frazier, eds. *Libertarian Handbook 1972* (Manchester, VT: Avenue Victor Hugo, 1972), 5–8.

77. Mark Frazier, "Anarchism: Revolutionizing the Right," *Harvard Crimson*, 12 March 1971, 5.

78. See Ronald E. Merrill, *The Ideas of Ayn Rand* (Chicago: Open Court, 1991), Ch. 7 for an overview of Rand's views of government and taxation. John Hospers's *Libertarianism* (Los Angeles: Nash, 1970) presents a conservative libertarian perspective.

79. See Watner, *Robert Lefevre*, Chapters 16–20.

80. One libertarian retreatist, Tom Marshall, described his life-style in an underground newsletter, *Vonu Life*, and encouraged others to do as he had done: leave Los Angeles and come to the remote Siskyou region of Southern Oregon. Getting few takers, he disappeared after 1974. In 1995, Jim Stumm published *Free Life*, a newsletter similar to *Vonu Life*. See R. W. Bradford, "The Mystery Man of the Libertarian Movement," *Liberty*, August 1987, 9, 44.

81. Frank S. Meyer, "Libertarianism or Libertinism?," *National Review*, 9 September 1969, 910; David Keene, "Libertarian into Anarchist," review of *Radical Libertarianism: A Right-Wing Alternative* by Jerome Tuccille, in *National Review*, 6 October 1970, 1065–6.

82. "Goldwater Aide Now a Radical," *New York Times*, 28 September 1969, 62(L); "Ideologues: You Know He's Right," *Newsweek*, 29 September 1969, 42; James Boyd, "From Far Right to Far Left – and Farther – with Karl Hess," *New York Times Magazine*, 6 December 1970, 48–9, 152, 154, 156, 159, 161, 164, 166, 168.

83. Stan Lehr and Louis Rosetto, Jr., "The New Right Credo – Libertarianism," *New York Times Magazine*, 6 December 1970, 24–5; 86–8, 93–4; James Dickinson, "Abolish Government," *National Observer*, 1 March 1971, 1, 18.

84. Jerome Tuccille, "A Split in the Right Wing," *New York Times*, 28 January 1971, 35(L); Murray N. Rothbard, "The New Libertarian Creed," *New York Times*, 9 February 1971, 37 (L); William F. Buckley, "The Conservative Reply," *New York Times*, 16 February 1971, 33(L).

85. Murray N. Rothbard, "Takeoff II," *The Libertarian Forum*, March 1971, 1, reprinted in *The Libertarian Forum (1969–1971)*.

4 THE ANTI-POLITICS OF MARKET LIBERALISM: THE LIBERTARIAN PARTY, 1972–84

1. Perhaps the most famour recent example of this type of thinking is Francis Fukuyama's much-discussed speculation on "The End of History?," *The National Interest* 16 (Summer 1989): 3–18.
2. Thomas Sowell, *A Conflict of Visions: Ideological Origins of Political Struggles* (New York: Quill, 1987), 31, 37, 115–17.
3. Murray N. Rothbard, "The President's Economic Betrayal," *New York Times*, 4 September 1971, 21 (L).
4. In early 1972 the Libertarian Party conducted a poll of its members to "serve as a guideline" in preparing the first party platform. The breakdown was as follows: "Isolationist" (50 percent), "Semi-Isolationist" (25 percent), "Rollback" (8 percent), "Pacifist" (2 percent), "Undecided (1 percent). "Platform Polls Shows Most LP Members are Objectivists," *Libertarian Party Newsletter*, 5 April 1972, 2.
5. Quoted in James T. Patterson, *Mr. Republican: A Biography of Robert A. Taft* (Boston, MA: Houghton Mifflin, 1972), 217.
6. Ibid., 482.
7. John B. Judis, *William F. Buckley, Jr.: Patron Saint of the Conservatives* (New York: Simon & Schuster, 1988), 42.
8. William F. Buckley, Jr., "The Party Stops at the Blue Sea," *Commonweal*, 25 January 1952, 392–3.
9. John Lewis Gaddis, *Strategies of Containment: A Critical Appraisal of Postwar American National Security Policy* (New York: Oxford University Press, 1982), 355–6.
10. Bennett Kovrig, *The Myth of Liberation: East Central Europe in U.S. Diplomacy and Politics Since 1941* (Baltimore, MD: Johns Hopkins University Press, 1973), 181–2.
11. David P. Calleo, *Beyond American Hegemony: The Future of the Western Alliance* (New York: Basic Books, 1987), 87–9.
12. *Renaissance News' Libertarian Who's Who at Convention '74*, 9, LPA (#10187-t), Box 2; David F. Nolan, "The Road to Liberty," *Reason*, May 1978, 39–41; David F. Nolan, "Present at the Creation," *New Libertarian Notes*, November 1974, 7–8; David Nolan, "In the Beginning ... A Brief Overview of the LP's First Years," LPA (#10187), Box 2.
13. Nolan, "In the Beginning. ... A Brief Overview of the LP's First Years"; David F. Nolan, "The Case for a Libertarian Party," *Individualist*, July/August 1971, 26, Walter Collection, Box 15.

14. Ed Crane, "How Now, Ayn Rand?," *LP News*, November/December 1973, 4; Ronald E. Merrill, *The Ideas of Ayn Rand* (Chicago: Open Court, 1991), 131, 138–9.

15. Dave F. Nolan to Murray Rothbard, 24 March 1972, 2, American Subject Collection, Box 3, Hoover Institution Archives, Stanford, CA. Hereafter cited as American Subject Collection.

16. "Temporary Platform of the Libertarian Party," LPA (#10187-S), Box 2, 6, 9.

17. "Hospers-Nathan 1972!," *Libertarian Party Newsletter*, June/July 1972, 1; Bob Haley, "The Libertarian Party Convention," *The Southern Libertarian Messenger*, July 1972, 2, LPA (#10187), Box 9.

18. "1972 Platform of the Libertarian Party," LPA (#10187), Box 2, 2.

19. Ibid., 3–11, passim.

20. For an overview of the diverse views of prominent libertarians in the early eighties on the morality of nuclear weapons see "Nuclear Disarmament: A Survey," *Individual Liberty*, October 1982, 1–6.

21. Murray N. Rothbard, *For a New Liberty: The Libertarian Manifesto*, rev. ed. (New York: Collier Books, 1978), 239; David Friedman, *The Machinery of Freedom*; *Guide to a Radical Capitalism*, 2nd ed. (La Salle, IL: Open Court, 1989), 135–43; Ayn Rand, *The Virtue of Selfishness: A New Concept of Egoism* (New York: Signet Books, 1964), 116–20.

22. Quoted in "The Libertarian Party, Pro and Con," *The Southern Libertarian Messenger*, November 1972, 1.

23. David F. Nolan, "Classifying & Analyzing Politico-Economic Systems," [reprint from *Individualist*, January 1971, 7], Evers Collection, Box 2.

24. David F. Nolan to Murray Rothbard, 24 March 1972, in American Subject Collection, Box 3; "Rothbard First Choice for Presidential Candidate, Greenspan, Kellems, Fitzgerald Make Strong Showing," *Libertarian Party Newsletter*, 6 May 1972, 3.

25. "David Nolan, "In the Beginning …. A Brief Overview of the LP's First Years."

26. (Los Angeles: Nash Publishing, 1971).

27. John Hospers, "The First Time: I Run for President," *Liberty*, November 1992, 27; *Renaissance News' Libertarian Who's Who at Convention '74*, 4–5.

28. Ibid., 30–3; Dave Nolan, "In the Beginning …. A Brief Overview of the LP's First Years; "Campaign News," *Libertarian Party Newsletter*, September, 1972, 1; "Campaign News," *Libertarian Party Newsletter*, October 1972, 1.

29. *Congressional Quarterly's Guide to U.S. Election* (Washington, DC: Congressional Quarterly, 1975), 307.

30. "Hospers Vote Projected at 5000+," *LP News*, November/December 1972, 1.

31. John Hospers, "The First Time: I Run for President," 33; Roger L. MacBridge, transcription of an interview by Norma Lee Browning, tape recording [n.d.], LPA (#10187-S), Box 1, 2–4.

32. Roger MacBride, "MacBride's March on Washington: An Interview with Roger MacBride," interview by Manuel Klasner, *Reason*, October 1976, 26–7.

33. Jack Mann, "The Presidency & Political Poetry," *Potomac*, 25 January 1976, 10.

34. Dan White, "Roger MacBride, '51, The Libertarian Candidate," *Princeton Alumni Weekly*, 26 April 1976, 12–13.

35. When in 1983 the Libertarians nominated David Bergland, widely perceived as an ultraist, MacBride left the Party and returned to the Republicans. In 1990 he joined the Republic Liberty Caucus, an organization of libertarians established in 1988 to work within the Republican Party. Roger Lea MacBride to Edmund Berkeley, Jr., 21 September 1983, LPA (#10187-N), "Correspondence 1979–1983, N.D."; Eric J. Rittberg, *Republican Liberty Caucus: Goals & Strategy for the '90s* (Tallahassee, FL: Republican Liberty Caucus, 1990), 2; "Note from the Editor," *Republican Liberty* II, no. 1 (Winter 1991): 2.

36. David F. Nolan, "The Road to Liberty," *Reason*, May 1978, 43; Edward E. Clark, transcription of an interview by Tom G. Palmer, tape recording, August 2, 1984, LPA (#10187-U), 4; *1974 Platform of the Libertarian Party*, LPA (#10187), Box 2, 1.

37. According to Bill Evers, this approach was pioneered in the "Berkeley Statement" of the Alliance of Libertarian Activists so that minimal statists and anarcho-capitalists could work together. Bill Evers, "From Goldwater to the Filthy Speech Movement: A Neglected Chapter in Libertarian History," Evers Collection, Box 36: 1, 7.

38. Robert Nozick, "An Interview with Robert Nozick," interview by Albert Zlabinger, *Libertarian Review*, 6 December 1977, 11.

39. *Program of the 1975 National Libertarian Convention*, LPA (#10187), Box 2, 8.

40. Kenneth L. Woodward, "Every Man for Himself," *Newseek*, 11 November 1974, 91.

41. *Renaissance News' Libertarian Who's Who At Convention '74*, 6.

42. Edward H. Crane, III, transcription of an interview by Tom G. Palmer, tape recording, 28 June 1984, LPA (#10187-U), 1.

43. Ibid., 3.

44. David Boaz, interview by author, tape recording, 3 July 1991, Dartmouth College, Hanover, NH.

45. Edward H. Crane, III, transcription of an interview by Palmer, 4–6; "LP Hires Director to Spur Organizing," *Libertarian Party News*, January/February 1975, 1; *Program of the 1975 National Libertarian Convention*, 10; "HQ Moves to Washington, D.C.," *Libertarian Party News*, September/October, 25.

46. Roger L. MacBride, transcription of an interview by Browning, 7–9.

47. "Its MacBride In '76," *Libertarian Party News*, September/October 1975, 1, 5.

48. Ibid., *1976 Platform of the Libertarian Party*, 11–12, LPA (#10187), Box 2, 11–12; Kathy McAdam, "Report on Libertarian Party National Convention," LPA (#10187), Box 2, 1.

49. Kathy McAdam, "Report on Libertarian Party National Convention," 2.

50. Roger Lea MacBride to Edward Crane, III, 23 September 1976, LPA (#10187), Box 3. Crane estimated in 1984 that MacBride had contributed over a number of years perhaps $500 000 to Libertarian Party activities. Edward H. Crane, III, transcription of an interview by Palmer, 8.

51. Edward H. Crane, III to Charles Koch, 4 May 1976, LPA (#10187), Box 2.

52. Charles G. Koch to "Rocky Mountain Oilmen," LPA (#10187), Box 5.

53. Peter N. Carroll, *It Seemed Like Nothing Happened: The Tragedy and Promise of America in the 1970s* (New York: Holt, Rinehart & Winston, 1982), 185.

54. Roger Lea MacBride, "Happy Days Are Here Again," *Reason*, January 1975, 30, 32.

55. "Rothbard: Timing is Right ...," *Libertarian Party News*, September/October 1975, 6–7.

56. Roger MacBride to Ralph Raico, 12 February 1976, LPA (#10187), Box 1.

57. "LP Standardbearers Travel to 30 States," *Libertarian Party News*, January/February 1976, 1, 12.

58. Roger MacBride, "How The Repression Of Political Ideas Is Managed In America," *Libertarian Review*, August 1977, 30.

59. Steven J. Rosenstone, Roy L. Behr, and Edward H. Lazarus, *Third Parties in America: Citizen Response to Major Party Failure* (Princeton, NJ: Princeton University Press, 1984), 21.

60. Robert H. Meier to Lee Weber, 25 March 1976; Edward Crane to Emile Franzi, 18 March 1976; Linda M. Webb to Porter Davis, 18 March 1976, LPA (310187), Box 1.

61. Edward H. Crane, III to Charles Koch, 22 June 1976, LPA (#10187), Box 2, 1976.

62. MacBride, "How The Repression of Political Ideas Is Managed In America," 29.

63. Herbert E. Alexander, *Financing Politics: Money, Elections, and Political Reform*, 3rd ed. (Washington, DC: CQ Press, 1984), 204–7.

64. "Legal Action Challenges Campaign Regulations," *Libertarian Party News*, January/February 1975, 1, 3; "Libertarians Join Buckley, McCarthy Against Campaign Act," LPA (#10187), Box 3.

65. "Supreme Court Decision Diminished Free Speech," *Libertarian Party News*, January/February 1976, 1, 8.

66. Steven V. Roberts, "McGovern Aide Rich and Modest," *The New York Times*, 26 June 1972, 24(N).

67. See correspondence in LPA (#10187), Box 1, "1975 Sept–1976 Oct, Corresp re Secret Service Protection."

68. Edward H. Crane, III to Carol Jennings, 28 May 1976, LPA (#10187), Box 2.

69. MacBride, "How The Repression of Political Ideas Is Managed In America," 31.

70. "Minutes of the Libertarian Party Executive Committee Meeting, February 1, 1976," LPA (#10187), Box 3; Roger MacBride, "How The Repression of Political Ideas Is Managed In America," 31.

71. "Transcript of Meet the Press, Sunday Oct 17, 1976," LPA (#10187), Box 3, 3, 22–3.

72. Ibid., 8–9.

73. Roger MacBride, "MacBride's March on Washington: An Interview with Roger MacBride," interview by Manuel Klausner, 29.

74. Transcript of *Firing Line*, 10 July 1976, "Would Anarchy Work?," LPA (#10187), Box 3, 3–4.

75. *Congressional Quarterly's Guide to 1976 Elections* (Washington, DC: Congressional Quarterly, 1977), 23; "MacBride Gets 183,000 Votes; Beats Maddox," *Libertarian Party News*, November/December 1976, 1; William Westmiller, "MacBride in .693; A Statistical Analysis of the California Vote and National LP Vote in the 1976 Election," LPA (#10187), Box 4, 8, 15.

76. P[aul] G[ordon], "Libertarian Lights," *Reason*, November 1984, 34–5; Michael Dunham, "When the Smoke Clears," *Reason*, March 1983, 33.

77. Richard White, *"Its Your Misfortune and None of My Own": A History of the American West* (Norman, OK: University of Oklahoma Press, 1991), 57–9, 576, 601–11.

78. Tom Palmer and Tom Avery, "The 1977 Libertarian Party National Convention," *Libertarian Review*, October 1977, 30.

79. Murray N. Rothbard, "The LP: Retrospect and Prospect," *The Libertarian Forum*, November 1976, 1, LPA (#10187), Box 7. More skeptical was E. Scott Royce, who pointed out that although the five-year-old Libertarian Party in 1976 ran 200 federal, state and local candidates, the Socialist Party in 1912 "could boast not 200 or even 1000 candidates, but 1,200 *elected* officials, including state legislators and 709 mayors." E. Scott Royce, "America's Third Largest Party: Failure!," *Reason*, August 1977, 20.

80. Ed Crane, "Pride In Our Accomplishments," *Libertarian Party News*, November/December 1976, 2.

81. Ibid., 2; Robert W. Poole, Jr., "Libertarian Realpolitik," *Reason*, August 1976, 6.

82. Bill Evers, "Reagan: Hubert Humphrey of the Right?" *Libertarian Party News*, November/December 1975, 7.

83. Edward H. Crane, III to Ronald Reagan, 19 January 1976, LPA (#10187), Box 1.

84. Ronald Reagan to Edward R. Crane, III, 19 February 1976, ibid.

85. Edward H. Crane, III to Joe Cobb, 16 January 1976, ibid.

86. Rinker Buck, "How Those Libertarians Pay The Bills," *New York*, 3 November 1980, 22.

87. Frank Smallwood, *The Other Candidates: Third Parties in Presidential Election* (Hanover, NH: University Press of New

England, 1983), 174; "Clark President Media Fact Sheet," LPA (#10187-W), Box 1, 1.

88. Ed Clark, "Campaign '80: Towards Freedom In Our Time," interview with Ed Clark, *The Libertarian Review*, October/November 1980, 18.

89. Edward Clark, transcript of an interview with Palmer, 1; Frank Smallwood, *The Other Candidates*, 175–6; "Clark President Media Fact Sheet," 1.

90. "The Liberty Interview: Ed Crane," interview by R. W. Bradford, *Liberty*, November 1990, 55–6; Ed Crane, "Taking Politics Seriously," *Libertarian Review*, August 1978, 27, 42; John A. Jenkins, "Free Thinkers," *TWA Ambassador*, March 1980, 82.

91. Chris Hocker, "Prop. 13 Tax Revolt: The California Tea Party?," *Libertarian Party News*, Summer 1978, 2; "Ed Clark Speaks Out On The Issues," *Ed Clark Governor*, Evers Collection, Box 41: 1–4.

92. Ed Clark to "Dear Libertarian," 10 February 1978, Evers Collection, Box 41: 1; "Libertarians Score Election Gains," *Frontlines*, December 1978, 1, 4, 6, PP 639; David F. Nolan, "Looking Back from 1988: How the LP Made History, *Frontlines*, December 1978, 2–3, PP 639; Murray N. Rothbard, "The Breakthrough Election," *Libertarian Review*, December 1978, 12–13.

93. Roger Lea MacBride, "Happy Days Are Here Again," 32.

94. Quoted in Everett Carll Ladd, Jr., and Seymour Martin Lipset, "Public Opinion and Public Policy," in *The United States in the 1980s*, Peter Duignan and Alvin Rabushka, eds (Stanford, CA: Hoover Institution Press, 1980), 65.

95. Leonard Liggio, "The Disenchanted Electorate: Capturing the Independent Voter," *Libertarian Review*, August 1978, 28–9.

96. Marshall Schwartz, "Libertarians in Convention," *Libertarian Review*, November 1979, 16.

97. David Koch to "Dear Delegate," 22 August 1980, LPA (#10187-N), "Correspondence 1979–1983, N.D.," 1; Edward H. Crane III and Chris Hocker, "Clark For President: A Report on the 1980 Libertarian Presidential Campaign," Evers Papers, Box 7: 24.

98. "Clark President Media Fact Sheet," Appendix B, p. i; Crane and Hocker, "Clark For President," 41–5. Copies of many of the white papers and briefing papers may be found in the following locations: LPA (#10187), Box 6; Evers Collection, Box 40; and Childs Collection, Box 28.

99. Crane and Hocker, "Clark For President," 18–19; Tom Palmer, "What the Clark Campaign Achieved: An Insider's View," *Frontlines*, December 1980/January 1981, 4–5, PP 639; Clark-Koch Top 900,000," *Libertarian Party News*, January/February 1981, 2. For documentation of Ed Crane's unavailing efforts to get Clark included in the 1980 campaign debates see LPA (#10187-W), Box 1.

100. David Boaz, Research Director for the Clark Campaign, states that the campaign staff knew – based on their own polling – that the projections generally were too high, but didn't publicly counter them

because they wanted to keep the press interested and activists motivated. David Boaz, interview by author.

101. Murray N. Rothbard, "The Clark Campaign: Never Again," *The Libertarian Forum*, September/December 1980, 1, 2, 7, Walter Collection, Box 13.

102. David F. Nolan, "Clark President: A Campaign Critique," LPA (#10187-P), 4, 8.

103. Friedrich A. Hayek, *Rules and Order*, vol. 1 of *Law, Legislation, and Liberty* (Chicago: University of Chicago Press, 1973), 38.

104. Because of such heresy, Rothbard in 1958 urged the Volker Fund to provide no support for the publication of Hayek's classic, *The Constitution of Liberty*. See Murray Rothbard to Kenneth S. Templeton, 24 January 1958 (and attached memorandum) and Murray N. Rothbard to Kenneth S. Templeton, 11 June 1960, Childs Collection, Box 32.

105. Jenkins, "Free Thinkers," 82; "Clark on Taxation and Spending," *Clark President News*, September/October 1980, 4, LPA 10187, Box 6; Crane and Hocker, "Clark For President," 41.

106. David Boaz recounts a conversation with *Washington Post* journalist T. R. Reid at the 1981 Libertarian National Convention. Reid asked Boaz how he was supposed to explain to his readers that a considerable faction within the Party wanted to elect a new National Chair who would repudiate the Clark campaign as having been too moderate. David Boaz, interview by author, 3 July 1991.

107. "200 Billion in One Year," *Clark President News*, September/October, 5; Ed Clark, "Campaign '80: Towards Freedom In Our Time," 22–4.

108. David F. Nolan to Jeff Daiell, 19 February 1981, Evers Papers, Box 6.

109. David Boaz, "Attacks on the Clark Campaign: Reviving the Big Lie," [manuscript submitted for *Caliber* convention issue] accompanying David D. Boaz to Roger L. MacBride, 7 August 1981, LPA (#10187-N), "Correspondence 1979–1983, N.D.," 6.

110. "The *Liberty* Interview: Ed Crane," 57.

111. Gerald M. Pomper, "The Presidential Election," in *The Election of 1980: Reports and Interpretations*, Marlene Michels Pomper, ed. (Chatham, NJ: Chatham House, 1981), 84–5; William Schneider, "The November 4 Vote for President: What did it Mean?," in *The American Elections of 1980*, Austin Ranney, ed. (Washington, DC: American Enterprise Institute, 1981), 247, 257–8.

112. "Human Events Airs Attacks on LP," *Frontlines*, December 1979/January 1980, 1, pp 639.

113. In 1986 Friedman described himself as a "Libertarian in Principle and [a] Republican on grounds of expediency." Friedman argued that "the Libertarian Party can serve a highly useful function provided that it sticks to principles and doesn't worry about electing candidates." "Milton Friedman: Libertarian in Principle, Republican for Expediency," *Stanford University News Service*, 18 April 1986, 1, Evers Collection, Box 39.

114. Moore, who subsequently served on Reagan's Council of Economic Advisors between 1985 and 1989, said in 1980 that he would only consider voting for Clark if Reagan clearly was going to win California. John Judis, "Libertarianism: Where the Left Meets the Right," *The Progressive*, September 1980, 37.

115. William S. Maddox and Stuart A. Lilie, *Beyond Liberal and Conservative: Reassessing the Political Spectrum* (Washington, DC: Cato Institute, 1984), 104; Crane and Hocker, "Clark For President," 41; Martin Anderson, *Revolution* (San Diego: Harcourt Brace Jovanovich, 1988), 165, 167–74.

116. Peter Collier, "The Next American Revolution," *New West*, 27 August 1979, 27–32; David Remnick, "The Lions of Libertarianism," *Washington Post*, 30 July 1984, E1, E4; James Allen Smith, *The Idea Brokers: Think Tanks and the Rise of the Policy Elite* (New York: Free Press, 1991), 219–23; W. John Moore, "Wichita Pipeline," *National Journal*, 16 May 1992, 1168–74.

117. Anne Groer, "Libertarian Lark," *The New Republic*, 3 October, 1983, 15–17; T. R. Reid, "Libertarians Pick Candidate for President; David Bergland Emphasizes Principle over Practicality," *Washington Post*, 4 September 1983, A17–18.

118. Doug Bandow, "Libertarian in the White House," interview by David Boaz, *Update*, January 1982, 4, 7, Walters Collection, Box 14; "Anderson, McClaughry Leaving White House," *Frontlines*, March 1982, 1, 5, PP 640; "Interview with Reagan Speechwriter Dana Rohrabacher," *Frontlines*, August 1982, 4, PP 640.

5 THE POLITICS OF MARKET LIBERALISM IN THE EIGHTIES: BLUE SMOKE AND MIRRORS?

1. Gillian Peele, *Revival and Reaction: The Right in Contemporary America* (Oxford: Clarendon Press, 1984), 5–13; Michael Schaller, *Reckoning with Reagan: America and Its President in the 1980s* (New York: Oxford University Press, 1992), 3–5, 51–9; Ed Clark, *For a New Beginning* (Aurora, IL: Caroline House Publishers, 1980), 9–19, 33–49, 104–11, 133–5.

2. Everett Carll Ladd, "The Brittle Mandate: Electoral Dealignment and the 1980 Presidential Election," *Political Science Quarterly* 96, no. 1 (Spring 1981): 3, 21; Gerald M. Pomper, "The Presidential Election," in *The Election of 1980: Reports and Interpretations*, Marlene Michels Pomper, ed. (Chatham, NJ: Chatham House, 1981), 89.

3. Quoted in William E. Leuchtenburg, *In the Shadow of FDR: From Harry Truman to Ronald Reagan* (Ithaca, NY: Cornell University Press, 1983), 230.

4. Martin Anderson, *Revolution* (San Diego: Harcourt Brace Jovanovich, 1988), 243.

5. US Bureau of the Census, *Statistical Abstracts of the United States: 1993*, 113th ed. (Washington, DC: US Government Printing Office, 1993), 328.

6. Quoted in *Reagan's First Year* (Washington, DC: Congressional Quarterly, 1982), 113–14.

7. For anthologies of market-liberal views produced by West coast think-tanks from which Reagan drew advisors see Peter Duignan and Alvin Rabushka, eds, *The United States in the 1980s* (Stanford, CA: Hoover Institution, 1980) and Michael J. Boskin, ed., *The Economy in the 1980s: A Program for Growth and Stability* (San Francisco: Institute for Contemporary Studies, 1980).

8. Murray Weidenbaum, "Reason Interview: Murray Weidenbaum," interview by Tibor Machan, *Reason*, September 1981, 43.

9. For an overview of supply-side economics by a convert see Lawrence B. Lindsey, *The Growth Experiment: How the New Tax Policy is Transforming the U.S. Economy* (New York: Basic Books, 1990).

10. David A. Stockman, *The Triumph of Politics: Why the Reagan Revolution Failed* (New York: Harper & Row, 1986), 92–6.

11. Paul Craig Roberts, *The Supply-Side Revolution: An Insider's Account of Policymaking in Washington* (Cambridge, MA: Harvard University Press, 1984), 93.

12. Steven M. Sheffrin, "Constitutional Principles and Economic Policy," in *Looking Back on the Reagan Presidency*, Larry Berman, ed. (Baltimore, MD: Johns Hopkins University Press, 1990), 100.

13. Richard M. Ebeling, "Will the Reagan Economic Program Work?," *Policy Report* 3, no. 4 (April 1981): 4.

14. David Boaz, "The Budget: Snipping at the Status Quo," *Libertarian Review* 10, no. 5 (May 1981): 20.

15. Murray N. Rothbard, "Do Deficits Matter?," *Reason*, December 1981, 65.

16. William Greider, *Secrets of the Temple: How the Federal Reserve Runs the Country* (New York: Touchstone, 1989), 381.

17. Richard K. Vedder and Lowell E. Gallaway, *Out of Work: Unemployment and Government in Twentieth-Century America* (New York: Holmes & Meier, 1993), 233.

18. Lindsey, *The Growth Experiment*, 105–13; William A. Niskanen, *Reaganomics: An Insider's Account of the Policies and the People* (New York: Oxford University Press, 1988), 315–16.

19. Robert D. Behn, "The Receding Mirage of the Balanced Budget," *The Public Interest* 67 (Spring 1982): 121–4 provides a discussion of the cumulative impact of forecasting errors.

20. Gary Robbins and Aldona Robbins, *Cooking the Books: Exposing the Tax and Spend Bias of Government Forecasts* (Lewisville, TX: Institute for Policy Innovation, 1995), 9.

21. Stockman, *The Triumph of Politics*, 122–5.

22. Ibid., 176–83, 276.

23. Sheldon Richman, "Reagan Pushes History's Largest Tax Increase," *Libertarian Party News* (September–October 1982): 1.

24. David Boaz, "The Reagan Budget: The Deficit That Didn't Have to Be," *Policy Analysis* (Washington, DC: Cato Institute, 10 August 1982), 38.

25. Quoted in John H. Makin and Norman J. Ornstein, *Debt and Taxes* (New York: Times Books, 1994), 166.

26. Joseph White and Aaron Wildavsky, *The Deficit and the Public Interest: The Search for Responsible Budgeting in the 1980s* (Berkeley: University of California Press, 1989), 196–7.

27. Ronald Reagan, *Public Papers of the Presidents of the United States, Book I: January 1 to July 2, 1982* (Washington, DC: Government Printing Office, 1983), 535.

28. Anderson, *Revolution, 136.*

29. Niskanen, *Reaganomics*, 13.

30. Ibid., 25.

31. *Reagan's First Year*, 35, 58–9.

32. Martin Feldstein, "American Economic Policy in the 1980s: A Personal View," in *American Economic Policy in the 1980s*, Martin Feldstein, ed. (Chicago: University of Chicago Press, 1994), 41–4.

33. Robert Capozzi, "Having Impact," *Update* 2, no. 12 (December 1982): 5; "Ex-White House Aid Now Fights System," *Update*, May 1983, 3, Childs Collection, Box 37; David Boaz and Edward H. Crane, "Introduction," in *Beyond the Status Quo: Policy Proposals for America*, David Boaz and Edward H. Crane, eds (Washington, DC: Cato Institute, 1985), 10–11.

34. Kevin Phillips, *The Politics of Rich and Poor: Wealth and the American Electorate in the Reagan Aftermath* (New York: Random House, 1990), 83.

35. Murray L. Weidenbaum, "The Changing Nature of Government Regulation of Business," *The Journal of Post Keynesian Economics* 2, no. 3 (Spring 1980): 345, 347.

36. John C. Schwartz, *America's Hidden Success: A Reassessment of Public Policy from Kennedy to Reagan*, rev. ed. (New York: W. W. Norton, 1988), 90–8.

37. Weidenbaum, "The Changing Nature of Government Regulation of Business," 356.

38. Charles L. Schultze, *The Public Use of Private Interest* (Washington, DC: The Brookings Institution, 1977), 6, 53.

39. William Tucker, "Environment/Reclaiming Conservative Ground," *The American Spectator*, February 1985, 17.

40. Murray N. Rothbard, "Property Rights and Pollution," *Cato Journal* 2, no. 1 (Spring 1982): 58, 87, 94–5.

41. Fred L. Smith, Jr., "A Free-Market Environmental Program," *Cato Journal* 11, no. 3 (Winter 1992): 468.

42. Richard N. L. Andrews, "Deregulation: The Failure at EPA," in *Environmental Policy in the 1980s: Reagan's New Agenda*, Norman

J. Vig and Michael E. Kraft, eds (Washington, DC: CQ Press, 1984), 161.

43. William Greider, *The Education of David Stockman and Other Americans* (New York: E. P. Dutton, 1982), 146, 156. The Dunkirk memorandum is included as an appendix.

44. Richard P. Nathan, "Institutional Change Under Reagan," in *Perspectives on the Reagan Years*, John L. Palmer, ed. (Washington, DC: Urban Institute, 1986), 130.

45. Larry Gerston, Cynthia Fraleigh and Robert Schwab, *The Deregulated Society* (Pacific Grove, CA: Brooks/Cole, 1988).

46. W. Kip Viscusi, "Health and Safety Regulations," in *American Economic Policy in the 1980s*, Feldstein, ed., 457.

47. James E. Hinish, "Regulatory Reform: An Overview," in *Mandate for Leadership: Policy Management in a Conservative Administration*, Charles L. Heatherly, ed. (Washington, DC: Heritage Foundation, 1981), 704.

48. Murray L. Weidenbaum, "Regulatory Reform Under the Reagan Administration," in *The Reagan Regulatory Strategy: An Assessment*, George C. Eads and Michael Fix, eds (Washington, DC: Urban Institute, 1984), 19.

49. George C. Eads and Michael Fix, *Relief or Reform?: Reagan's Regulatory Dilemma* (Washington, DC: Urban Institute, 1984), 6.

50. Ibid., 39.

51. Norman J. Vig, "The President and the Environment," and J. Clarence Davies, "Environmental Institutions and the Reagan Administration," in *Environmental Policy in the 1980s: Reagan's New Agenda*, Vig and Kraft, eds, 87, 148–9.

52. Walter A. Rosenbaum, *Environmental Politics and Policy*, 2nd ed. (Washington, DC: CQ Press, 1990), 25.

53. Viscusi, "Health and Safety Regulation," in *American Economic Policy in the 1980s*, Feldstein, ed., 483.

54. Gerston, Fraleigh and Schwab, *The Deregulated Society*, 175, 181, 184–93; W. Kip Viscusi, "Health and Safety Regulation," in *American Economic Policy in the 1980s*, Feldstein, ed., 460, 486, 493.

55. Robert Poole, Jr., "Rhetoric is Not Enough," *Reason*, May 1983, 8; Doug Bandow, *The Politics of Plunder: Misgovernment in America* (New Brunswick, NJ: Transaction Books, 1990), 204.

56. David Vogel, *Fluctuating Fortunes: The Political Power of Business in America* (New York: Basic Books, 1989), 166; James C. Miller, III, *The Economist as Reformer: Revamping the FTC, 1981–1985* (Washington, DC: American Enterprise Institute, 1989), 2, 8.

57. James C. Miller, III, *Fix the U.S. Budget!: Urgings of an "Abominable No-Man"* (Stanford, CA: Hoover Institution, 1994), xiii–1; Miller, *The Economist as Reformer*, viii, 1.

58. Miller, *The Economist as Reformer*, 26–7, 36.

59. Ibid., 65–7.

60. Thomas F. Walton and James Langenfeld, "Regulatory Reform under Reagan – The Right Way and the Wrong Way," in *Regulation and the Reagan Era: Politics, Bureaucracy and the Public Interest*, Roger E. Meiners and Bruce Yandle, eds (New York: Holmes & Meier, 1989), 49.

61. Walter E. Williams, *The State Against Blacks* (New York: McGraw-Hill, 1982), 75–88. See also Clint Bolick, *Grassroots Tyranny: The Limits of Federalism* (Washington, DC: Cato Institute, 1993), 146–7.

62. Miller, *The Economist as Reformer*, 43–53.

63. William F. Shugart, II, "Antitrust Policy in the Reagan Administration: Pyrrhic Victories?," in *Regulation and the Reagan Era*, Meiners and Yandle, eds., 90.

64. Miller, *The Economist as Reformer*, 48–50.

65. Niskanen, *Reaganomics*, 120.

66. Thomas Gale Moore, "Reagan's Regulatory Record," in *To Promote Prosperity: U.S. Domestic Policy in the Mid-1980s*, John H. Moore, ed. (Stanford, CA: Hoover Institution, 1984), 252.

67. Milton Friedman, *Bright Promises, Dismal Performance: An Economist's Protest* (San Diego, CA: Harvest/HBJ Books, 1983), 364–9.

68. Stockman, *The Triumph of Politics*, 155.

69. Niskanen, *Economics*, 140.

70. Robert Crandall, "Import Quotas and the Automobile Industry: The Costs of Protectionism," *The Brookings Review* (Summer 1984): 16.

71. Daniel Klein, "Taking America for a Ride on a Harley," *UPdate* (March 1964): 6 in LPA (10187), Box 8.

72. See in particular Murray N. Rothbard, *For a New Liberty: The Libertarian Manifesto*, rev. ed. (New York: Collier Books, 1978), Chs 10–12; William D. Burt, *Local Problems: Libertarian Solutions* (Washington, DC: Libertarian Party, 1979); and Robert W. Poole, Jr., *Cutting Back City Hall* (New York: Universe Books, 1980).

73. Robert Poole, Jr., "Keeping Ahead of the News," *Reason*, May 1983, 55.

74. "The Making of a Privatization Boondoggle," *Newsweek*, 21 September 1987, 57; Stuart M. Butler, *Privatizing Federal Spending: A Strategy to Eliminate the Deficit* (New York: Universe Books, 1985), 28; William A. Donahue, review of *The Enabling State: Modern Welfare Capitalism in America* by Neil Gilbert and Barbara Gilbert, *Society* (May/June 1990): 111.

75. Patrick Cox, "Land Sales Man," *Reason*, November 1982, 49: Steven H. Hanke, "The Privatization Debate: An Insider's View," *Cato Journal* 2, no. 3 (Winter 1982): 660–1; "Getting Land Sales Out of the Rut," *Reason*, May 1983, 21.

76. Robert H. Nelson, "Privatization of Federal Lands," in *Regulation and the Reagan Era*, Meiners and Yandle, eds, 143–4, 154–8.

77. President's Commission on Privatization, David F. Linowes, Chairman, *Privatization, Towards More Effective Government*:

Report of the President's Commission on Privatization (Urbana: University of Illionois Press, 1988), xiv–v; Peter Young, "Privatization: Better Services at Less Cost," in *An American Vision: Policies for the '90s*, Edward H. Crane and David Boaz, eds (Washington, DC: Cato Institute, 1989), 252–3. The work of the President's Commission on Privatization may be followed in the Annelise Graebner Anderson Collection, Hoover Institution Archives, Stanford, CA.

78. Oliver Letwin, *Privatising the World: A Study of International Privatization in Theory and Practice* (London: Cassell Educational Ltd, 1988), 12–13.

79. James Tobin, "Reaganomics in Retrospect," in *The Reagan Revolution?*, B. B. Kymlicka and Jean V. Matthews, eds (Chicago: Dorsey Press, 1988), 85.

80. Milton and Rose Friedman, *Tyranny of the Status Quo* (San Diego, CA: Harcourt Brace Jovanovich, 1984) 2, 9, 165.

81. Berman, *America's Right Turn*, 118; Larry M. Schwab, *The Illusion of a Conservative Reagan Revolution* (New Brunswick, NJ: Transaction Publishers, 1991), 128, 181.

82. *Statistical Abstracts of the United States: 1993*, 328, 445.

83. Charles Schultze, "Budget Policy," in *American Economic Policy in the 1980s*, Feldstein, ed., 284.

84. Calculated from data provided in Rose Gutfeld, "White House Tempers Its Outlook But Still Presents Fiscal Optimism," *Wall Street Journal*, 6 January 1987, 11 (E).

85. *Statistical Abstracts of the United States: 1993*, 343.

86. Milton Friedman, "Why Liberalism is Now Obsolete," interview by Peter Brimelow, *Forbes*, 12 December 1988, 161; Milton Friedman and Rose Friedman, "The Tide in the Affairs of Men," in *Thinking About America: The United States in the 1990s*, Annelise Anderson and Dennis L. Bark, eds (Stanford, CA: Hoover Institution Press, 1988), 463; "Serfdom USA" [a symposium], *Policy Review* 69 (Summer 1994): 17.

87. Murray N. Rothbard, "Ronald Reagan: An Autopsy," *Liberty*, March 1989, 14–15.

88. Lindley H. Clark, Jr., "Reaganomics Reassessed: What Went Right – and Wrong," *Wall Street Journal*, 24 September 1987, A26 (E).

89. "The American 80's: Disaster or Triumph?" [a symposium], *Commentary*, September 1990, 21.

90. David A. Stockman, "Budget Policy," in *American Economic Policy in the 1980s*, Feldstein, ed., 270.

91. Miller, *Fix the U.S. Budget!*, 158.

92. R. Emmett Tyrrell, Jr., *The Conservative Crack-Up* (New York: Simon & Schuster, 1992), 216–17, 244.

93. "Where We Succeeded, Where We Failed: Lessons from Reagan Officials for the Next Conservative Presidency" [a symposium], *Policy Review* 43 (Winter 1988): 46; Martin Anderson, *Revolution*:

The Reagan Legacy (San Diego, CA: Harcourt Brace Jovanovich, 1990), xlix.

94. Robert L. Bartley, *The Seven Fat Years and How To Do It Again* (New York: Free Press, 1992), 169.

95. Lawrence B. Lindsey, *The Growth Experiment: How the New Tax Policy is Transforming the U.S. Economy* (New York: Basic Books, 1990), 79, 115, 119–22.

96. Lowell Gallaway and Richard Vedder, "The Distributional Impact of the Eighties: Myths vs Reality," *Critical Review* 7, no. 1 (Winter 1993): 63, 71–3.

97. William A. Niskanen, "The 'R' Word," review of *Revolution*, by Martin Anderson, *Liberty*, January 1989, 60. Other market liberal assessments of the Reagan program include David R. Henderson, *The Truth about the 1980s* (Stanford, CA: Hoover Institution Press, 1994); Richard B. McKenzie, *What Went Right in the 1980s* (San Francisco: Pacific Research Institute for Public Policy, 1994); and Edward S. Rubenstein, *The Right Data* (New York: National Review, Inc., 1994), 203–305.

98. Herbert Stein, *Presidential Economics: The Making of Economic Policy from Roosevelt to Reagan and Beyond* (Washington, DC: American Enterprise Institute, 1988), 403.

99. For several examples see Alan S. Blinder, *Hard Heads, Soft Hearts: Tough-Minded Economics for a Just Society* (Reading, MA: Addison-Wesley, 1987), 3–4; Benjamin M. Friedman, *Day of Reckoning: The Consequences of American Economic Policy* (New York: Vintage Books, 1989), 20; and David P. Calleo, *The Bankrupting of America: How the Federal Budget is Impoverishing the Nation* (New York: Avon Books, 1992), 36.

100. Feldstein, "American Economic Policy in the 1980s: A Personal View," in *American Economic Policy in the 1980s*, Feldstein, ed., 25; Don Fullerton, "Inputs to Tax Policy-Making: The Supply-Side, the Deficit, and the Level Playing Field," in *American Economic Policy in the 1980s*, Feldstein, ed., 176; Bartley, *The Seven Fat Years And How To Do It Again*, 169–71.

101. Anderson, *Revolution*, 132, 152; Norman B. Ture, "To Cut and To Please," *National Review*, 31 August 1992, 36; Paul Craig Roberts, "'Supply-Side' Economics – Theory and Results," *The Public Interest* 93 (Fall 1988): 29.

102. Robert Heilbroner and Peter Bernstein, *The Debt and the Deficit: False Alarms/Real Possibilities* (New York: W. W. Norton, 1989), 24–7.

103. Daniel Patrick Moynihan, *Came the Revolution: Argument in the Reagan Era* (San Diego, CA: Harcourt Brace Jovanovich, 1988), 154.

104. Fred I. Greenstein, "Ronald Reagan – Another Hidden-Hand Ike?," *PS: Political Science and Politics*, 23, no. 1 (March 1990): 12.

105. Stockman, *The Triumph of Politics*, 68–9, 133. In a 1991 National Bureau of Economic Research conference Stockman denied Moynihan's charge but acknowledged that the deficits indeed had the

effect that Moynihan described. "Summary of Discussion," *American Economic Policy in the 1980s*, Feldstein, ed., 287.

106. Paul Craig Roberts, "'Supply-Side' Economics – Theory and Results," 30.
107. Stockman, *The Triumph of Politics*, 69.
108. McKenzie, *What Went Right in the 1980s*, 268–9.
109. John C. Goodman and Gerald L. Musgrave, *Patient Power: Solving America's Health Care Crisis* (Washington, DC: Cato Institute, 1992), 456–8.
110. James M. Buchanan and Richard E. Wagner, *Democracy in Deficit: The Political Legacy of Lord Keynes* (New York: Academic Press, 1977), 21.
111. Makin and Ornstein, *Debt and Taxes*, 183–6, 277, 281.
112. Aaron Wildavsky, *How to Limit Government Spending* (Berkeley: University of California Press, 1980), 36.
113. Hugh Heclo, "Reaganism and the Search for a Public Philosophy," in *Perspectives on the Reagan Years*, Palmer, ed., 50.
114. Lou Cannon, *President Reagan: The Role of a Lifetime* (New York: Simon & Schuster, 1991), 109, 114, 153, 185.
115. David Stockman, "Budget Policy," in *American Economic Policy in the 1980s*, Feldstein, ed., 272.
116. Seymour Martin Lipset, "The Economy, Elections, and Public Opinion," in *To Promote Prosperity: U.S. Domestic Policy in the Mid-1980s*, John H. Moore, ed. (Stanford, CA: Hoover Institution Press, 1984), 405. For an elaborate documentation of this point and evidence that this "bifurcated" condition continued through the eighties see Linda L. M. Bennett and Stephen Early Bennett, *Living with Leviathan: Americans Coming to Terms with Big Government* (Lawrence: University of Kansas Press, 1990).
117. James Q. Wilson, "The Dilemmas of Conservatism II," *The American Spectator*, March 1982, 13, 14.
118. Stein, *Presidential Economics*, 309.
119. Niskanen, *Reaganomics*, 24.
120. Martha Derthick and Paul J. Quirk, *The Politics of Deregulation* (Washington, DC: Brookings Institution, 1985), 36, 54, 112.
121. A. James Reichley, *Conservatives in an Age of Change: The Nixon and Ford Administration* (Washington, DC: Brookings Institution, 1981), 269, 399–400.
122. Gerston, Fraleigh and Schwab, *The Deregulated Society*, 42–53.
123. Robert Wood, *Whatever Possessed the President? Academic Experts and Presidential Policy, 1960–1988* (Amherst, MA: University of Massachusetts Press, 1993), 144–5; Paul Krugman, *Peddling Prosperity: Economic Sense and Nonsense in the Age of Diminished Expectations* (New York: W. W. Norton, 1994), 70–5.
124. Roberts, *The Supply-Side Revolution*, 63.
125. Walter Dean Burnham, "The Reagan Heritage," in *The Election of 1988: Reports and Interpretations*, Gerald M. Pomper, ed. (Chatham, NJ: Chatham House, 1989), 15.

126. Bernard H. Siegan, *Economic Liberties and the Constitution* (Chicago: University of Chicago Press, 1980); Richard A. Epstein, *Takings: Private Property and the Power of Eminent Domain* (Chicago: University of Chicago Press, 1985).

127. Richard Vigilante, "Beyond the Burger Court," *Policy Review* 28 (Spring 1984): 23–5; Virginia I. Postrel, "Banned from the Bench?," *Reason*, April 1989, 12.

128. Jeffrey Rosen, "Overqualified," *The New Republic*, 4 April 1994, 42.

129. Jane Shaw, "Breaking New Ground," *Policy Review* 33 (Summer 1985): 77.

130. Delgaudio, "Refugee Economist in America", pp. 454–60; Karen I. Vaughn, *Austrian Economics in America* (Cambridge: Cambridge University Press, 1994), 71, fn. 17, 117–20; Lawrence H. White, *The Methodology of the Austrian School Economists*, rev. ed. (Auburn, AL: Ludwig von Mises Institute, 1984), 27; Murray N. Rothbard, "Austrian Economics – Boom, Sell-Out and Revival," *American Libertarian*, March 1989, 6; Peter J. Boettke, "The Story of a Movement," *Freeman*, May 1995, 322–6.

131. Gregg Easterbrook, "Ideas Move Nations," *The Atlantic Monthly*, January 1986, 66; Quoted in John Kenneth White, *The New Politics of Old Values*, 2nd ed. (Hanover, NH: University Press of New England, 1990), 139.

132. Bolick, *Grassroots Tyranny*, 7.

133. W. John Moore, "Local Right Thinkers," *National Journal*, 1 October 1988, 2455; John K. Andrews, "So You Want to Start a Think Tank," *Policy Review* 49 (Summer 1989): 63, 65. See William D. Eggers and John O'Leary, *Revolution at the Roots: Making our Government Smaller, Better and Closer to Home* (New York: Free Press, 1995) for a review of efforts to bring the market revolution to the state and local level.

134. W. John Moore, "Wichita Pipeline," *National Journal*, 16 May, 1992, 1168–74.

135. Ed Crane, "Crane urges L. P. to Learn Issues and Take Initiative," *Libertarian Party News*, June–July 1977, 1; "Cato Shifts Gears," *Frontlines*, September 1979, 1–2, PP 639; J. Allen Smith, *The Idea Brokers: Think Tanks and the Rise of a New Policy Elite* (New York: The Free Press, 1991), 221. Overviews of Cato policy prescriptions in the eighties can be found in two volumes edited by David Boaz and Edward H. Crane: *Beyond the Status Quo: Policy Proposals for America* (Washington, DC: Cato Institute, 1985) and *An American Vision: Policies for the '90s* (Washington, DC: Cato Institute, 1989).

136. Leonard P. Liggio memo to Chris Hocker, 3 March 1982, 10.

137. Edward H. Crane and William Niskanen, "Message from the President and the Chairman," *Cato Institute 1988 Annual Report* (Washington, DC: Cato Institute, 1989), 4–5.

138. Quoted in Thomas G. Paterson, J. Garry Clifford and Kenneth J. Hagan, *American Foreign Policy: A History/1900 to Present*, 3rd ed. (Lexington, MA: D. C. Heath, 1988), 272.

6 THE FUTURE POLITICS OF MARKET LIBERALISM: "ARE WE A PERMANENT MINORITY?"

1. Alonzo L. Hamby, *Liberalism and Its Challengers: FDR to Bush,* 2nd ed. (New York: Oxford University Press, 1992), 339, 384–5.
2. Paul H. Weaver, "The Intellectual Debate," in *Assessing the Reagan Years,* David Boaz, ed. (Washington, DC: Cato Institute, 1988), 415.
3. Burton Yale Pines, *Back to Basics: The Traditionalist Movement That is Sweeping Grass-Roots America* (New York: William Morrow, 1982), Chs. 5–6; Rebecca Klatch, "Complexities of Conservatism," *America at Century's End,* Alan Wolfe, ed. (Berkeley: University of California Press, 1991), 367–71; Jerome L. Himmelstein, *To the Right: The Transformation of American Conservatism* (Berkeley: University of California Press, 1990), 99–108.
4. Seymour Martin Lipset and Earl Raab, "The Election and the Evangelicals," *Commentary,* March 1981, 27.
5. Irving Kristol, *Two Cheers for Capitalism* (New York: Basic Books, 1978).
6. Irving Kristol, "Reason Interview: Irving Kristol," interview by Tibor Machan, *Reason,* January 1983, 40–4.
7. Irving Kristol to Roy A. Childs, Jr., 13 February, 1979, Childs Collection, Box 7, "R.A.C. Correspondence."
8. James Q. Wilson, "The Dilemma of Conservatism," 16.
9. George F. Will, *Statecraft as Soulcraft: What Government Does* (New York: Simon & Schuster, 1983), 93–4.
10. Robert Nisbet, "Still Questing," *The Intercollegiate Review* 29, no. 1 (Fall 1993): 44–5.
11. Russell Kirk, "Libertarians: The Chirping Sectaries," in *Freedom and Virtue: The Conservative/Libertarian Debate,* George W. Carey, ed. (Lanham, MD: University Press of America, 1984), 120.
12. Murray N. Rothbard, "Frank S. Meyer: The Fusionist as Libertarian Manque," in *Freedom and Virtue,* Carey, ed., 98.
13. Ronald Reagan, *Public Papers of the Presidents of the United States, 1983; Book I-January 1 to June 29, 1983* (Washington, DC: United States Government Printing Office, 1985), 363; Ronald Reagan, *Public Papers of the Presidents of the United States, 1984; Book II-June 30 to December 31, 1984* (Washington, DC: United States Government Printing Office, 1987), 1167.
14. Barry W. Lynn, "Civil Liberties: Whatever Happened to Limited Government?" in *Assessing the Reagan Years,* Boaz, ed., 372–3; Steve Bruce, *The Rise and Fall of the New Christian Right: Conservative Protestant Politics in America 1978–1988* (Oxford: Clarendon Press, 1990), 136.
15. William A. Niskanen, *Reagonomics: An Insider's Account of the Policies and the People* (New York: Oxford University Press, 1988), 288.

16. Dinesh D'Souza, "Thinking Ahead Conservatively," *The American Spectator*, 8 August 1985, 13.

17. "What Conservatives Think of Reagan" [a symposium], *Policy Review* 27 (Winter 1984): 18–19.

18. Paul Gottfried and Thomas Fleming, *The Conservative Movement* (Boston, MA: Twayne Publishers, 1988), 62–3.

19. Paul H. Weaver, "Ideas in American Politics," in *Left, Right and Babyboom: America's New Politics*, David Boaz, ed. (Washington, DC: Cato Institute), 91.

20. Gary Dorrien, *The Neoconservative Mind: Power, Culture and the War of Ideology* (Philadelphia, PA: Temple University Press, 1993), 228–9, 362–3; Hamby, *Liberalism and Its Challengers*, 300.

21. John B. Judis, "The Conservative Wars," *The New Republic*, 11 and 18 August 1986, 15–16.

22. M. E. Bradford, "On Being a Conservative in a Post-Liberal Era," *The Intercollegiate Review* 21, no. 3 (Spring 1986): 15.

23. Judis, "The Conservative Wars," 16; Jeffrey Hart, "Gang Warfare in Chicago," *National Review*, 6 June 1986, 32.

24. Jacob Weisberg, "Hunter Gatherers," *The New Republic*, 2 September 1991, 14–16.

25. Milton Mueller, "The Neoconservative in the White House," *Libertarian Review*, November/December 1981, 9; Ed Crane, "Reagan Never Meant What He Said," *Washington Post*, 19 August 1982; Robert W. Poole, Jr., "Strategic Options for the LP," *Caliber*, October–November 1981, 11 in Evers Collection, Box 3.

26. David Bergland, "Bergland Committee Report," *Libertarian Party News*, November 1984/February 1985, 11.

27. Don Ernsberger, "Election Viewpoints," *Libertarian Party News*, November 1984/February 1985, 15.

28. Mike Holmes, "Is the LP in Trouble?," *American Libertarian*, October 1986, 6 and "LP Membership Down 20% From 1985," *American Libertarian*, April 1987, 1 in Karl Peterjohn Collection, Box 5, Hoover Institution Archives, Stanford, CA. Hereafter cited as Peterjohn Collection.

29. Ronald E. Paul to Frank Fahrenkopf, 8 January 1987, Evers Collection, Box 16, 2.

30. Ron Paul, "AL Interview: Ron Paul," interview by Mike Holmes, *American Libertarian*, July 1987, 1–2, 6, 8, Peterjohn Collection, Box 5.

31. Murray N. Rothbard, "Victory and Defeat in Seattle," *American Libertarian*, September/October 1987, 3; Chester Alan Arthur, "The Libertarian's Quandary," *Liberty*, August, 1987, 39.

32. Randy Langhenry, "Paul/Marrou Picked to Lead LP in '88," *Libertarian Party News*, September/October, 1987, 6.

33. Chester Alan Arthur, "High Noon for the Libertarian Party?," *Liberty*, January 1989, 19.

34. Murray N. Rothbard, "Life or Death in Seattle," *Liberty*, August 1987, 39.

35. Arthur, "High Noon for the Libertarian Party?," 22, 24.
36. M. E. Bradford, "Collaborators with the Left," *Policy Review* 57 (Summer 1991): 78, 81.
37. For examples of Rockwell's argument and skeptical libertarian responses see Llewellyn H. Rockwell, Jr., "The Case for Paleo-Libertarianism," *Liberty*, January 1990, 34–8; Llewellyn H. Rockwell, Jr., and Jeffrey A. Tucker, "Ayn Rand is Dead," *National Review*, 28 May 1990, 35–6; and "Libertarianism: Paleo and Con" [a symposium], *Liberty*, March 1990, 44–50.
38. Thomas Fleming, "The New Fusionism," *Chronicles*, May 1991, 11; Justin Raimondo, *Reclaiming the American Right: The Lost Legacy of the Conservative Movement* (Burlingame, CA: Center for Libertarian Studies, 1993), 220–37; David Frum, *Dead Right* (New York: New Republic Books/Basic Books, 1994), 124–58.
39. Patrick Buchanan, "America First – and Second, and Third," *The National Interest* 19 (Spring 1990): 81.
40. Adam Meyerson, "The Limits of Tyranny," *Policy Review* 56 (Spring 1991): 2; Owen Harries, "Drift and Mastery, Bush-Style," *The National Interest* 23 (Spring 1991): 5.
41. Frum, *Dead Right*, 157.
42. William E. Simon to Edward H. Crane, 8 April 1991, Childs Collection, Box 7.
43. The Cato Institute lost $750 000 in contributions as a consequence of its stand on the Gulf War. New donors such as Coca-Cola, Citibank, Shell Oil, Philip Morris and Toyota helped fill the gap. John J. Fialka, "Cato Institute's Influence Grows in Washington as Republican-Dominated Congress Sets Up Shop," *Wall Street Journal*, 14 December 1994, A14 (E).
44. Edward H. Crane to William E. Simon, 15 April 1991, Childs Collection, Box 7.
45. John B. Judis, "Crackup of the Right," *The American Prospect* 3 (Fall 1990): 41.
46. Michael Duffy and Dan Goodgame, *Marching in Place: The Status Quo Presidency of George Bush* (New York: Simon & Schuster, 1992), 79, 90, 99.
47. Fred Barnes, "Bush's Big Government Conservatives," *The American Spectator*, April 1990, 14.
48. "Sophomore Slump: Mid-Term Grades for the Bush Administration" [a symposium], *Policy Review* 55 (Winter 1991): 32–3; Burton Yale Pines, "Bull Moose Revolt: George Bush and the Shadow of William Howard Taft," *Policy Review* 55 (Winter 1991): 5.
49. Rush Limbaugh, "Why Liberals Fear Me," *Policy Review* 70 (Fall 1994): 4; Dan Balz and Ronald Brownstein, *Storming the Gates: Protest Politics and the Republican Revival* (Boston: Little, Brown, 1996), 170; James Atlas, "The Counter Counterculture," *The New York Times Magazine*, 12 February 1995, 34; Fred Barnes, "Right Back," *The New Republic*, 5 July 1993, 20; Peter Brimelow, "Our Customers are Weird," *Forbes*, January 31 1994, 102; R. W. Bradford, "How We

Started 'Liberty'," *Liberty*, September 1992, 57–8; R. W. Bradford to "Friend of Liberty," 12 July 1994 [circular].

50. R. Hal Williams, "'Dry Bones and Dead Language': The Democratic Party," in *The Gilded Age*, rev. ed., H. Wayne Morgan, ed. (Syracuse, NY: Syracuse University Press, 1970), 143; Walter Dean Burnham, "Party Systems and the Political Process," in *The American Party Systems: Stages of Political Development*, 2nd ed., William Nisbet Chambers and Walter Dean Burnham, eds (New York: Oxford University Press, 1975), 287–9; 298–301.

51. "Voters Throw a Party," *Wall Street Journal*, 11 November 1994, A14(E); R. W. Apple, Jr., "1994 Isn't Forever," *New York Times*, 10 November 1994, A14(N); Thomas B. Edsall, "Revolt of the Discontented," *Washington Post*, 11 November 1994, A31; John B. Judis, "The New Era of Instability," *New York Times*, 10 November, 1994, A15(N).

52. David M. Ricci, *The Transformation of American Politics: The New Washington and the Rise of Think Tanks* (New Haven, CT: Yale University Press, 1993), 73.

53. William S. Maddox and Stuart A. Lilie, *Beyond Liberal and Conservative: Reassessing the Political Spectrum* (Washington, DC: Cato Institute, 1984), 4–6, 35, 68.

54. William A. Niskanen, "Why Our Democracy Doesn't Work," *The Public Interest* 116 (Summer 1994): 94–5.

55. Burton Yale Pines, "America's New Bargain with Washington," *Policy Review* 62 (Fall 1992): 23.

56. Will now concluded that the modern welfare states was an "overbearing, overreaching, underachiever that can not write – or adhere – to a budget." George F. Will, "Economics and Politics in Washington, D.C.," *World Capitalism Review* 1, no. 3 (July 1993): 10.

57. Frum, *Dead Right*, 4.

58. Ralph Reed, "Casting a Wider Net: Religious Conservatives Move Beyond Abortion and Homosexuality," *Policy Review* 65 (Summer 1993): 32; Ralph Reed, "Conservative Coalition Holds Firm," *Wall Street Journal*, 13 February 1995, A14(E).

59. Dick Armey, "Freedom's Choir: Social and Economic Conservatives are Singing the Same Song," *Policy Review* 67 (Winter 1994): 29.

60. William Kristol, "The Future of Conservatism in the U.S.," *The American Enterprise* 5, no. 4 (July/August 1994): 37.

61. John C. Green and James L. Guth, "The Sociology of Libertarians," *Liberty*, September/October 1987, 10; "Opinion Survey Results Surprising," *Individual Liberty*, May 1979, 1–2, Walters Collection, Box 3; "Who We Are, What We Think," *Frontlines*, May 1983, 1–2, PP 640; "The Liberty Poll: Who We Are and What We think," *Liberty*, July 1988, 37–9, 46–8.

62. Doug Bandow, "Libertarians and Christians in a Hostile World," *Liberty*, July 1992, 34; William L. Anderson, "Onward Christian Soldiers?," *Reason*, January 1994, 28–34; Peter Schrag, "The Great School Sell-Off," *The American Prospect* 12 (Winter 1993): 34.

63. Peter G. Peterson and Neil Howe, *On Borrowed Time: How the Growth in Entitlement Spending Threatens America's Future* (New York: Touchstone, 1988), 393.

64. Jonathan Rauch, *Demosclerosis: The Silent Killer of American Government* (New York: Times Books, 1994), 12.

65. Jonathan R. Macey and Geoffrey P. Miller, "The End of History and the New World Order: The Triumph of Capitalism and the Competition between Liberalism and Democracy," *Cornell International Law Journal* 25 (1992): 297–8.

66. James L. Payne, "Where Have All the Dollars Gone?," *Reason*, February 1994, 17–19.

67. Richard McKenzie and Dwight R. Lee, *Quicksilver Capital: How the Rapid Movement of Wealth Has Changed the World* (New York: Free Press, 1991), 87–90.

68. David Osborne and Ted Gaebler, *Reinventing Government: How the Entrepreneurial Spirit is Transforming the Public Sector* (New York: Plume, 1993) and Al Gore, *Creating a Government That Works Better and Costs Less: The Report of the National Performance Review* (New York: Plume, 1993) represent liberal efforts to come to terms with downsizing pressures.

69. Richard Cornuelle, "The Power and Poverty of Libertarian Thought," *Critical Review* 6, no. 1 (Winter 1992): 6.

70. For sympathetic studies of these market or non-profit alternatives to state-provided welfare, see David Beito, "Mutual Aid for Social Welfare: The Case of American Fraternal Societies," *Critical Review* 4, no. 4 (Fall 1990): 709–36; Marvin Olasky, *The Tragedy of American Compassion* (Washington, DC: Regnery Gateway, 1992); and Richard C. Cornuelle, *Reclaiming the American Dream: The Role of Private Individuals and Voluntary Associations*, with an afterword by the author (New Brunswick, NJ: Transaction Publishers, 1993).

71. The literature on privatization of public services is extensive. Overviews include E. S. Savas, *Privatization: The Key to Better Government* (Chatham, NJ: Chatham House Publishers, 1987), William T. Gormley, Jr., ed., *Privatization and Its Alternatives* (Madison: University of Wisconsin Press, 1991), and William D. Eggers and John O'Leary, *Revolution at the Roots: Making our Government Smaller, Better and Closer to Home* (New York: Free Press, 1995).

72. Ernest van den Haag, "The Political Threat to the Market Economy," Hayek Collection, Box 86: 5.

73. George Stigler, "Why Have the Socialists Been Winning?," Hayek Collection, Box 87: A-8.

74. Robert Skidelsky, *The Road from Serfdom: The Economic and Political Consequences of Communism* (New York: Allen Lane/The Penguin Press, 1995), ix.

75. Robert Heilbroner, "After Communism," *The New Yorker*, 10 September 1990, 98.

76. John Lewis Gaddis, "The Tragedy of Cold War History: Reflections on Revisionism," *Foreign Affairs* 73, no. 1 (January/February 1994): 152.

77. Milton and Rose Friedman, "The Tide in the Affairs of Men," in *Thinking About America: The United States in the 1990s*, Annelise Anderson and Dennis L. Bark, eds (Stanford, CA: Hoover Institution Press, 1988), 455.

78. Friedrich A. von Hayek, *Hayek on Hayek: An Autobiographical Dialogue*, Stephen Kresge and Leif Wenar, eds (Chicago: University of Chicago Press, 1994), 125, 152; F. A. Hayek, "The Best Book on General Economics in Many a Year," review of *Knowledge and Decision* by Thomas Sowell, in *Reason*, December 1981, 48.

79. Hayek, *Hayek on Hayek*, 128; Vaughn, *Austrian Economics in America*, 66, fn. 8.

80. Murray N. Rothbard, 1926–1995" [a symposium], *Liberty*, March 1995, 26; Peter Brimelow, "No Water Economics," *Forbes* 6 March 1989, 91.

81. Gordon Tullock, *Rent Seeking* (Brookfield, VT: Edward Elgar 1993), 17.

82. Alfred L. Malabre, Jr., *Lost Prophets: An Insider's History of the Modern Economists* (Cambridge, MA: Harvard Business School Press, 1994), Ch. 5 provides a good overview of both the rise and decline of the influence of Friedman's monetarism.

83. Alfred E. Kahn, "Applications of Economics to an Imperfect World," *American Economic Association* 69, no. 2 (May 1979): 1.

84. Theodore J. Lowi, *The End of Liberalism: The Second Republic of the United States*, 2nd ed. (New York, W. W. Norton, 1979); T. Grieder, *Secrets of the Temple* (London: Pocket Books, 1989), 96.

85. Friedman, "The Tide in the Affairs of Men," in *Thinking About America*, Anderson and Bark, eds, 463.

86. Ibid., 465; Milton Friedman, *Why Government is the Problem* (Stanford, CA: Hoover Institution Press, 1993), 16.

87. Bennett Harrison and Barry Bluestone, *The Great U-Turn: Corporate Restructuring and the Polarizing of America* (New York: Basic Books, 1988), 170.

88. Walter Dean Burnham, "The 1980 Earthquake: Realignment, Reaction, or What?," in *The Hidden Election: Politics and Economics in the 1980 Presidential Campaign*, Thomas Ferguson and Joel Rogers, eds (New York: Pantheon Books, 1981), 127.

89. Jeffrey R. Henig, "Privatization in the United States: Theory and Practice," *Political Science Quarterly* 104, no. 4 (Winter 1989): 669.

90. Peter F. Drucker, *The New Realities: In Government and Politics, in Economics and Business, in Society and World View* (New York: Perennial Library, 1989), 4, 61.

91. Quoted in Thomas J. DiLorenzo, "Classroom Struggle: The Free Market Takeover of Economics Textbooks," *Policy Review* 40 (Spring 1987): 44, 49.

92. Seymour Martin Lipset, "The Death of the Third Way," *The National Interest* 20 (Summer 1990): 36. One indication of the growing influence of market-liberal ideas outside the US was the number of overseas free-market think-tanks. See Arthur Seldon, *Capitalism* (Oxford: Basil Blackwell, 1990), 404–6.

93. "A New View of the Electorate," *American Enterprise* 5, no. 3 (May/June 1994): 91.

94. Richard L. Berke, "Victories Were Captured by G.O.P. Candidates, Not the Party's Platform," *New York Times*, 10 November 1994, B1(N); Gerald F. Seib, "Voters, Having Changed Congress, Now Want Congress to Change Washington," Poll Indicates," *Wall Street Journal*, 11 November 1994, A16(E).

95. "New House Speaker Envisions Cooperation, Cuts, Hard Work," *Congressional Quarterly Weekly*, 12 November 1994, 3297.

96. For a post-1994 election analysis skeptical of Republic claims of a mandate to downsize the state see Clyde Wilcox, *The Latest American Revolution? The 1994 Elections and Their Implications for Governance* (New York: St Martin's Press, 1995), 20–1.

97. Norman P. Barry, *On Classical Liberalism and Libertarianism* (London: Macmillan, 1986), 65.

98. "Politics of the Professoriate," *The American Enterprise* (July/August 1991): 87.

99. Amitai Etzioni, *The Moral Dimension: Toward a New Economics* (New York: Free Press, 1988), 31. Etzioni edits the communitarian journal, *The Responsive Community*. Offering an alternative to liberalism, communitarian ideas have garnered considerable attention in the last decade. Scholarly evaluations include Robert Booth Fowler, *The Dance with Community: The Contemporary Debate in American Political Thought* (Lawrence: University Press of Kansas, 1991), a generally sympathetic treatment, and Stephen Holmes, *The Anatomy of Antiliberalism* (Cambridge, MA: Harvard University Press, 1993), a sharp indictment. See William A. Schambra, foreword to Robert A. Nisbet, *The Quest for Community: A Study in the Ethics of Order and Freedom* (San Francisco: ICS Press, 1990), vii–xix for a discussion of how both Republicans and Democrats have tried to appropriate the term "community."

100. Friedrich A. Hayek, *The Mirage of Social Justice*, vol. 2 of *Law, Legislation and Liberty* (Chicago: University of Chicago Press, 1976), 87.

101. Friedrich A. Hayek, *The Political Order of a Free People*, vol. 3 of *Law, Legislation and Liberty* (Chicago: University of Chicago Press, 1979), 54–5.

102. F. A. Hayek, *Studies in Philosophy, Politics, and Economics* (Chicago: University of Chicago Press, 1967), 194.

103. George Gilder, *Wealth and Poverty*, rev. ed. (San Francisco: ICS Press, 1993); Donald McCloskey, "Bourgeois Virtue," *The American Scholar* 63, no. 2 (Spring 1994): 187–91.

104. Peter L. Berger, *The Capitalist Revolution: Fifty Propositions about Prosperity, Equality and Liberty* (New York: Basic Books, 1986), 206.

105. Noting the increased influence of libertarians in Republican ranks after November 1994, E. J. Dionne, Jr. suggested that the libertarians had supplanted the marxists as the "world's leading Utopia builders." E. J. Dionne, Jr., "Libertarians' Lure," *Washington Post*, 6 December 1994, A19. The Cato Institute's President insisted on the practicality of libertarian goals in Edward H. Crane, "Give Me Liberty, Not Utopia," *Washington Post*, 11 January 1995, A17.

106. James M. Buchanan, *What Should Economists Do?* (Indianapolis: Liberty Press, 1979), 282.

107. Roy A. Childs to Irving Kristol, 13 April 1983, Childs Collection, Box 7.

108. Murray N. Rothbard, "The LP: Retrospect and Prospect," *The Libertarian Forum*, November 1976, 3, LPA (10187), Box 7.

109. Jan Narveson, *The Libertarian Idea* (Philadelphia, PA: Temple University Press, 1988), 334–5.

110. Joseph Mark Hazlett, "An Analysis of American Minor Parties: The Libertarian Party as a Case Study" (Ph.D. dissertation, University of Tennessee, 1987), 202–7; Tim W. Ferguson, "The Reason for Reason's Influence," *Wall Street Journal*, 2 October 1991), A12(E); Warren Weaver, Jr., "Cato Institute Marks 10 Years," *New York Times*, 19 May 1987, B6(L); John J. Fialka, "Cato Institute's Influence Grows in Washington as Republican-Dominated Congress Sets Up Shop," *Wall Street Journal*, 14 December 1994, A14(E).

111. E. J. Dionne, Jr., *Why Americans Hate Politics* (New York: Simon & Schuster, 1991), 260.

112. Everett Carll Ladd, "The 1992 Election's Complex Message," *The American Enterprise* (January/February 1993): 51.

113. *Reviewing the Revolution: Conservative Success in the 104th Congress* (Washington, DC: Heritage Foundation, 1996) provides an optimistic assessment of the Republican Party's accomplishments during the 104th Congress.

114. Richard B. McKenzie, "Clinton Confidential," *Reason*, November 1996, 40.

115. "President's Address to Congress on the State of the Union," *New York Times*, 24 January 1996, A14(L).

116. The search for a new public philosophy threatens to become more than just a cottage industry. Some of the recent debate can be followed in Robert N. Bellah, Richard Madsen, William M. Sullivan, Ann Swidler and Steven M. Tipton, *The Good Society* (New York: Alfred A. Knopf, 1992); Mickey Kaus, "Paradigm's Loss," *The New Republic*, 27 July, 1992, 18–20; A. Lawrence Chickering, *Beyond Left and Right: Breaking the Political Stalemate* (San Francisco: ICS Press, 1993); Paul H. Weaver, "Do-Good Libertarianism," *Reason*, May 1993, 61–3; William A. Schambra, "The Rediscovery of Citizenship," *Policy Review* 69 (Summer 1994): 32–8; Daniel B.

Klein, "Libertarianism as Communitarianism," *Freeman*, December 1994, 685–9; Amitai Etzioni, ed., *Rights and the Common Good: The Communitarian Perspective* (New York: St Martin's Press, 1995); Robert D. Putnam, "Bowling Alone: America's Declining Social Capital," *Journal of Democracy*, 6, no. 1 (January 1995): 64–77; Dan Coats, Gertrude Himmelfarb, Don Eberly and David Boaz, "Can Congress Revive Civil Society?" [a symposium], *Policy Review: The Journal of American Citizenship* (January/February 1996): 25–33; Joel Kotkin, James Payne, Glenn Loury, "What's Wrong with the … Left, Center, Right," *The American Enterprise* (January/February 1996): 30–9; Michael J. Sandel, *Democracy's Discontent: America in Search of a Public Philosophy* (Cambridge, MA: Harvard University Press, 1996).

Index